Triple Takes on
Curricular Worlds

TRIPLE TAKES
ON
CURRICULAR
WORLDS

❦

MARY ASWELL DOLL
DELESE WEAR
MARTHA L. WHITAKER

STATE UNIVERSITY OF NEW YORK PRESS

Published by
State University of New York Press, Albany

Printed in the United States of America

For information, address State University of New York Press,
194 Washington Avenue, Suite 305, Albany, NY 12210-2384

Production by Christine L. Hamel
Marketing by Susan Petrie

Library of Congress Cataloging-in-Publication Data

Doll, Mary Aswell.
  Triple takes on curricular worlds / Mary Aswell Doll, Delese Wear,
Martha L. Whitaker.
       p. cm.
  Includes bibliographical references and index.
  ISBN 0-7914-6721-X (hardcover : alk. paper)
  1. Curriculum planning—Study and teaching (Graduate)—United States.
2. Curriculum planning—Study and teaching (Higher)—United States.
3. Interdisciplinary approach in education—United States. 4. Critical
pedagogy—United States. I. Wear, Delese. II. Whitaker, Martha L.,
1948– . III. Title.
  LB2806.15.D63 2006
  375'.0071'1--dc22

                                                        2005015253

  ISBN-13: 978-0-7914-6721-3 (hardcover : alk. paper)

                    10 9 8 7 6 5 4 3 2 1

Contents

Foreword

MARLA MORRIS

I assure you, reader, that this book will make you think differently about your own curricular world(s). This foreword is meant only to spark interest, not to steal fire. So I will try not to steal fire. Rather I write this foreword to help readers get ready to look forward, not to fore-cast. Here I would like to fore-tell (for forewords are about telling about the book one is about to read) readers that *Triple Takes on Curricular Worlds* is a brilliant and ground-breaking book that will knock your socks off. This is a book that is un-for-gettable. If readers, however, are looking for a for-mula for curriculum, they are barking up the wrong tree. This book is an intellectual exploration of what it means to live in curricular worlds from the perspective of three women who work in radically different kinds of intellectual institutions.

What an interesting book. Indeed. What I like about this book is that these authors have interesting ideas about words. Words such as boundaries, disgrace, distance, fear, forgiveness, light and mothers inform their curricular worlds. Readers will do a double take on each triple take as they are delighted, shocked, saddened, and made joyful by the seriousness and—yet—the playfulness of the text-at-hand. Read and read again the concepts that web together this text, reader. You will be delighted. The woven fabric of the three voices touch on issues relevant not only to scholars of curriculum but to scholars and students across the disciplines as well. Autobiography, politics, medicine, literature, philosophy and religion, as they relate to curricular worlds, enliven and embolden the text in provocative ways. Curricular worlds are the sites that both teachers and students inhabit, yet the authors suggest that teachers and students must rethink their habits and undo them, to think differently and more metaphorically about issues such as difference and alterity.

Each section of the book is indeed a triple play as the bases are loaded with rich, metaphoric, and deep insight. Mary Aswell Doll, Delese Wear, and Martha Whitaker write deliciously about the possibilities of the progressive educative dream. These writers continue Dewey's call for progressive thinking that allows students and teachers to become public intellectuals as they explore their own curricular worlds against the backdrop of the sociopolitical landscape. Readers, get fired up and get ready to steal the bases for the home run! *Triple Takes* is the home run of curriculum scholarship.

Introduction

MARY ASWELL DOLL
DELESE WEAR
MARTHA L. WHITAKER

With *Triple Takes on Curricular Worlds* three educators representing three different academic disciplines write on a broad range of concepts not usually found in the field of curriculum studies: Boundaries, Disgrace, Distance, Fear, Forgiveness, Light, Mothers. Two chapters directly address curriculum issues: Teaching, and Curriculum. The concepts are considered separately by each educator, such that each is discussed from three distinct viewpoints, or "takes," to form nine chapters in all. Delese Wear teaches medical education in a midwestern university system; Martha Whitaker teaches elementary education in a western university; and Mary Doll teaches liberal arts in a southern art college. The chapters allow each writer to reflect from her personal as well as professional background. Each articulates from her distinct perspective but in a way that occasionally overlaps with the other writers. The book is grounded in what Maxine Greene (1995) calls "perspectival sight," arising from different domains, different bodies, different projects.

An intriguing aspect of the book is that the concepts we write on are rarely addressed in curriculum theorizing. The worlds we inhabit individually and collectively with our students involve more than traditional curricular concerns. Like those cultural and feminist studies that inform our work, we draw on a wide range of fields—aesthetic, spiritual, political—to produce the knowledge required to teach, to live. We think that the book will offer new, sometimes startling understanding of the selves educators bring to work. We think, because it dares to write from night thought as well as from day thought, it is out of the bounds of traditional books on curriculum while yet being intricately associated with the teaching and learning moments that face students and teachers on a daily basis. And so we offer five unique aspects to this work.

First, we are committed to the premise that curriculum theory is an interdisciplinary enterprise. The interdisciplinary structure of the field, and especially the strong influence of the humanities and the arts, makes curriculum theory a distinctive specialization within the broad field of education. Not only do the three of us represent three branches of education, but we draw on a wide variety of sources within those branches in discussing our topics. Delese focuses on health and doctor/patient issues that have important ramifications for educators in the social sciences. Martha bolsters her work with elementary teachers by references to philosophy and religion. Mary's literary references provide her theoretical frame to demonstrate how the humanities, especially literature, address curricular concerns. It is our intention to suggest that the curricular worlds we inhabit through our interdisciplinary approaches will make education more accessible to a wide audience.

Second, we think this book gives the promise to what Rorty (1989) means by "conversation" and what Pinar (1995, p. 848) means by "complicated conversation." Our chapters web our various selves with the networks that surround us, not unlike a rhizomatic structure with connections growing ever outward. Perhaps our intertwining life stories will invite readers to interpret their own teaching, learning, and living. That, in any case, is our wish. The chapters deliberately employ an autobiographical method to complicate, enrich, and nuance the theories we endorse. Believing with Bill Pinar and Madeleine Grumet (1976) that the root of curriculum is *currere*, we see the tracing of our ideas as of a piece with the running of our own lives; consequently, we offer ourselves as part of our study. This autobiographical method asks us to slow down, to remember, but not to cling. Then, slowly, and in our own terms, we analyze our experiences of the past in order to understand more fully, with more complexity and subtlety, our submergences in the present. Without self-reflexivity, what coin is there in words? With the intention of examining our own voices, lest we become voyeurs of our students (Ellsworth, 1989), we write about our own motives, intentions, suspicions, hesitations, and lostnesses with the purpose of going beyond the bounds of such dry curriculum issues as assessment or classroom management. Our triple takes can be read as a kind of conversation that the reader is invited to listen in on as a necessary fourth component.

Third, and related to the second point, is our interest in how each of us uses our work in memory and reflection to engage the serious issues of our time: terrorism, power, technology. Examining our own histories, as one way of confronting historical and contemporary dimensions of our country's ideological and economic forces, keeps us focused on the personal which is political. What is it for us to be living in a country that calls itself the greatest superpower in the world but that forgets the lessons of history—not to mention the teachings of the classics? We are mindful of the hubris of our leaders who allow disinformation to justify war and colonialism. The topics we have selected attempt to look at the present from the lens of the past, with the idea of complicating today's spin or tomorrow's headlines. Curriculum theory provides a space where we from our various backgrounds can search for more complete understanding of the intersections between private and public lives for ourselves as well as for our students.

Fourth, we are concerned with issues of social justice, particularly as women who live, work, and theorize in a patriarchal culture. Mindful of the situatedness of our own subjectivities, each of us attempts to confront our own class and identity assumptions as these have affected the way we teach and work and think lest we perpetuate the stances we critique. Proceeding with caution, we search for visions that fall short of grand theories while daring to claim to shed light on the paths we travel as educators—as women. We hope that by raising our voices and speaking personally we can serve as a countering example to the increasingly strident voices and zipzap wizardry of postmodern technology.

Fifth, we seek a different understanding in an age where information is more prized than wisdom. And surely it is wisdom that should be the point of the educational enterprise. There are other ways of thinking about education than the ways currently in fashion that trumpet testing and accountability, forcing us into ever more narrow thinking. We urge attention to smaller matters, not narrow thinking. We urge suchness in the manner of the Zen master who says, "You should therefore cease from practice based on intellectual understanding . . . and learn that backward step that turns your light inwardly to illuminate your self" (in Waldenfels, 129). We hope our readers will find places in the writings that invite reflection, response, and reaction.

ONE

Boundaries

INTRODUCTION

Mary

WE LIVE IN AN increasingly boundary-conscious world, despite this being the next millennium, despite the discourse on otherness and difference, despite the best teaching in the field of curriculum studies to the contrary. Our quagmire in Iraq and in trouble spots around the globe indicates this. We Americans, led by an administration that touts itself as the supreme arbiter of dispute and injustice, commit boundary crossings in order to maintain world supremacy, fight terrorism, and plunder oil fields not within our boundaries. Martha, writing of the history of oppression in Sri Lanka by foreign rule, observes that boundaries are necessary for the colonial enterprise. In order—yes, in Order—I believe the phrase is "to liberate" oppressed people, colonists devise political strategies to justify invasion. The classical liberal idea of "liberation" necessarily carries the boundary baggage: wealthy foreigners go into (preemptively strike) lands afar and disrupt the life patterns of indigenous people. The boundary is between colonizer and colonized, wealthy and (often) poor, third world and first world, them and us—all for noble sounding goals. "In the name of progress and development, boundaries are held in place by ideological markers," Martha observes. Trouble is, rich oil fields or other glittering natural resources are seldom mentioned as the idea behind invasion. If I sound bitter, it is because I am appalled by the headlines—"More soldiers die in Iraq"—that have been the continual mantra since Saddam was toppled.

Boundaries, Delese argues, are ingrained in our systems, especially our medical system, as a management device of "socialization." Early on in their training, medical students are introduced to a little procedure that many of us

5

may not know: the lesson of "the first patient." This is a cadaver—dead flesh—on which students can carve, amputate, and inspect. Students are implicitly trained to think of their patients as metaphoric cadavers. Patients become embalmed Its, objectified by the medical gaze. Further citing the thick boundary that separates doctors from patients, Delese deconstructs the signification of the white coat. Meant to convey sanitation, immunity, and professionalism, the coat literally invests the wearer with title, power, and authority—all the labels of whiteness. I often amuse myself by reimagining the protocol of naming, which goes along with the white coat. Doctor comes into examination room, "Hello, Mary, my name is Dr. Robert Wilson." Patient responds, "Hi there, Rob. My name is Dr. Doll."

In our classrooms, boundaries tend to be strictly enforced, especially for elementary students or cadaver trainees. What this means is that the process of differentiating Them from Us reinforces the stereotypes that prop up gender, class, identity, and power boundaries. Fixed boundaries reify. Classroom architecture abets in this process: even in the art culture, where I teach, the podium occupies a phallic central position, in front of which are chairs neatly lined in rows. What this instantiates, of course, is the false belief that the one who stands knows more, is mightier, deserves obedience from those who sit. One talks, others listen.

My take on boundaries, like that of my collaborators, questions line drawing. I discuss the figures of trickster, fool, jester, and clown in earlier societies, whose function it was to trouble the middle region between borders. Between the standing and the sitting lies a fertile space. This is the territory of greatest potential movement that draws on the very energy of that which it seeks to exclude. Border figures like fools unfix categories and taunt rigidity, the sort that believes we must be carefully taught (as the song goes) to hate the people our grandparents hate. Indeed, in the new millennium there still exist stone-age attitudes, even literal stoning. Something there is that loves a wall. We should be so lucky in today's strife-ridden world to encourage a permeability of boundaries. We should be so lucky to act more knowingly, like fools.

THROUGH THICK AND THIN:
BOUNDARIES IN MEDICINE

Delese

> He longed to soothe her, not with drugs, not with advice, but with simple, kindly words.
> —Chekhov, "A Doctor's Visit" (2003, p. 176)

A border is a margin, edge, brink, rim, brim, or simply the line that separates two things. Some of these boundaries are useful, even necessary, as when a mother says protectively to her child, "Now don't go out into the street," or when a zoning board protects citizens' safety and aesthetic sensibilities by not allowing malls or gas stations within a certain distance from their homes. Sometimes boundaries are drawn to distinguish between health and illness, as in "borderline hypertension," referring to "the dividing point between two separate spaces or anything indicating a limit or confine. It is where one stops and the other begins, or simply the edge, the point at which a defined entity stops" (Sommers-Flanagan, Elliot, & Sommers-Flanagan, 1998, p. 38). When applied to humans rather than physical objects, boundaries take on meanings that have more to do with appropriate and inappropriate expectations and interactions within a relationship; here, the doctor-patient relationship.

Volumes have been written about the boundaries between "the" doctor and patient. I highlight the word "the" because "the" relationship is usually treated as a unitary, nonspecific dyad regardless of the context and uniqueness of both doctor and patient (feeble attempts at cultural differences notwithstanding). Even in the first, nonclinical year of medical school, students are taught about the sacredness and obligations inherent to the doctor-patient relationship, and the dangers that can arise if the relationship is not tethered to the twin gods of objectivity and reason. But like the hyphen in the phrase itself separating doctor and patient, the relationship as conceived by medical educators has everything to do with boundaries, a preoccupation with getting "too close," with maintaining "professional distance" images that conjure up, literally, a kind of invisible but rigidly constructed border or boundary separating the doctor from the person for whom she is providing care.

The composition of these boundaries can be thick, or thin, or a mixture of both. The thickness of our boundaries is part of who we are. The person with thick boundaries is able to focus clearly on one thing, keeping other things at bay. She makes a distinction between thought and feeling, between reality and fantasy, waking and dreaming (Hartmann, 1997). Moreover, a person with thick borders

> has a definite sense of personal space around himself or herself, and tends to have a clear autonomous sense of self, never losing him/herself in a relationship. This person will usually have a very solid sense of group identity and of sexual identity, saying something like: "Men are men, women are women." . . . This person will prefer well-demarcated, hierarchical social structures, and often sees the world in terms of black and white with few shades of gray. (p. 149)

In a word, this is doctors and their boundaried/bounded selves, distinct from their patients, distinct from all others in the health professions. As one of the most penetrating forms of socialization in North American culture, medical education makes those boundaries even more impenetrable regardless of the boundaries students arrive with. As Berger and Luckman wrote almost forty years ago in *The Social Construction of Reality* (1966), the educational/training experience of three professions—the military, the religious life, and medicine—operate as primary socializations. That is, the values, beliefs, world views, and standards inherent to these professions eventually transcend the socialization of initiates' families. Once in, the us (doctors) and them (patients, all other health care professionals, the "laity") boundaries begin to appear.

In medicine it is no accident that dissecting cadavers occurs during the initial weeks of medical training: a well-documented rite of passage that breaks a cultural taboo against cutting human flesh, with the cadaver becoming students' "first patient," one that is utterly compliant, one that makes no demands, one that asks no questions. Diane Roston (1986) recognized what was going on in the anatomy lab when she, a first-year medical student, wrote: "Now student,/to anatomy:/cleave and mark this slab of/thirty-one-year-old caucasion female flesh,/limbs, thorax, cranium, muscle by rigid muscle/dissemble this motorcycle victim's every part/(as if so gray a matter/never wore a flashing ruby dress)" (1986).

Limbs, thorax, cranium, and muscle by rigid muscle are studied for two years, structures found here on slabs but also in texts, slides, and power points separated from living humans. Interaction with patients is limited, and practice is done on actors—"coached" patients as they're called in medicine—so that students learn facile, scripted responses to patients as they are learning to do histories and physicals: fake responses to fake patients. Later during bedside teaching rounds in the third year, students peer down on accommodating "real" patients whose bodies become the object of their inquiry, the props for their teachers, ground zero of the medical gaze. Even as they touch, probe, listen, palpate, cut, and repair, inside and outside bodies, they do so with a growing psychic distance between themselves and patients. No place here for someone who questions what has been established as "good," "normal," and "natural." These are labels at the core of medical reasoning.

But as part of the professional initiation into a doctorly identity, U.S. medical students are seduced into believing that if they get too "close" to a patient (what does this mean? interested in? disclosing personal information to? suffering with?), their judgment might falter as the required "clinical distance" between doctor and patient is compromised. In addition, if they become too close to their patients, their personal lives will suffer as they become workaholics who bring their psychic "work" home with them. Moreover, by the time students begin to see patients during their third year of medical school, patients have become part of the vast mass of humanity known as "the laity"; that is, there are doctors, and there are all others.

Medicine, as it is enacted in the United States, is grounded in paternalism, a positioning that requires boundaried hierarchies. Such paternalism is enacted in astonishing overt ways in clinical settings where many clinical faculty still locate themselves and convey this to students as the ones who know, patients as the ones who do not know and the ones who do not need to know. Anatole Broyard, the *New York Times Book Review* editor who chronicled his own dying in a series of essays, had trouble with these boundaries and spent much time dissecting the doctor's persona, watching the relationship unfold with his critic's eye. "I think," he wrote in "The Patient Examines the Doctor" (1992),

> that the doctor can keep his technical posture and still move into the human arena. The doctor can use his science as a kind of poetic vocabulary instead of using it as a piece of machinery. . . . I see no reason why he has to stop being a doctor and become an amateur human being. Yet many doctors systematically avoid contact. I don't expect my doctor to sound like Oliver Sacks, but I do expect some willingness to make contact, some suggestion of availability. (p. 44)

Broyard offers an astonishing (for doctors, anyway) suggestion regarding boundaries and the necessity of keeping them rigid. Instead of distancing themselves from suffering as a protective move, Broyard suggests that doctors need to "save" themselves and can do so by "dissecting the cadaver of their professional persona." That is, the doctor

> must see that his silence and neutrality are unnatural. It may be necessary to give up some of his authority in exchange for his humanity, but as the old family doctors knew, this is not a bad bargain. In learning to talk to his patients, the doctor may talk himself back into loving his work. He has little to lose and everything to gain by letting the sick man into his heart. If he does, they can share, as few others can, the wonder, terror, and exaltation of being on the edge of being, between the natural and the supernatural. (p. 57)

Abraham Verghese, a doctor, writer, and reflective observer of the profession, similarly wonders at these emotional boundaries that are constructed during training, particularly the fact that while patients are encouraged to express their most intimate selves to doctors, doctors are socialized to hide their feelings behind their title, power, and authority. "Despite all our grand societies, memberships, fellowships, specialty colleges, each with its annual dues and certificates and ceremonials," he writes, "we are horribly alone." He continues:

> The doctor's world is one where our own feelings, particularly those of pain and hurt are not easily expressed. . . . We trust our colleagues, we show propriety and reciprocity, we have the scientific knowledge, we learn empathy, but we rarely expose our own emotions. There is a silent but terrible collusion to cover up pain, to cover up depression; there is a fear of blushing, a

machismo that destroys us. The Citadel quality to medical training, where only the fittest survive, creates the paradox of the humane, empathetic physician . . . who shows little humanity to himself. The profession is full of "dry drunks," physicians who use titles, power, prestige, and money . . . physicians who are more comfortable with their work identity than with real intimacy. . . . It is not individual physicians who are at fault as much as it is the system we have created. (Verghese, p. 341)

Of course, boundaries in medicine have to do not just with liminal space, but with the physical space between doctors and patients. The white coat worn by doctors in most clinical settings represents, literally, a boundary between themselves and their patients. First conceived with the concept of aseptic surgery, which originated in the United States around 1889, the white coat's purpose was to protect doctor and patient from cross-contamination. In subsequent years, white coats gave doctors the appearance of scientists, which in the United States validates the practice of medicine. Later, when patients were moved from home to hospitals for care, whiteness became associated with medical institutions. Couple those with Western cultural meanings associated with whiteness life, purity, innocence, superhuman power, goodness, and it is easy to see how the white coat became the favored garment for doctors. All over the United States as medical schools welcome entering classes, white-coat ceremonies are enacted when senior students or faculty give neophytes a white coat, initiating them into the profession. The so-called white-coat ceremony is intended to impress upon medical students the importance of compassion and humility in the midst of the high-tech, bottom-line-oriented practice of today's medicine.

What we don't impress upon students during such ceremonies is that the white coat also marks boundaries, symbolizing caregiving hierarchies and spheres of practice, the social and economic privilege of doctors, and medicine's well-established practices (not unlike those of the law or the priesthood) in determining membership in the profession. What we don't impress upon students is that the white coat is only an article of clothing, and that their bodies underneath are as complicated, variable, and imperfect as the bodies they'll be caring for. To link a white coat to a mythologic, Welbyized image of a physician who is always decisive, who is "immune" to variations in economic and social status, race, ethnicity, national origins, and sexual desire; to differences in body type, size, appearance, and hygiene; and to variations in family structure, religion, occupation, political beliefs, and moral life sets students up not just for failure but also for guilt, cynicism, and denial when the ideal fails to materialize (Wear, 1998).

In fact, wearing a white coat, the occupational clothing of a prestigious group with substantial power over human lives, may actually promote thick boundaries between doctors and patients rather than the opposite. Doctors may become the coat, sometimes keenly aware of and sometimes unconscious of the way persons respond to them with deference, respect, shyness, self-consciousness, or even silence. A medical student, upon donning the occupational clothing of her profession, quickly recognizes that it establishes her "right to a given status without her need to prove herself" (Joseph, 1986).

But if the white coat represents a boundary between doctor and patient in a face-to-face interaction, the boundaries between clinical and nonclinical settings represent something even more impenetrable. Hospitals, clinics, and doctors' offices are fortresses; they constitute medical turf. Patients are allowed in at regularly scheduled intervals, to interact with doctors, using protocols determined by doctors, answering questions determined relevant by doctors, and in general acting and responding in ways determined appropriate by doctors. In addition, patients are vulnerable because of what ails them; they are their illnesses and symptoms. Never mind their lives outside the fortress; Proust said that his doctor did not take into account the fact that he had read Shakespeare (Broyard, p. 47). That is, the boundaries between doctors and patients are multiple, separating doctors and all others by doctors' real and perceived power, knowledge, social class, and status.

What does a doctor with thin boundaries look like? John Stone (1980) shows us in a poem. The narrative voice is a doctor at the home of one of his former (maybe current) patients, we don't know. What we do know is that six or seven years before, he had performed surgery on her heart, a valve replacement or some such thing. Today he is visiting her—is it a house call, or is he just stopping by to say hey? Whatever the reason, protocols and hierarchies and power differentials change: "Here, you are in charge," he thinks.

He Makes a House Call

Six, seven years ago
when you began to begin to faint
I painted your leg with iodine

threaded the artery
with the needle and then the tube
pumped your heart with dye enough

to see the valve
almost closed with stone.
We were both under pressure.

Today, in your garden,
kneeling under the sticky fig tree
for tomatoes

I keep remembering your blood.
Seven, it was. I was just beginning to learn the heart

inside out.
Afterward, your surgery
and the precise valve of steel

and plastic that still pops and clicks
inside like a ping-pong ball.
I should try

chewing tobacco sometimes
if only to see how it tastes.
There is a trace of it at the corner

of your leathery smile
which insists that I see inside
the house: someone named Bill I'm supposed

to know; the royal plastic soldier
whose body fills with whiskey
and marches on a music box

How Dry I Am;
the illuminated 3-D Christ who turns
into Mary from different angles;

the watery basement,
the pills you take, the ivy
that may grow around the ceiling

if it must. Here, you are in charge of figs, beans,
tomatoes, life.

At the hospital, a thousand times
I have heard your heart valve open, close.
I know how clumsy it is.

But health is whatever works
and for as long. I keep thinking
of seven years without a faint

on my way to the car
loaded with vegetables
I keep thinking of seven years ago

when you bled in my hands like a saint.

Let us praise the opportunity for patients to "be in charge"; let us praise caregivers with thin boundaries!

BOUNDARY LESSNESS

Mary

In the film *A Beautiful Mind* the John Nash character, played by Russell Crowe, gives an incredibly real performance of a man's belief that he can decode enemy messages and the secret meanings of numbers so as to save the world. A mathematical genius, Nash studied patterns in nature. His genius extended beyond the boundary of normal perception; he saw what mere mortals did not. That, in any case, was the outward Nash, whose slip into madness didn't seem mad at all. At first. Gradually, we learn that the formulae he scratches on windows and on pieces of paper all over his study walls are not normal. Nash is schizophrenic.

What Sylvia Nasar, author of the biography of John Forbes Nash, Jr., tells us is that the disease, schizophrenia, is misunderstood. It can be a "ratiocinating illness" that allows for a "heightened awareness, insomniac wakefulness and watchfulness" not overt disorientation or confusion (1998, p. 18). Because of seeming rational explanations by a patient, the disease is not easily discernible. But eventually, the boundary between sanity and madness dissolves: "His longstanding conviction that the universe was rational evolved into a caricature of itself, turning into an unshakable belief that everything had meaning, every thing had a reason, nothing was random or coincidental" (Nasar, p. 19). Nash had no defense against the onslaught of the alien voices in his head. Even the viewer of the film is sucked into the voices and connivinces, believing them to be true. The condition is that of a swamped and invaded ego, one of the dangers threatening the psyche when the ego has no firm boundary to separate it from the dynamic energy of the unconscious (Harding, 1963, p. 230).

Edgar Allan Poe's characters come to mind in this regard. Their skill at ratiocination is such that they can explain away their repressions, until the "return of the repressed" causes disintegration of the ego. Poe's frequent use of the fallen house as metaphor for the self demonstrates an early, pre-Freudian understanding that the house of the self collapses when the ego's wall crumbles to the demands of the id. Another example of the loss of ego control, this time to the demands of the super ego, is seen in Katherine Mansfield's story, "The Daughters of the Late Colonel." Two sisters, maiden ladies, are indistinguishable one from the other, having been suffocated all their lives by an overbearing father, the late colonel. Mansfield suggests that without the protection of an ego able to discern difference and erect boundaries, the result is the preemption of the center of consciousness. Only when the old man has died do the sisters begin to experience a sort of life on their own terms. But their experience is faltering, their behavior childish, and their imaginations stunted by years of obedience to an outside force so powerful as to snuff out the daughters' individuality. The two are glomed into each other's self so much that they even fantasize in the same manner and complete each other's half sentences.

An opposite problem of psychic boundaries too directed by id or super ego is that of the ego boundary too absolute. Samuel Taylor Coleridge uses the metaphor of a walled-in garden to give expression to this idea of the hermetically sealed ego. In his "Kubla Khan" a picture is given of an emperor who erects a pleasure dome among "enfolding spots of greenery" through which runs a sacred river. We can interpret the river as the life force itself. But unless the sacred river is connected to the larger cosmic ocean, the spirit will die—or, in Coleridge's symbology, will become a cave of ice. When the ego hardens, the boundary around it is so rigid that access to life-giving forces is blocked. Similarly, Jack London's arctic tundra suggests a landscape frozen off from the springs beneath it. London's world rebels against the romance of nature. In "To Build a Fire," the unnamed man believes too much in the power of his mind and too little in the power of the wild. The latter, with its deep spring buried below, causes the freezing death of one who lacks imagination. Too, in her classic *The Yellow Wallpaper*, Charlotte Perkins Gilman shows that the wife's postpartum depression is worsened when she is cut off from the outside world. The situation is that of virtual imprisonment—inside her ego, inside her room. The wallpaper, with its bars and smooches, becomes a metaphor of the imprisoned woman closed off from sanity and closed inside her own increasing psychosis. Her dominating, overly "kind" doctor-husband exacerbates the problem by sedating her, denying her social intercourse, keeping her in an attic room with a nailed-down bed, and forbidding her access to journal writing. This "mad woman in the attic" has no recourse to defenses of any kind. But in an amusing feminist twist, Gilman suggests that the wife's madness is actually the beginning of escape, since she is able, finally, to see her husband not as an overly kind man but, simply, as "that" man—like any other impediment to autonomy. Similarly, she is able to see, in the phantom woman behind the bars in the yellow wallpaper, a replica of herself as a prisoner.

The above examples reveal a two-fold nature of psychic boundaries in Western culture: either the boundary is not well established, in which case the ego is invaded; or the boundary is too well established, in which case the ego is insulated. The idea of the boundary in archaic societies was seen as a magical defense against chaos. Well before the advent of ego psychology, early cultures thought of boundaries as physical necessities for safe social functioning. Anything foreign was regarded as an enemy that required warding off by clear delineations like moats, walls, ditches, labyrinths, or stones. Mircea Eliade summarizes traditional ideas about these matters:

> In archaic and traditional societies, the surrounding world is conceived as a microcosm. At the limits of this closed world begins the domain of the

unknown, of the formless. On this side there is ordered . . . space; on the other, outside the familiar space, there is the unknown and dangerous region of the demons, the ghosts, the dead and of foreigners. (1961, p. 37)

What to the primal mind was the threat of formlessness is to the modern mind the invasion by the unconscious—each threat of sufficient danger to require the erection of a boundary: either literally or psychically.

Now, I ask what would it be to think differently about boundaries? Myths, for instance, configure boundaries differently. They are completely permeable, allowing for easy passage to and fro. Recall the way Greek gods and goddesses on Mount Olympus frequently mingled in human affairs. Zeus was forever assuming disguises so as to seduce human maidens. Ulysses gained access to the Underworld. Psyche, a mortal, ascends to the gods' domain, Mount Olympus, upon completion of her nonmortal tasks. As Edith Hamilton describes the miracle of Greek mythology, it is a "humanized world, men freed from the paralyzing fear of an omnipotent Unknown. . . . The terrifying irrational has no place in classical mythology" (1942, pp. 9, 10). In Navajo myths, a truly cooperative community of humans and gods ensured that each fulfilled and completed the other. Far from irrationalizing the other, mythic understanding welcomes a mingling energy.

The Navajo Emergence Myth (n.d. Centerpoint) is case in this transgressive point. Pot Carrier, along with eight ants and beetles, exists in the dark underworld seen as a house of four chambers. Moving from the first to the second chamber, he discovers that he has forgotten his pots, so he must go back down to retrieve them. The myth tells of other incidents of confusion and disorder before the house of the self can be constructed: there is much moving about, restlessness, hithering and thithering. The notion of boundaries is nonexistent. Instead, selfhood is achieved by moving beyond the confines and engaging with foreignness.

Border figures, like clowns, tricksters, tramps, and fools, also show a disregard for boundaries, since boundaries ring off chaos from order and flatten out the world. In fact, it is the bringing of chaos into order, disturbing the status quo, that delights these figures. Jamake Highwater (1981) comments that the extraordinary is regarded by Native Americans as gifted and sacred. The clown performs a spiritual ceremony with his foolishness because of his intuition of another reality (p. 175). Similarly, Paul Radin's (1956) research on the trickster figure reveals its disdain for boundaries. Adding disorder to order provides an experience of what is not permitted, expanding the idea of wholeness. Tricksters, clowns, and fools reaffirm their vital connection with boundaries, making boundaries themselves subject to vitality. By so doing, these figures invert assumed beliefs, showing the utter arbitrariness of established value systems (Willeford, 1969, p. 136).

One of these assumed values is the idea of a fixed identity, boundaried we might say. Someone once wittily remarked that her multiple personalities gave her access to "the party within." Exactly. Today I am studious; tomorrow, silly; this moment I am happy; the next, sad. And what I was like forty years ago has absolutely no meaning for what I am like today! Another of these assumptions is that reality and rationalism go together. John Nash's wry comment is appropriate here. In his Nobel autobiography he wrote about the two worlds he occupied. On the boundary of both, he remarked: "rational thought imposes a limit on a person's concept of his relation to the cosmos" (in Nasar, p. 295).

A very different idea of boundaries is seen not only in myth but in ancient Eastern thought and modern Buddhism. What early Western societies thought of as threat, this other strand of thinking envisions as opportunity. The unknown is not regarded as enemy but as energy, not as witchcraft but as wisdom. Ego is a hindrance to the embrace of the unknown, and so ego must dissolve into the river of cosmic consciousness. Laotzu expresses this idea, so foreign to Western ears: "A man at his best, like water, / Serves as he goes along" (in Bynner, 1980, p. 29). Romantic poets like Coleridge image water as that which cannot be contained; its flow erases boundaries. To Western thinking, boundarylessness creates confusion, if not disease. But con-fusion, like dis-ease, brings things together and calls into question the very nature of objects, people, and the world as understood by the discriminating mind. Labels, like boundaries, limit understanding; fusions, like water, expand.

In my younger years I lived by boundaries. I took my gender training seriously and behaved like the lady I was supposed to be. I smiled, crossed my legs, married, and produced progeny. I joined clubs, held office, took notes. I was praised for my good efforts and told never to change. But change I did and cross boundaries I did. I am now in a relationship with a woman twenty-two years younger than I. People find this unsettling. What can we possibly have in common? But if you know Marla, you know she has an old soul. And what does age have to do with it, anyway? I eschew labels for they diminish my personhood, shrink me into a convenience that others can understand. There is nothing convenient to understand about my life change. Yes: confusion calls into question the nature of things. And people. If boundaries are crossed, confusions arise. So be it. One of the basic functions of the fool, trickster, and clown is to question labels, even those basic ones like "good," "normal," and "natural." These are, really, wash-out ideas that need to be flushed down the drain.

I would like to end by referencing Jamaica Kincaid, one of the most boundary-crossing writers I have encountered in my recent reading. Frankly, she confuses me; that is why I read her. All of her major work revolves around her mother: just as her life unfolds, she enfolds her mother's life. What I think I see her doing is attempting to separate herself from her mother's powerful influence—an ego-strengthening program. But as she attempts to do this, she is also, at the same time, emptying out her ego in a Buddhist move to become egoless, boundaryless, and so to engage not her literal mother but the cosmic mother. This process is described in her book "At the Bottom of the River," a title that suggests a sense of de-evolving along with the water creatures so as to acquire a fluid consciousness. Consider this remarkable passage:

> I stood up on the edge of the basin and felt myself move. But what self? For I had no feet, or hands, or head, or heart. It was as if those things—my feet, my hands, my head, my heart—having once been there, were now stripped away, as if I had been dipped again and again, over and over, in a large vat filled with some precious elements and were not reduced to something I yet had no name for. I had no name for the thing I had become, so new was it to me, except that I did not exist in pain or pleasure, east or west or north or south or up or down, or past or present or future, or real or not real. (1992, p. 80)

How close this merging of all things is to the Buddhist notion of emptying out so as to be present to the suchness of things in the entire cosmos! Emptying the willing mind, the ego, allows one to be open to the transmission of energies, the currents beneath the mainstream. In the flow of things, there are no names or labels, no categories, no boundaries. Formlessness for Laotze is unending motherhood, the way of life (in Bynner, 40). The thought might terrify. The thought might en-trance. The thought might stretch the boundary.

RE-VISIONING BOUNDARIES

Martha

Children need boundaries, I tell my preservice teachers. Emotional safety. The sense that someone is in charge. And, of course, this is true in a classroom of thirty young students. Create the boundaries together, I tell them. Engage students in the process because it is the right thing to do, because they do have rights, and because it prepares them for effective participation in the democratic process. After class I call myself on the carpet. How could I have discussed this with students without troubling the idea that boundaries operate all around us in oppressive ways? I revisit the idea of boundaries myself so that I can examine it with my students in ways that will allow us to work together to push back the boundaries of our understanding. I fear this must be handled with care, for boundaries are often dangerous places.

In the classroom, boundaries are typically defined and enforced by the teacher. Little or no input from the students needed. Top-down directives. The metaphorical is almost visible: Do not cross this line. It's this way in the world beyond the classroom, too. Look historically at any country where capitalism has woven its way into the social and economic order and watch a new boundary develop predictably. Private and public become separate spheres

(Nicholson, 1980) and the shared work of subsistence existence is restructured in increasingly dramatic ways. Someone (male) begins to seek work on the land of another. Someone else (female) must stay at home, tend the garden, the household, and the children. Housewife/Breadwinner. Ideology in support of the economic winners. The boundary between the private and the public sphere—invisible and taken-for-granted. Whether work is carried out on one side or the other has tangible results for the worker. Sparks fly if you suggest this presumably immutable boundary of gender is a continuum, is fluid. To intimate that a person's location on one side or the other is culturally constructed, externally determined—sacrilege! Political and economic forces and ideological constructs are always at work shifting boundaries in ways that shape lives and labor to promote and eventually maintain the social relations preferred by the economically privileged.

Boundaries abound. All forms of "ethnic difference" (nonwhiteness) lie on one side of the boundary. Who drew this line? There is the boundary between those who have a home and those who are homeless. Shelter-dwellers and refugees in the United States, Afghanistan, Rwanda, Palestine. The words of cultural critique flow easily when speaking about rigid, oppressive boundaries, but look historically and see that, over time, the shifting of these boundaries has been subtle and elusive. And it could be that it is in this subtle and elusive shifting that the power is held fast. I need to track them down, examine their movement across time in a particular place. Can I invite my students to identify how ideological conceptions, signs, if you will, have been pressed into the service of those who have a vested interest in the location and movement of boundaries? Power, Foucault (1982) reminds us, circulates. To think of it as fixed and easily identified and acknowledged is to miss the boat.

Monarchies and warlords wielded their power straightforwardly. The divine right of kings was flaunted, not hidden. Boundaries were clear. Peasants struggled, regardless of gender. Royalty lived, well, like royalty—whether they were kings or queens. When lands were colonized, no one had to guess who held the power. But with the advent of colonization, as Western society claimed "enlightenment," a new set of classical liberal ideals were touted as egalitarian and liberating. Political methodology merged with academic interests and, eventually, business, until a network of power circulated in less clearly identifiable ways. Boundaries, while still rigid, blurred into the background as ideology shaped the modern subject, white and "other," male and female, meritorious and derelict. To trace the intrusion and expansion of Western ways in a particular place may shed light on how shifting boundaries operate oppressively. Perhaps there will be connections between disenfranchisement within that specific location and the marginalization of various subjectivities in other settings where people deploy discourse (Foucault, 1980) in both oppressive and empowering ways.

*Revisiting the Boundary between Private
and Public in Sri Lanka: A Cautionary Tale*

To suggest there was an idyllic time of equity and peace in any culture is suspect. Sri Lanka provides a case in point. There have always been contentious
divisions between groups of people in Sinhala (early Sri Lanka) and from the
early centuries of the millennium until the 1600s, the struggle for power and
control was obvious.

> From the late third century AD to the middle of the twelfth century, Sin-
> hala was dominated by Tamil kings and by a succession of invaders from
> southern India. Native princes regained power briefly in the late twelfth cen-
> tury and again in the thirteenth century. From 1408 to 1438 Chinese forces
> occupied the island of Sinhala, which had been partitioned into a number of
> petty kingdoms. (Sri Lanka/Encarta, 2001)

Today the population of Sri Lanka is approximately 19.5 million. About 74
percent of the population of Sri Lanka is Sinhalese, 18 percent are Sri Lankan
Tamils and Indian Tamils, and the remaining are descendants of Moors
(Arabs), Burghers (Dutch), Malays, and Veddas (Sri Lanka/Encarta).

The Sinhalese and Tamils are two distinct nations which have inhabited
this "teardrop island" south of India for more than two thousand years. Conflict between these two nations, although present across time, has gradually
escalated since the British granted independence to the country, then called
Ceylon, in 1948. This political clash has ranged from struggle over legislating
a national language to violent rioting and police action which began in the late
1970s and rose to tragic, genocidal proportions by 1984 when more than five
hundred Tamils were killed in anti-Tamil riots, and Tamils in the south and
on plantations fled to the north (Ponnambalam, 1983). Centuries of colonial
disregard for humanity and environment left the people and the land with little to work with. When the damage had been done, the final in a series of
"mother countries" left the scene—pulled back her boundaries.

Today, civil war rages between the Liberation Tigers of Tamil Eelam and
the current Sinhalese-dominated government. Child conscription is escalating
among the Tamils and thousands of people are among the "disappeared" (Jayasinghe, 2002). This island environment, devastated by centuries of rapacious colonization, is unable to provide enough work for the economy to remain viable.
First men and now women have been forced to outsource their labor to gulf
countries for low and undependable wages (Joseph, 1998). The devastation and
death toll resulting from the recent December 2004 tsunami disaster seems
especially cruel in the face of the tenuous conditions of the land and the people.

Amid this extreme social turmoil, can any conclusions be drawn about the
significance of boundaries in our everyday lives? Can we understand, in some

small way, how power has circulated and influenced the material circumstances of the people of Sri Lanka as labor patterns created and recreated
social relations? Learn about how power operates in discursive ways (Foucault,
1980)? Can revisiting the shifting boundary between the public and the private spheres in Sri Lanka help me understand the marginalization according
to ethnicity, gender, sexual preference, and socioeconomic status that exists in
other contexts? Will it allow me to revision boundaries, understand ideological constructs and political strategies more clearly, and reorganize my orientation to boundaries in empowering ways? The journey through time begins.

Kinship and Labor in Early Sri Lanka

While definitive evidence concerning kinship and labor patterns in prefeudal
Sri Lanka is unavailable, some scholars have speculated that binna marriage,
in which the daughter and her husband live in her parents' household, might
be an extension of an earlier matriarchal system of property ownership and
descent. Early foreign travelers all noted the fact that women often had more
than one husband. This polyandry "bears similarity to the system of matri-
archy of the Nayars of South India, some of whom migrated to Sri Lanka in
ancient times" (Grossholtz, 1984).

    What of boundaries in this long time past? Determining which labor pat-
terns during these early times were "private" and which were "public" is difficult. Being viewed as in control of reproductive contributions to the society
(giving birth, gathering food and water, and eventually planting and harvest-
ing) might have given women's labor honor and standing in the community
that is unlike our modern day conceptions. In addition to lineage being traced
through women, their reproductive rights included polyandry and looseness of
the marriage norm (Mies, 1986). Hunting forays and war between kinship
groups were part of men's contribution to the group. While men and women's
labor may have been valued differently, we have no reason to believe one sort
of contribution dominated another. Rigid definitions of public and private
were unnecessary.

    How often I think of feminism and collaborative gender relationships as
a modern idea. I often assume that prior to Mary Wollstonecraft society had-
n't even conceived of such noble ideals as equitable levels of respect and power
for all members of society. Relatively new forays into archeology and anthropology tell another tale (Eisler, 1987). Ancient Sri Lanka was likely a more
hospitable culture for women than the United States in the nineteenth century. And so I wonder, how can I speak to my students of racism, sexism,
homophobia, and economic oppression in ways that remind them that these
discriminatory beliefs and practices have been exacerbated, not quelled, by the
many "advancements" of our modern, technological society? Romanticizing
the distant past is pointless, but noticing that long ago there was an absence

of boundaries in the allocation of daily work, and attempting a response that connects us with the past, may matter.

I want my students to understand the connections between who labors in what ways: When they are teachers, will they make the decisions about the labor force of the classroom? Old habits die hard. Teachers do the creative work, the thinking, the organizing, the planning. Students reproduce information—their preferences, interests, ability to choose, lie dormant, perhaps atrophying. In an equitable, viable community, work is shared and boundaries blur. Behavioral boundaries? One wonders if they do not emerge from the value of shared daily experience. Adults who respect the wisdom of children and who have important information and skills to share with them receive respect without a word. Guidelines are negotiated, agreed upon, for the good of the community. Shared labor blurs boundaries and role definitions and structures a more equitable environment.

Feudal Sri Lanka

During early feudal times, a system of communal use of lands defined the living patterns of the people of Sri Lanka. Villages were likely self-sufficient, a system of public plots: one for paddy growing, one for house and vegetable gardening, and one for alternating agriculture. This village pattern persisted into the twentieth century in some of the isolated areas of north central Sri Lanka, and the essentials of this social and economic system were little disturbed by the advent of kingships (Grossholtz, 1984). The allocation of land from the king came with a requirement of service. This meant that each citizen contributed to the construction of the water supply (an elaborate and sophisticated irrigation system) and the maintenance of roads and temples.

Kinship patterns remained oriented to the village, each consisting of paddy land and house lots with vegetable gardens and the right to use forest lands for chena cultivation. Chena land consisted of forest plots which families cleared and used to grow fruits, vegetables, or other crops for three or four years. After this time the land would be allowed to rest for approximately seven years. Ancestral lands were passed from generation to generation. Families worked together to cultivate the land. The labor of women and, during peak seasons, children was vital. Kurakkan (finger millet) was the principal food crop of the chena. Women were responsible for the labor-intensive work of reaping this nutritional crop that could be stored for up to ten years. Paddy cultivation which was predominantly handled by men was less reliable due to its dependence on sufficient rainfall. Still, everyone's labor was needed to reap daily food from the soil and, we might expect, everyone's labor was valued. "Cultivation rights were available to everyone; society was communal in nature and organized to benefit and care for all its members" (Grossholtz, 1984).

Where land remains plentiful and its careful use is maintained by communities who have a vested interest in its yield, social structures are not subjected to the sort of strain that leads to extremely inequitable reordering of social relations. Certainly there were boundaries between royalty and peasants, but within the communities themselves remnants of earlier days of subsistence living persisted.

Nevertheless, a boundary began to emerge between the private, close-to-home activities (reproduction and care of the family members) and the public sphere which acknowledged the right to use certain land. Decreasing availability of land for cultivation, combined with a stronger presence of religious patriarchal ideology, led to an increase in the need to control women's sexuality. Women's lives became increasingly restricted and descent was traced through male lineage. Economic necessity, however, kept these restrictions from limiting women's involvement in cultivating the land. While a sexual division of labor existed, women still had considerable control over the efforts to supply their family's subsistence needs. Women's labor remained an essential part of the sphere that was beginning to be defined as public (away from home).

Concerns for property rights and the male domination of religious experience in the United States have influenced our perceptions of whose work matters and whose voice should be heard. When I consider the gradual erosion of women's rights in Sri Lanka in the distant feudal era, can I feel a kinship with women no longer with us? Women's lives, then and now, began to be reshaped by ideological perceptions that privilege male inheritance and facilitate collaboration among religious, political, and business interests.

How are the expectations and discourse of classrooms today shaped by these subtle notions of whose labor is acknowledged and whose is marginalized? What gender-laden traditions are reflected in the messages about gender-appropriate school and life experiences? Boys line up here, girls there. The difference matters, obviously. I need some boys to help me carry the tables down to the auditorium. Will you girls wipe up the sink area? We have fire-*men* visiting the school today. I need a helper to befriend our new student— Sarah, you're so good at helping. . . . And so the labor is divided in subtle ways and the public/private boundary finds its way into the classroom. School is not the equitably accessible bridge from the private to the public sphere that we often imagine. It is, in fact, a place where implicit lessons are learned about boundaries and one's place on either side of the divide. Virginia Woolf's warnings about dangerous bridge-crossing that requires us to embrace the very values and beliefs that constrict lives ring in my ears (Woolf, 1938). Boundaries do create security—but for whom?

Western Intrusion: Portuguese and Dutch Colonization

Marco Polo said it well: ". . . in good sooth the best island of its size in the world." Sri Lanka's beauty and bounty, however, were endangered. The early

Westernization of Asia marked the beginning of the end of the legendary spice trade that brought the Portuguese to the coast of Sri Lanka in 1505. For one hundred and fifty years the Portuguese carried on a brutal assault on the Sinhalese in an attempt to control the island and its resources and to locate fortresses for international military purposes in the harbor of Sri Lanka.

During the time of the Portuguese occupation of Sri Lanka, subtle changes in labor occurred. Products of the island were collected and shipped to Europe and the Portuguese officials collected land taxes, death duties, and revenues from the sale of exports. Resources were manipulated (i.e., the burning of cinnamon) in such a way that Sri Lankans had to sell their labor as a minimally paid commodity. The boundary between public and private shifted as Sri Lanka's trade market was dismantled through the mismanagement of resources and a brutal unwillingness to consider the history and the culture of the people of the island (Grossholtz, 1984). This, coupled with internal disruptions, violence, and the deterioration of the tank irrigation system for paddy rice cultivation, left the native people impoverished and vulnerable.

Ironically, the Sri Lankans believed the Dutch promises to rid them of the dreadful woes that had accompanied the Portuguese occupation. From 1640 until 1796 the Dutch pressed the Sri Lankan's economic and political circumstances into further ruin. The Dutch claimed the king's right to all the land but took none of the king's obligations to provide land and the right to labor. Laboring conditions in the public sphere, increasingly separate from the private, deteriorated to the point of becoming intolerable. The Dutch continued and elaborated the Portuguese practice of forcing the cinnamon peelers to work for pay. The colonizer's counterpart to the king's required service became full-time labor, even forced labor without pay in labor camps. The caste of cinnamon peelers, called chalia, were compelled to work in these camps. They resisted in various ways. Some fled to the interior of the island (Kandy) while others resorted to marrying their children to nonchalia caste persons. Famines swept the land periodically and because the internal economy had been crushed, whole families sold themselves into slavery. Western views of gender resulted in men and women being included differently in these new international schemes. Women were expected to work as unpaid or poorly paid appendages to male laborers. Family and village boundaries, informal yet indicative of safe haven, dissipated as the best option for survival could sometimes be found away from kin. Meanwhile, the Dutch East India Company realized a typical profit of 80 percent on their investments in Sri Lanka. Grossholtz (1984) refers to "an arbitrary theft of the goods and labor of Sri Lanka."

Rape and pillage come to mind. Removal of dignity. Impregnation of an alien and hostile way of life. In a way never before imagined, family ties were replaced by connections with strangers for the sake of survival. The harmony of an earlier time—communal use of the land, shared goals, the expectation of social responsibility, shared wisdom from intergenerational ties—was disrupted. Boundaries become rigid when the goals of those who hold the power undermined timeless values. Boundaries established with violence force the question, Why the boundaries in our schools? Between the school and the world? Between classrooms? Between administration, teachers, and students? Between students? Boundaries abound. Grade levels, ability groups, enclosed rooms, narrow and prescribed curriculum all create increasingly rigid boundaries. For whose good?

The Extreme End of Colonial Sri Lanka: British Rule

In 1796, the British began what was to be the capstone of colonization, the true beginning of the country's conversion to capitalism. They governed Sri Lanka until 1947, their rule coinciding temporally with the industrial revolution in Europe. England needed raw materials for British industry, markets where they could sell their manufactured goods, and an outlet for capital created by their domestic wage labor. Their plans for their colonies were even more expansive than those of the Portuguese or Dutch. No longer affecting changes on existing trade patterns or concentrating their efforts only on the island's periphery, they penetrated the central regions, eventually claiming rights to all land and labor.

The imposition of the plantation economy dealt a final blow to the village structure of Sri Lanka. Roads were built and the land was sold without regard to traditional uses and economic patterns. The labor of the native people was appropriated for the building of roads that eventually brought an end to what had been the isolated location of the Kandyan resistance in the central region of the island. Life in these regions had been ravaged during the Portuguese and Dutch rule by the destruction of the local economy and the obliteration of the irrigation system. The people were impoverished. With no understanding of their complicity in the difficulties these Native Sri Lankan's faced daily, the British justified the use of Sinhalese and Tamil forced labor by critiquing their unwillingness to participate in British development as "indolence" (Grossholtz, 1984).

The roads built throughout the country enabled plantation owners to travel and send goods back and forth as needed for their production purposes. The first plantations were dedicated to the production of coffee. Particularly brutalizing to the village system was the Crown Lands Ordinance (1840): "All forest, waste, or uncultivated land was to be presumed to be the property of the Crown until contrary is proven." All chena areas were now the property of the Crown. Land in the Kandyan highlands was the first to be sold and virtually all of it was sold to foreigners, who could purchase up to four thousand acres of land, tax free for five years. Land sales to indigenous persons were restricted to one hundred acres. Eventually, the villages were partitioned and sold, including chena land. The transfer of land rights from native to foreign lands and the reconceptualization of labor and land use was complete.

Native Sri Lankans now sold their labor as their only resource available to them. Still, they resisted these new forms of labor. Aware that their land had been confiscated under a spurious rationale, they were nevertheless pushed to work in exploitative jobs on the coffee, tea, and rubber plantations, roads and water systems that offered little hope, despite the rhetoric of colonizers.

Boundaries between the wealthy colonizer and the indigenous people of Sri Lanka were never more clear. The depth of division between these two groups became the defining dynamic of life. Just as the homeless on U.S. streets are deemed lazy—unwilling to work hard enough to remedy their situation—the resistant behavior of Sri Lankan laborers was mistaken for lack of initiative. The boundary between public and private worlds still existed but the most salient boundary was the boundary between colonizer and colonized. When the British withdrew and Sri Lanka became independent, social relations of the people of the island that had startled Marco Polo with its beauty and bounty were in such a state of chaos that social turmoil has marked Sri Lankan life. The outsourcing of the labor of indigenous people has become commonplace, though fraught with exploitative and abusive practices. Assisted by the boundary adjustments, powerful colonizers took what they chose from a land and a people they never understood.

What shall I tell my teacher education students about boundaries? The glib teacher lore is beginning to pale as I consider the importance of crossing boundaries, erasing boundaries, standing against boundaries. Can I reinstate the relationships that diminish the need for boundaries—intergenerational community, social responsibility, common goals, respect for the environment? What boundaries do I draw each day? At what cost? Draw a boundary between schools that succeed and those that fail, between students who "make it" and those who don't? Accountability becomes the watchword. And how do our perceptions of who's making it and who isn't, create boundaries within the walls of individual classrooms?

Boundaries Revisited

What if our students thought differently about boundaries? What if we thought deeply together about privilege and poverty as we discuss classroom communities? What lessons might we learn? Dewey (1938) reminds us:

> The institutions and customs that exist in the present and that give rise to present social ills and dislocations did not arise overnight. They have a long history behind them. Attempts to deal with them simply on the basis of what is obvious in the present is bound to result in the adoption of superficial measures which will only render existing problems more acute and more difficult to solve. (p. 77)

I want to invite my students to dredge a little deeper with me as we think of their opportunities to be cultural workers. Learn from Sri Lankan and other boundary stories and think seriously about boundaries in our communities and classrooms. Can I make explicit what has been part of the null curriculum? Can I infuse important yet ignored learning into our daily schoolwork? Eisner (1979) provides the example of politics and economics as untapped possibilities for classroom attention. Helping students develop a critical eye regarding the boundary making of politicians and economists—that might be a worthy goal. Cognizant of the powerful effects of work allocation on social relations, can I reconstruct labor and relationships within the classroom? Can schools with permeable walls be created where community members enrich the life within and children enrich and learn from life without?

Thinking differently about boundaries changes my mind. I have to adjust my commitments. I want to work with my students, drawing new mental boundaries that allow us to imagine a bond with Sri Lankan women forced to decide between laboring abroad (thus, hardly knowing their children) and living in dreadful poverty. Can we feel connected to the human suffering of the growing number of homeless among us? Will we think differently about life in our classrooms if we realize that the current boundaries between socioeconomic classes, between genders and ethnic groups, between the gay and the straight among us are all asymmetrical? That they create false binaries that blur the particularities of lived experience?

What new thoughts will allow me to consider what we have in common across boundaries and how we might take the risk of crossing and resisting those boundaries, restructuring the social dynamics that hold them in place? What would our classrooms be like if boundary work were central to curriculum? More importantly, what world could we and our children make if we believed that our time together could lead to rethinking and restructuring boundaries? We need new and empowering cross-historical and cross-cultural boundaries that allow us to regroup our alliances with an eye toward new coalitions and a commitment to a world where we join hands across old boundaries, erasing oppressive power and revisioning new possibilities.

TWO

Curriculum

INTRODUCTION

Mary

TEACHING LITERATURE, I often get the complaint from undergraduates, "I just can't relate to this." Conversely, they say, "I really liked this because I could relate." How ordinary, unsophisticated, sophomoric, moronic is this idea that that which is familiar is only that to which I can relate. Something in the equation is so not postmodern. What the relating is about, of course, is usually heteronormativity, Eurocentrism, phallologism, or any other "ism" of any established norm that prevents mind travel.

And so I try to introduce texts in the curriculum I design for my literature students with the explicit purpose of jolting complacency and that other "cy" that undergraduates come girded with: normalcy. I continue to be shocked, however, when my art students in a required English elective want fiction to end happily, or, if not, to tie up loose ends. I have to remind myself that today's art is, more often than not, sequential design, a form of art that requires linearity. Complications are introduced in my students' story boards for plot development and thrill: emotions that appeal to the satisfaction of reason's urgings. But I ask, with Derrida, "Is the reason for reason rational?" (1983, p. 9). Art that appeals to reason's satisfaction with logic, conclusion, and relation is not doing the work that curriculum should be doing. If curriculum is to heed Bill Pinar's challenge to be a "complicated conversation" (1995, p. 848), then curriculum workers should, at the very least, unseat the ready expectations that students bring to a text. Take them for a ride. Unmoor the anchor. Set sail.

27

The problem my students have with good (i.e., complicated) literature is that it refuses their goad. That is, the texts I teach introduce situations that require students to examine biases, walk in the shoes of others, become uncomfortable, get lost, throw away the guide, forego google. Curriculum that fights the "gentle coercions toward normalization" (Gough, 2003, p. 42) meet resistance from those who view art as standpoint theory. If resisters understand clearly a particular point of view, they can say with confidence that they either relate or do not relate with the text. But if curriculum does its job, all texts should work toward introducing contradictory standpoints that defy easy classification. All texts should dispel the too-easy assumption that there is such a thing as a norm, an ending, a relation to the privilege that grounds "ism" in secure locations. Curriculum should, as Marla Morris (2003) puts it, be undecidable. This casting off from the sure land of normalcy will put students inside the flow of *currere*, perhaps even encourage an "autobiographics of alterity" (Pinar, 2002, p. 43) instead of relationism.

Delese encounters the relation issue with her medical students. Students are supposed to relate to a wide variety of patients from a diverse set of backgrounds. Medical curriculum explicitly sets "competency" as its goal, defining competency as respect for alterity by a series of other-directed knowledges. But while becoming competent is the expressed goal, with neutrality and rationality as the pathways to that goal, nothing in the training of doctors addresses how medical students are supposed to set aside, ignore, or overcome their individual biases when treating people from other cultures. Delese finds that the lack of critical analysis in medical curriculum has allowed the term "competency" to be a mask that can too easily serve as a cover for disrespect.

Martha sees the normalizing power of curriculum as downright abusive to the individuality of students. The "No Child Left Behind" doctrine—far from encouraging an autobiographics, or alterity—is a testing movement that clamps down, not opens out. We should ask, with Martha, testing for what? A curriculum that is grounded in theories of Western rationality only is a curriculum that is afraid of possibility for otherness.

I propose what could be called a curriculum of hyphens, by offering the figure of the Harlequin as metaphor. Could this be the possibility Martha seeks? With his multicolored patches and antic behaviors, the Harlequin is a single figure whose essence is multiplicity, a mixture of genders, nationalities, and reactions. He/she/it has astounded audiences since medieval times, occurring most recently in the philosophy of Michel Serres. It is time curriculum take notice of what politics, history, and literature celebrate in the Harlequin. I suggest that the Harlequin's archetypal importance can prod life into the dead ideas that tend to keep curriculum from following its more natural coursings *(currere)* with motley, movement, and surprise.

DOING CURRICULUM IN THE MEDICAL ACADEMY

Delese

This is why we need the writer in opposition . . . who writes
against power, who writes against the corporation or the state or
the whole apparatus of assimilation. We're all one beat away from
becoming elevator music.

—DeLillo (1993, p. 290)

In medical education, curriculum work is tethered almost exclusively to the
nuts-and-bolts objectives-content-instruction-evaluation paradigm. This orientation is linked to the conception of curriculum as an institutionalized practice of development, in contrast to how curriculum theorists now view curriculum as a critical, hermeneutical practice aimed at understanding (Pinar et
al., 1995). Thus, little critical inquiry generally occurs into the social effects of
the curriculum on medical students, particularly the formal curriculum. When
we wring our hands about a medical student's negative attitude (pick one: a
sense of entitlement, lack of compassion, cynicism), we rarely look to the curriculum we've constructed ourselves—the content of lectures, seminars, syl-
labi, or case studies; the organization of basic science and clinical knowledge;
evaluation methods—for sources of such attitudes. Instead, we believe the cul-
prit is the hidden curriculum—those nasty power-driven temper tantrums in
surgery suites witnessed by students; the messages about equity and justice
sent to them by learning medicine almost exclusively on poor, uninsured
"house patients"; the sorting machines of particular specialities that still limit
the number of women who can enter certain fields. Certainly all those factors
do influence the kinds of doctors we're educating, but they do not explain the
depth and breadth of the complex forces at play in the medical environment
that try to wash away the eager altruism of most entering medical students . . .
forces that all too often succeed.

Medical educators, then, rarely think about the medical curriculum as a
symbolic representation, one that includes "institutional and discursive practices, structures, images, and experiences" that can be analyzed, among other
ways, politically, autobiographically, phenomenologically, or racially (Pinar et
al., 1995, p. 16). Volumes of critical interrogation of medical education have
been written from outside the discipline, including the fields of sociology
(Freidson, 1986; Mishler, 1984; Waitzkin, 1991), feminist studies (Sherwin,
1992; Tong, 1996; Wolf, 1996), philosophy of science (Harding, 1991), even
literature (Nelson, 1997). Yet a similar search for understanding the medical
curriculum—itself nothing if not political—rarely occurs within academic
medicine itself. My interpretation of this lack is simple: The culture of medicine still views itself as sitting above the rest of the culture, identifying most

strongly with the objective and neutral posturing of science. Teaching bio-chemistry or physiology, cardiology or gynecology is viewed as an apolitical action. That is, there is a discrete body of knowledge in these domains—the best that's been thought and funded—and it's *scientific knowledge* for god's sake, agreed upon by experts around the world! What's to understand about how curriculum arising from these domains is developed?

Recent moves toward the addition of multiculturalism into the curriculum offer an engrossing, if not disturbing, example of a curriculum project in medical education whose utter lack of critical analysis by its developers indicates the arrested growth of the field in medicine. Academic medicine limited its response to teaching culture by adding courses, workshops, or lectures variously dubbed as cultural awareness, cultural diversity, or (most often) cultural competency. In the monolithic, slow-to-move, elephantine medical curriculum, any such approach is an important move, particularly given the huge cultural rifts between doctors and their patients. But medicine's view of culture in any of these approaches is so limited, so uncritical, that their sole use as vehicles for understanding the complex interplay between medicine and culture can actually deepen these very rifts.

For example, cultural competency approaches do not require medical students from dominant racial groups to think, for example, about their African American patients' experiences of living in a racist culture, how medicine has failed the poor, or how common practices and procedures normalize heterosexuality and pathologize other sexual identities. Cultural competency approaches do not require medical students to reflect on how their own biases are likely to spill over seemingly undetected into their interactions with patients, nor do they ask medical students to identify how the biases of medical institutions are in a synergistic relationship with the curriculum itself.

But this is the age of "competency," which has turned the attempt to understand and respect patients into categories to be "mastered"; that is, if Mexican American then this, if Jehovah's Witness then that. Yet such understandings are not data sets resulting from various "trait" lectures on race, national origins, religion, social class, or sexual orientation that ultimately lead to stereotyping, overgeneralizing, and viewing differences as deficiencies (Ford, 1999, p. 9). Ford argues that understanding patients' social and cultural environments is not a competency at all but rather "a process of becoming . . . a perspective or a shared frame of reference from which reality is perceived . . . a way of being, perceiving, thinking, and acting in the world in ways that symbolize the equal respect of all humanity" (1999, p. 4).

But when "competency" is what we're after, students remain focused on patients who are not white, middle class, U.S. born, English speaking, heterosexual, or Judeo-Christian, and not on themselves and their selective reality as they posture as "neutral" and "objective" in their interactions with patients unlike themselves. Patricia Williams (1998) suggests that the "racial divide" in the United States is exacerbated by a "welter of little lies":

> White people are victims. Poor Bangladeshies are poor because they want to be. Poor white people are poor because rich Indians stole all the jobs under the ruse of affirmative action. There is no racism in the marketplace. . . . Immigrants are taking over the whole world, but race makes no difference. . . . If some people are determined to be homeless, well then let them have it, if being homeless is what they like so much. (p. 10)

When interviewing patients based on "traits" they have memorized via cultural competency approaches, what do students "do" with these "little lies" circulating around them and their patients? If the formal curriculum doesn't deal with them directly, these biases take up residence in the hushed (but oddly informally sanctioned) hallway talk among students and residents, particularly in the shorthand they use to categorize particular kinds of patients (e.g., "teeth to tattoo" ratios).

Like much in medical education, cultural competency approaches purport to be "rational," based on the belief that culture is something to be learned and tested for evidence of its "mastery." The *OED* defines competence as "*sufficiency of qualification; capacity to deal adequately with a subject*" [italics added]; *Webster's Third International Dictionary* defines it as "the quality or state of being functionally adequate or of having sufficient knowledge, judgment, skill, or strength." As such, competence is hardly an appropriate descriptor for how well one understands, respects, and values cultural differences among all of us. In fact, such an undertaking involves far more than "adequate" or baseline cognitive and analytic skills that enable one to understand the central beliefs, values, practices, and paradoxes of counterpart or nondominant cultures; it also has an *emotional* component—the "ability to assume genuine interest in, and to maintain respect for, different (especially counterpart) values, traditions, experiences, and challenges" (Koehn & Rosenau, 2002, p. 110). How can "competence" and "genuine interest" be used in the same breath? Moreover, maintaining respect for patients whose cultural beliefs and behaviors are often antithetical to one's own, particularly when one is *not* interested in or respectful of such beliefs and behaviors, is not addressed in current cultural competency curricula. Yet facing these lapses in respect is a challenging, never-to-be complete task, one that involves unlearning biases and prejudices. Such work is not amenable to the whole notion of competency. Instead, it is the self-critical, reflective work individuals must engage in repeatedly, honestly, and concurrently with the narrow cognitive component of cultural competency (Wear, 2005).

Thus, current cultural competency curricula tries to tell medical students that differences among patients based on race, ethnicity, national origins, social class, physical or intellectual abilities, sexual identity, or religious beliefs can be known, understood, and respected to maximize their efforts at restoring and maintaining health. What these curricula do not say, but what students learn, is that cultural competency can be more or less mastered or achieved by learning cultural "data sets" without confronting and working against the all-too-real effects of their biases on persons from nondominant cultures who live in a white-dominated, heterosexist, religiously intolerant, rabidly nationalistic and currently xenophobic culture. In fact, this hidden dimension "raises questions about an institution primarily composed of members of the dominant class (and primarily serving that class) to interpret and read signs of illness and health in nondominant persons, not to mention nondominant persons' relationships to their communities" (Stanford, 2003, p. 34). Moreover, this hidden dimension shaping medical students as part of an intense socialization into the profession may lead them to a view of patients that is actually narrow, unreflective, even *dis*respectful. But there is hope.

Megan Boler, author of a critical study of emotions and education, urges all of us whose project is teaching to engage with our students "in critical inquiry regarding values and cherished beliefs, and to examine . . . *how one has learned to perceive others*" (1999, p. 176, italics added). If we look beyond the simplified data students learn to "unearth" patients' social, political, economic, emotional, and spiritual worlds by various cultural competency approaches (designed by and for doctors), we find a vast world of unspoken, unacknowledged "values and cherished beliefs" students use in their history taking and questioning strategies, many of them taught or reinforced by their medical education. Learning to look and think beyond the data—from the indoctrinations of medical education to the multiple and often messy beliefs one carries at all times—is part of what Boler calls a pedagogy of discomfort.

But this is only the first step. A pedagogy of discomfort moves beyond past reflection, for to reflect only diminishes the difficulties and paradoxes of the social world into an "overly tidy package that ignores our mutual responsibility to one another" (Boler, p. 177). Not moving past reflection, she argues, may bring about some honest self-assessment of biases but nothing more, with no significant changes to oneself or how we view or treat others. A pedagogy of discomfort moves beyond self-scrutiny into spheres of power, where unlike cultural competency approaches, we examine how the world is shaped by the dominant culture. For medical students, this involves not only the dominant U.S. culture but also the daunting medical culture that instructs them in all kinds of unspoken ways how to treat patients from nondominant cultures—particularly those who are economically disadvantaged, those who don't "take care" of themselves, persons who are obese, and those who don't do what their doctors tell them; in short, those who don't look, think, and act like privileged doctors. Boler calls this selectivity "inscribed habits of (in)attention" built on social and economic hierarchies (p. 180).

If medical educators were to adopt a pedagogy of discomfort even while using cultural competency approaches for the critical health data such approaches can provide, medical students would be urged to recognize the selectivity of what they see, the kinds and amount of attention they give patients based on who they are, and the systematic gaps built into health care based exclusively on how much money a patient has. They would examine how we all have selective sight, learned through families, educational experiences, religion, and a medical curriculum that is motivated to construct the world in particular ways. Most medical students come from middle-range or economically privileged classes (AAMC, 2001); most would uneasily recognize that they have great incentives to remain privileged, that the world view they have is based on their social status and medical training, and that the way they explain poverty and the health problems associated with it are based on selective sight arising from their social status (Wear, 2005). Similarly, medical educators engaged in a pedagogy of discomfort may recognize that the curriculum focuses squarely on a doctor-patient relationship that keeps doctors firmly in charge of questioning, of "managing" patients, of determining what's normal and what's not, and of determining the very meaning of health and illness.

Doing curriculum in the medical academy should involve a pedagogy of discomfort for all of us as we scrutinize a medical curriculum that purports to educate skilled, caring, empathic doctors even as it relentlessly sorts, categorizes, normalizes, and pathologizes, hailing objectivity and scorning subjectivity at every turn. As part of a faculty that conceives, builds, and evaluates the medical curriculum, I cannot deny some complicity with keeping things alive that work against educating students to that end. With my colleagues in gross anatomy, infectious disease, surgery, and radiology, I cocreate institutional and discursive practices, build structures, select images, and mandate experiences for students. But in that process, and always traveling alongside my students, I hope I am sometimes able "to spoil a good party and break an encompassing circle, to travel from the safe to the unsafe," creating difficulties everywhere (Williams, 1991, p. 129).

MOTLEY TOPICS: TOWARD A HARLEQUIN CURRICULUM

Mary

Throw away the lights, the definitions,
And say of what you see in the dark
That it is this or that it is that,
But do not use the rotted names.
   —Stevens, "The Man with the Blue Guitar"

I am grateful to Bill Reynolds for drawing my attention to the figure of the Harlequin and its significance for curriculum studies. Like a circle within a circle, Bill relies on Michel Serres's (2000) meditation on the Harlequin to reimagine understanding. Like a Harlequin's coat, Serres writes, understanding lies at the intersection or interference of things, in patches here and there. While a structuralist mindset yearns for the whiteface of unity, clarity, and order, understanding is so much more colorful and fluid and works seamlessly. Reynolds along with Serres argues for—nay—celebrates—poststructural multiplicity as "an attempt to avoid setting up binary oppositions" (Reynolds, unpublished manuscript, p. 10), searching instead for "spaces to do curriculum studies that help to create different worlds that are not so cruel" (p. 11). Elsewhere, Bill joyfully exclaims, "Curriculum studies IS not this or that. Defining it leads to this or that" (Reynolds, 2003, p. 94). A musician as well as a curriculum theorist, Bill Reynolds is something of a man with a blue guitar, urging an embrace of motley. The new explorations and knowledges that he finds among recent scholarship—into fields as various as science fiction (Weaver et al., 2003) or Holocaust studies (Morris, 2001a)—energize thought because they "do not use the rotted names."

Perhaps it is odd to introduce a sixteenth-century comedic figure, the Harlequin, in today's cruel new world. Stuck as we seem to be in a quagmire of literalism that equates, for instance, shock and awe with military air strikes, we are experiencing politically, socially, culturally, spiritually, and educationally the fallout from an arrogant belief that might is right because America is first.

Wallace Stevens, Pulitzer prize-winning poet of the last century, wrote about a similar conundrum in the middle of World War II. Meditating on the Platonic figure of the noble charioteer driving two horses of the soul, Stevens asks why that figure, which for centuries had inspired thought, became in the 1940s a mere emblem. What stands between the figure and us? he wonders. What has caused this blockage? His answer is a rousing condemnation of what war does to consciousness:

> The spirit of negation has been so active, so confident, and so intolerant . . . we live in an intricacy of new and local mythologies, political, economic, poetic, which are asserted with an ever-enlarging incoherence. This is accompanied by an absence of any authority except force. (Stevens, 1951, p. 17)

Stevens's excoriation continues. He equates the disenobling of the emotions of shock and awe with the pressure of external events. It is the poet's role, he insists, to make poetic imagination ours so that we can live our lives better, more contemplatively. Speaking as an elitist, Stevens somewhat humorously qualifies who "we" might be: "not a drab, but . . . a woman with the hair of a pythoness" (p. 29).

I don't think Bill Reynolds would call himself an elitist. But perhaps I may, for a few pages, become the Medusa figure Stevens addresses and wonder with him and with Bill how potent figures of the past can provide the necessary force to create supreme, life-enhancing fictions. What better time to bring back the spirit of the Harlequin, whose love of disorder, illogic, and disarray can offer new meaning, indeed new life, to the phrase "shock and awe"; and can inspire, thereby, new explorations for curriculum!

The Harlequin gained fame in the sixteenth century in France and northern Italy, most appropriately for those associated with the annual curriculum theorizing conference, in Bergamo, with the Commedia dell'Arte. As a stock comic figure, Arlecchino, the Zany, was associated with a dance called the Bergamasque. His costume, motley, showed that he belonged to no particular nationality and seemed to have no specifics of any kind, either of gender or identity or race (Welsford, 1966, p. 293). His ambiguity was further suggested by his cap, decorated with an animal's tail or bunch of feathers; and his bat, serving as wand or cudgel. Clearly, his chameleon nature and ribald behavior caused laughter. But his black mask had an eerie, slightly sinister aspect that can be heard in a variation of his name, "hellequin" (Miller, 1995, p. 75). In the Middle Ages, the hellequin figure was the leader of a ghostly, ghastly ghoulish troupe of clowns and comic actors who dropped out of sight on the stage through a trap door called "la chappe d'Hellequin" or the jaws of hell (Miller, p. 76). The hellequin survived his descent, of course, suggesting association with mythological heroes like Hercules or Hermes who easily could traverse regions not traveled by landlocked mortals.

At the end of the seventeenth century, Harlequin becomes less of an acrobat and more of a clown, using extravagant fantasy known as pantomime. And by the 1800s Harlequin's motley was further transformed into a costume of sparkling silk and spangles, with a black mask that made him invisible (Welsford, p. 302). I suppose that the Harlequin romances of Barbara Cartland fame derive from the eighteenth-century costume suggesting fantastic, if gaudy, escapism into a bejeweled other world.

The Harlequin, thus, is an old world figure of just enough stability despite its manifold variations through time to suggest archetypal significance. Carl Jung describes archetypes as supraordinate or over-life-sized figures which express "man as he really is, not as he appears to himself" (1977, pp. 185–86). Jung equates this figure with the "self" or the unconscious, as distinct from the ego. External, objective figures and symbols, such as the clown or Harlequin; geometric figures like the circle or square; animal parts like a fox tail or bird feathers represent this impersonal component of the human personality. But these external representations are, Jung says, indefinite, making a comprehensive description of the human personality impossible (p. 187). With motley, cap, and bat or scepter, Harlequin is the clown-fool-jester-acrobat part of ourselves; with mask, he cavorts with the devil and plays devilish tricks on our presuppositions. With Pierrot, the whitefaced clown, he shows the dual nature of all beings: male *and* female, human *and* animal, mortal *and* immortal, scary *and* silly ("silly"—a word that originally meant "blessed" [Willeford, 1969, 10]). This bonding with *and* suggests two sides of one archetype, like Picasso's Harlequin and Chaplin's clown. Call *and* an "extra-being, inter being" (Deleuze and Parnet, 1977, p. 57). Call *and* the "andswer" that keeps the questions coming, refusing to stop: the *and* that opens up, troubles, disrupts. "AND flows into IS," Bill Reynolds says (2003, 95).

For those who are uncomfortable with slap-stick and ribald humor (Harlequin's bat was many things—phallus, scepter, magic wand, stick to slap with), the Harlequin is shocking; he is awful. *And* that is the point. David Miller reminds us that "all genuine comedy is anarchic and iconoclastic. . . . It is challenging assumptions, testing limits, crossing boundary lines, disabusing any public of its most firmly held beliefs" (1995, p. 71). To connect too literally with the Harlequin is to miss the point. He stands before us to disillusion us from our illusions. His pratfalls inspire awe. And so, as Serres urges, "Gaze with all your eyes" on this figure "everywhere unexpected" and let your heart start beating (2000, p. viv).

These life-affirming qualities of the Harlequin archetype are among the reasons it is an appropriate trope for curriculum studies in a time that equates doubt with despair. I surmise that three features of this figure are pertinent to my discussion. In the following citations from literary works, I find that the archetype of the Harlequin, even in modern times, resists the modernist urge to adhere to either-or definitions. To do such would be to submit to "the rotted names." Rather, consistent with its own ancient history, the Harlequin's enduring features include motley associations with androgyny, underworld chaos, and movement.

In Colette's short short story "The Secret Woman," for instance, Harlequin appears as his alter-ego Pierrot, played not by a male actor but by a female. The story involves a married couple, politely bored with one another's roles as man and wife, especially as these roles stifle eros. Marriage, Colette implies, exists on a lie enacted by social constraints. The setting is a costume party at which both husband and wife appear, unknown to each other, each in disguise. The opening sentence sets the tone, "He had been looking for a long time at the sea of masks in front of him, suffering vaguely from the mixture of colours and from the synchronization of two orchestras which were too close" (Colette, p. 38). The unnamed husband is transported into a world of make-believe, where a vibrancy of color, sound, and movement cause him to suffer vaguely. His long-slumbering erotic self is being disturbed. The "sea" of masks unmoors him from his too-secure land-locked role of The Man. Here at the ball all is mixture and slippage, sound and frenzy. Here is carnival, life. What then catches the husband's eye is "someone."

> He turned round and saw someone sitting astride the balustrade, wearing a
> long and impenetrable disguise, looking like Pierrot because of the smock
> with vast sleeves, the loose trousers, the headband and the plaster-white
> colour which covered the small area of skin visible below the fluffy lace of the
> mask. The fluid fabric of the costume and the cap, woven of dark purple and
> silver, shone like the conger-eels that you fish for at night. (p. 39)

Colette's water imagery, echoing the earlier phrase "sea of masks," is notice-
able in this passage. Pierrot's fabric is "fluid" and shiny like an eel. Eels are
particularly primal fish which, because they have no ventral fins, resemble
snakes. They slither. The husband wonders who the costumed creature is.
Shortly, he recognizes his wife as this Pierrot, transformed from wifely deli-
cacy into slippery sorcery. He watches "half stifled with surprise, waiting and
nightmare" (p. 39) as she moves through the crowd, flirting first with men,
then with a woman, all costumed. Colette ends the story on a highly ambiguous note, with a long, slithering, one-hundred-sixteen-word sentence describ-
ing the husband's presuppositions about his wife: that she would go back
home, "restored to her irremediable solitude and immodest innocence" (p. 41).
Oh? I think Colette is playing a trick on the reader. The sibilant sentence constructions and sea imagery play around and within the edges of this story, lap-
ping at the husband's anxious prudery. As Wallace Stevens writes, "the sea is
a form of ridicule" (1972, p. 146). Just so.

One of the Harlequin's features is to create a new world of spiritual freedom (Willeford, 1969, p. 325). Here in a few short pages, Colette captures
what Karl-Josef Kuschel calls "a poetics of postmodernity, which is a poetics
of the 'as if,' a wink of the eye, and agreement over the degree of deception
which one will accept" (1994, p. 36). Lying—or rather, recognizing the lie of
social constructions—is a theme of this story. Husbands and wives sustain a
lie about their true desires, Colette suggests. So which is the greater lie: the lie
of social norms? or the lie of fantasy? The carnival outside the world of the
"kept" spouse puts a mirror up to marriage. Colette's romance does not so
much offer alternative realities as it underscores "the fictionality of the 'real'
and the unreality of the culture" (Elam, 1998, p. 204).

Integral to Harlequin—and his paired other, Pierrot—is doubleness,
blurring, ambiguity, androgyny and vitalism. Here is a story of desire born
through the mask. What Reynolds (2003) calls the "vitalistic perspective" of
Deleuze's notion of "lines of flight" (1995, p. 96) is suggested by Colette's several sea references and to the story's new Eve, capable of creating a force that
bursts the pipe of social constraints.

Lest we get too upperworldly in this discussion of the Harlequin and think
that revitalizing the curriculum is only a matter of rethinking gender (it is that,
partly) or complexifying identity (it is partly that) Joseph Conrad puts us
straight (!). The kind of Harlequin energy found in *Heart of Darkness* revisits a

more archaic side of this archetypal figure: underworldiness. If Colette praises the vitalism of sexual energy, Conrad warns of the vitalism of the underworld and Harlequin's particular relation to chaos. But rather than opposites, these variations show what Umberto Eco (1990) calls "a slight degree of non-coincidence between the resemblances" (p. 30). We can view the Harlequin, then, as an ironic postmodern figure with "wondrous eccentricities" (Serres, p. xiii) that extend, Serres playfully imagines, down to the tattoos on his skin (p. xv). Essence, in other words, is itself mottled.

Conrad's novelette is a story with a lie. The story, you recall, concerns the plunder of African Congo ivory resources by European hunters, notably by Mr. Kurtz. One lie has been unearthed by Adebayo Williams (2000) and others decrying Conrad's portrayal of native Africans as savages. Another lie is what Marlow feels compelled to tell the fiancée of Mr. Kurtz, that the last words on Kurtz's dying lips were her name. The lie allows the fiancée to live in her white world unaware of the horrors of colonialism. I have often wondered about the Harlequin's presence inside this story, a presence that seems more an afterthought than a necessity. The Harlequin gives rise to a third lie.

Marlow, recall, is about to meet Kurtz for the first time when he comes across a strange, out-of-place figure:

> His aspect reminded me of something I had seen—something funny I had seen somewhere. As I maneuvered to get alongside, I was asking myself "What does this fellow look like?" Suddenly I got it. He looked like a harlequin. His clothes had been made of some stuff that was brown holland probably, but it was covered with patches all over, with bright patches, blue, red, and yellow—patches on the back, patches on the front, patches on elbows, on knees; coloured binding around his jacket, scarlet edging at the bottom of his trousers; and the sunshine made him look extremely gay and wonderfully neat withal, because you could see how beautifully all this patching had been done. A beardless, boyish face, very fair, no feature to speak of, nose peeling, little blue eyes, smiles and frowns chasing each other over that open countenance like sunshine and shadow on a wind-swept plain. (Conrad, 1986, p. 90)

Conrad's earlier description of the map of Europe with patches of blue, red, yellow, orange, and purple (p. 36) echo the patches on the Harlequin's coat, suggesting that this Harlequin figure is a map himself, from everywhere and nowhere. He inspires astonishment in Marlow: "His very existence was improbable, inexplicable, and altogether bewildering. He was an insoluble problem . . . and there he was gallantly, thoughtlessly alive, to all appearance indestructible solely by the virtue of his few years and of his unreflective audacity" (p. 91). This boyish youth is a devotee of Kurtz, the madman; Marlow cannot square the devotion the boy owes Kurtz with the clownish aspect of his clothes. After an exchange of words, the episode disappears and is never referred to again. Like Marlow, the reader is left wondering: What on earth?!

The hellequin of Medieval times was allowed escape from the jaws of hell by a trap door, coming back alive, and astonishing the audience. Call this shock and awe: comedy as a drama of life over death. But the medieval audience, despite its laughter and delight, knows that what it sees is not "true"; the Harlequin lies. Does Conrad imply that the Harlequin figure, in the hell of Kurtz's Congo, has been untouched? Does he stand before Marlow as a lie? If that is a possibility of this strange interlude in Conrad's tale of darkness, there seems to be a profundity here that perhaps can explain what Umberto Eco means when he says his theory of signs is a theory of lies (1976, p. 6). For just as the map of brightly colored patches on the walls of the Belgium counting house belies the horror of colonialism, so does the grinning youth in motley belie his association with the monster Kurtz. Harlequin is profound, inspiring shock and awe, not because he defies death but because his happy reappearance from the jaws of hell is a lie. The lie is that we *can* make sense of that which we cannot understand, that interpretation can verify things for us. James Guetti in his essay on Conrad makes this point about interpretation that reverberates for the poststructuralist curriculum:

> The story as the account of a journey into the center of things . . . poses itself as the refutation . . . that meaning may be found within, beneath, at the center. At the end of the search we encounter darkness, and it is no more defined than at the beginning of the journey and the narrative; it continues to exist only as something unapproachable. The unapproachable is, however, tremendously "significant." (in Conrad, p. 20)

It would seem that "significance" is found with the unapproachable Harlequin, who disabuses us from ascribing to the significations around us a clarity that does not exist.

My final discussion of the Harlequin figure in literary works is with Wallace Stevens's poem "The Comedian as the Letter *C*," which utilizes the quest motif of traditional literatures but with a poststructuralist twist. Traditionally, the quest pattern involves the journey of a hero, usually male, out from the territory of home into a wilderness region where an ensuing battle tests the hero, proves his mettle, and enables him to return triumphant, usually with a boon or trophy, to prove the fact of conquest and to save the homeland. The heroic quest is what gives war its mighty name, its righteous cause, its dependence on distinguishing good from evil. But all those words, Stevens implies, use "the rotted names" to defend a reality of wish based on a fantasy of fact. The quest pattern, as old as Homer's *Iliad* and as modern as Joyce's *Ulysses*, depends on heroics and is definitely end-based. Stevens counters this tradition with highly original, sometimes maddeningly obtuse, language that tells a different story of movement and that uses a Harlequin in place of a hero. The poem is mock, it is ironic, it is comedic. The butt of all its wordings is romanticism, modernism, and realism. To that end (!) Stevens takes the reader on a rollicking ride through the Americas in a prepoststructuralist "wilderness of differences," of which, according to Harold Bloom, few other texts partake (1977, p. 72). (I think of Virginia Woolf's *Orlando* in this regard).

The questing figure in the poem is Crispin, one of the many words with the letter *C* that sound as backdrop throughout the six sections. This is Comedy with the letter *C*, where the Harlequin thrives. Early on we meet him: "Crispin,/the lutanist of fleas, the knave, the thane,/The ribboned stick, the bellowing breeches, cloak/Of China, cap of Spain, imperative haw/Of hum" (Stevens, 1972, p. 58). Here is Crispin, the Harlequin in motley, surrounded by words that suggest color, sound, and movement: "His mind was free/And more than free, elate, intent, profound/And studious of a self possessing him/That was not in him in the crusty town/From which he sailed" (p. 63). Further, Stevens describes Crispin's voyaging as "An up and down between two elements,/A fluctuating between the sun and moon,/A sally into gold and crimson forms" (p. 65). With this kind of oscillation between opposites, Crispin serves the Harlequin function of destabilizing forms and undercutting reason or fact by chance and imagination. Indeed, Crispin's venture is "curriculum for the marvelous sophomore"/. . . allowing him to "see how much/Of what he saw he never saw at all" (p. 66). I take those lines to be Stevens's comment on the possibilities inherent within a curriculum, or journey, that enables new seeing because of an astonishment at the is-ness of what comes before the eyes.

Helen Vendler calls Stevens "a poet of the midworld" (1969, p. 47). His verse, she says, "trembles always at halfway points, at the point of metamorphosis" and of "the transitional moment" (p. 47). This is Harlequin country—Serres's "instructed third" that prompts Bill Reynolds to ask, "Why should we go backwards towards a restoration when we can go, move, and travel forward in the middle?" (unpublished manuscript). Crispin's up/down voyages and plans take us to the middle region. This is the place, Vendler continues, of "mutual accommodation of the self and the world and in the nature of things" (p. 54). No matter how many words we say or facts we hold up as evidence, the "thing" is always slightly beyond our conceptual grasp. As Stevens puts it, "The plum survives its poems" (1922/1972, p. 70).

I leave us gazing on the Harlequin with shock and awe. He has seemed a creature of utter irreality, leaping the gaps of our constructed world with unbounded ease. He is a disturbance to prudes, a knave to thought, a jostling festival with his motley and mask. We gape, open mouthed. What is that sense of menace behind the black mask? Why the Pierrot accompaniment? Darn him: he refuses to settle down into one neat form, driven as he is to reformulate and unsettle my assumptions. This allusive figure has even spawned a complex, coined by Dr. David C. McClelland. The "Harlequin complex" refers to demon lovers that women dream when confronted with death (Willeford, p. 246). These multiple manifestations of the Harlequin wrench us away from ourselves. He is ambiguity with a capital H. And perhaps that is the point of curriculum, through which a river runs (Reynolds, 2003). We should keep the river running through the curriculum so as to avoid the sort of "crude stereotyping, rigid defenses, and general lack of insight that accompanies a low tolerance for ambiguity" (Levine, 1985).

Harlequin, you upset the status quo; you are ec-static. May all our sophomores be marvelous in your company!

CURRICULUM: ABUSE OR POSSIBILITY?

Martha

Curriculum has been envisioned in myriad ways and the merits of various approaches have been dissected and described. To dare to teach is to weave a fabric of curriculum—regardless of how consciously or unconsciously the crafting proceeds. But, of course, it is not only teachers who care deeply about the content and pedagogy of schools. Those with vested interests in what teachers say and do each day—politicians, corporations, parents, educational bureaucrats—leave their mark. Despite the close proximity and intimate relationship between teachers and what is taught, threads and tones that contradict and ignore lived experience appear in the tapestry that emerges as teachers, students, and content come together.

The struggle over what is to be taught in our classrooms comes as no surprise. Educational literature is replete with extensive analyses. From the "Bible Wars" of Philadelphia in the mid-nineteenth century when violence in the streets erupted over the issue of separation of church and state, to the battle between opposing notions of progressivism in the early twentieth century, to the challenges of today's trend toward restrictive content shaped by test prep and sanctions, we have always known, at some level, that power circulates in either menacing or empowering ways in our curricular decisions. We can, if we choose, play it safe in our academic discourse and ignore the power of curriculum to exclude and disable. Sounds harsh, I know, but I have no more patience for soft words and pleasant critiques. These are difficult times.

My work with preservice and inservice teachers has shifted dramatically in the last year as a result of the context of our experiences. It's not that the content of the curriculum that brings us together has changed dramatically. What is new is the wide-eyed engagement of students, their intense interest in the history of school reform, their sense that we are poised on the precipice of historic change as the fragile social contract that has kept public schools alive seems truly threatened. They wonder aloud about their chosen career. Will the requirements and restrictions of current reform rob them of their opportunity to teach in ways they believe are best for children? How, they ask, will they be able to administer tests to second language learners, knowing that every test is, undeniably, a language test? My students are idealistic. They want to teach inclusively, help students read the world as well as the word (Freire, 1994). The last thing they want to participate in is abuse.

Abusive curriculum stands in the way of well-intentioned teachers moving toward the challenging yet invigorating goal of making spaces for living a dream of community and social justice. It fills the spaces with facticity, leaving no room for imagination and metaphor. Personal engagement? Perspective taking? Empathy? Under current thinking, unnecessary, dismissed as romanticism (Hirsch, 1996). At a very daily, practical level, science, social studies, visual and dramatic arts, music, and inclusive literary experiences are being marginalized and/or excluded by an intense focus on decoding words and implementing algorithms. In many schools, recess is eliminated as the pressure to demonstrate competence on measures that are narrow and developmentally and culturally insensitive increases. I am envisioning curriculum as abuse because it is the only way I know to create the clarity necessary to nurture the hope of curriculum as possibility. Abuse creates a fog that is difficult to penetrate. But the clear skies that emerge for those who persist are exceptionally blue. Difficult times call for penetrating metaphors.

Abuse. Emotional abuse. The abuser, pushed to a controlling posture by his or her own insecurities, aims to control others, to exert power in ways that bolster a sense of importance where he or she is the center of the universe. Perpetrators of emotional abuse are narcissistic (Evans, 1996, NiCarthy, 1990). The target of the emotional abuse is manipulated, isolated, degraded, and exploited until a sense of self is diminished, even destroyed. Individuals who are targeted lose perspective; their view of the world is warped. They come to believe they are undeserving. Stress builds as clarity fades and is replaced with feelings of self-doubt and inadequacy. Eventually the abused may come to live according to these misperceptions. They may even pattern their own behavior toward others after the abusive strategies that have been used to oppress them, perpetuating the cycle of abuse. Thus, the path to healing can only begin with new knowledge, a clarified understanding of how the abuser has exerted control. But this knowledge is hard to come by.

Control over another is most effective when executed subtly, even when controlling behaviors are intermittently aggressive. Sometimes controlling behaviors are tempered with expressions of affection and overtures of seeming support. A pattern of reasonableness and normalcy is established. I am reminded of Flax's (1993) description of legitimate rule as that which characterizes most political regimes:

> A mode of legitimation is a set of practices and beliefs in and through which people come to believe their rulers have the right to exercise power over them. . . . People's habitual participation . . . allows power to circulate. . . . Its adherents are not even aware of its effects. . . . This is the most effective method of wielding power, since it requires the least wielding of force. (p. 41)

The abuser, mirroring the establishment of legitimate political rule, creates a situation in which the victim accepts the appropriateness of being dominated.

Most relationships are characterized by occasional hostility and efforts to manipulate the other. All the more reason that it is difficult to identify emotional abuse and to name it as such. But it is this naming that is the landmark moment that can begin to liberate, can result in the target individual walking away from the perpetrator toward a chance to rebuild confidence and a sense of personal purpose (Evans, 1996; NiCarthy, 1990). Naming can only occur when the patterns that have held fast can be examined from a perspective that questions what has been taken as normative. Information is needed from outside the destructive relationship. A view from elsewhere. A chance to see with new eyes.

But this is a chapter about curriculum and it may seem I have strayed from the topic. Or, if the reader is well versed in the historical and contemporary conflicts over curriculum, connections may be forming, comparisons may be emerging. For, as I stated unapologetically from the start, curriculum, with all its normalizing power and despite the good it does accomplish, has also functioned as abuse since its inception. And now I would add that current trends that have been described as "narrowing of the curriculum," "victory for the radical right," "neoliberalism," and "neocolonialism" (Apple, 2001; Giroux & McLaren, 1994; McLaren, 1998) might also be named, using a word that captures the subtlety and destructive force of curricular power more clearly—abuse. Emotional abuse. Abuse that destroys in the same silent and debilitating manner that characterizes individual, emotionally abusive relationships. Upon close examination, the similarities flow freely.

Like the emotional abuser described in psychological tomes, a curriculum that is exclusive and technical, grounded in theories of Western rationality, develops from intense insecurity and the need to control. The greater the sense of chaos and threat to the power of the status quo, the more tightly curriculum has been crafted. In today's rapidly diversifying world, multicultural demographics in the United States and an increasing paranoia about the many who are considered Other by those entrenched in Eurocentrism have raised the sense of political and personal insecurity to new heights (Apple, 2001; Spring, 1998). Strident warnings about imminent threats pepper the airwaves. Those in power have wielded these warnings in an unprecedented manner; we read, watch, and listen as the media drama, strategically shaped for us, unfolds in our living spaces through crafted conversations. Great pains are being taken to provide the mainstream with a sense of security. And the curriculum, central to the legitimizing institution of school (Gramsci, 1971), is one vehicle for constructing a story that pacifies, that establishes as normative a narrative that reflects only one perspective—the view of the abuser.

You see, those who hold the power in our society, those who feel so threatened by any suggestion that everyone should have a place at the table, a voice in the government, their perspective included, are determined to remain at the center of the universe. Satisfied only by maintaining their centrality and supreme subjectivity, abusers manage to convince others, including the abused, that what they say is right and proper—legitimate. Efforts from progressive politicians and educators to decenter the privilege that is enjoyed by so few have been decidedly limited in their ability to affect systemic change.

Isolated from perspectives other than those enshrined in the abusive curriculum, students' (and teachers') subjectivity is absent from the content and process of schooling. They begin to see a world in which they do not belong and they may come to believe a narrative that does not include their stories. Gradually, their desires and impulses are suppressed and they accept a diminished view of themselves and an inflated view of Western, masculine accomplishments and values. Manipulated and exploited in this way, they come to believe they are undeserving. The stress that marks their daily school experiences is internalized (Trueba, 1989) as they struggle to progress in a system that is dependent upon their failure (Kozol, 1991). For only through the submission or failure of the abused can the abuser truly maintain superiority and privilege.

Eventually, the abused participate in their own oppression as they internalize a destructive yet pervasive view of the world. Students may accept and eventually pass along to others the dominant values of intense competition and rugged individualism and the content rarely examined for omissions or misrepresentations. Teachers become participants in promoting hegemonic perspectives, and in this way the curriculum abuses teachers as well as students (Grumet, 1988).

This curricular travesty reflects the social narratives that are woven throughout our national rhetoric. Consider the public's acceptance of such misleading slogans as "No Child Left Behind." Shored up by participation in the fast-paced worlds of both school and society, the socialization processes instill in students (and teachers) an ethic of patriotism that implicitly prohibits dissension or protest. Increasingly, all that matters is what counts—what can be measured through standardized tests. Incessant talk of school failure leads toward the complete condemnation of public schools and an unprecedented level of advocacy of the privatization of education. Differentiated schooling opportunities and egregious unfairness in funding persist, grounded in the eugenics movement of the 1920s and 1930s (Stoskopf, 1999). This context of schooling pervades students' experiences. Abuse is accepted as normative, legitimate, appropriate.

Students sacrifice self and subjectivity and agree to the rules of school when young. Eventually, however, many decide to live outside the school system. Like emotionally abusive relationships, the only way students can escape is to leave. But leaving is not a response that is inherently liberating, although it can become a platform for healing. Only through a reconfigured understanding of the way power has been used against them can victims begin to recover subjectivity and their rightful place as significant members of the human race. But this reconfiguration is unlikely, at best. Flax (1993) asserts that "[t]here can be no exercise of power without its concomitant production of truth. Legitimate power requires grounding in and justification by a set of rational rules." Curriculum actively teaches those rules through its omissions and inferences.

When students can no longer endure the abuse of curricular experience, becoming "push-outs," the effects of the abuse stay with them, despite their decision to leave. They can only regain the power that comes from understanding their own subjectivity by learning and producing new "truths" about themselves and their world. The chance of this happening in the world of truncated options available to students who don't complete school is slim. And for this reason, the abusive curriculum, the very vehicle of legitimation that has oppressed, must be changed *radically* to expose the historic and contemporary abuses of power that are currently morphing into global practices of economic and social dominance. Only with new knowledge can avenues of opportunity, bolstered by solidarity, begin to emerge within the curriculum and within the lives of students. Only then can curriculum become possibility.

Possibility. The word captures all we can hope for in curriculum. Curriculum has held our attention for generations because those who think seriously about education understand its inherent possibility. Maxine Greene's (1993) call for a return to the search for Dewey's great community, her call to rise to the challenge of coming together without losing each person's unique way of being in the world challenges our educational imagination. More recently, Carlson (2003) calls us to become cosmopolitan intellectuals, working across boundaries toward an unknown public good while respecting the particularities of individual communities. Their words carry radical implications for curriculum reform.

Think of the possibilities. A curriculum that is representative. Inclusive. Informative. A view from elsewhere. A view from many positions. A chance to see with new eyes. Dialogue. Engagement. What stands in our way? Abuse. Emotional abuse. The belief that what is accepted as normative is immutable. Naming the struggle *can* be the beginning of our reclamation of the educative process. Yes, the struggle continues to be immense. But if we name it and hold that renaming steadily within our consciousness as we do our work, we may be less likely to accept partial solutions. More inclined to strike out in strategically radical ways. More willing to cross boundaries and work with others who also view curriculum as possibility. More able to see the subtle patterns that creep insidiously into our daily activities and interactions despite increased understanding. Old habits die hard and patterns of abuse are difficult to dislodge. But there have always been dissident voices and they are energized by difficult times.

Never before has the need for new curricular vision been so urgent. Like survivors of emotionally abusive relationships, educators and citizens who want radical change must make a daily commitment to honing heightened consciousness. Reading the subtexts of experience, reading the world (Freire, 1970), and feeling the emotional pain that is inevitable when unpacking and working to reverse abusive dynamics is exhausting but exhilarating work. Challenging times call for explicit language that can guide us toward clarity and a commitment to new, expansive, inclusive curricular possibilities. Resources abound (Whitaker, 2004). The future is waiting. The possibilities are endless.

THREE

Disgrace

INTRODUCTION

Martha

How does one use words to explore the disgraceful oppression perpetrated by naming, reasoning, intimidation: the colonization of land, minds, and hearts? There seems to be no defensible linguistic option. Even Derrida is caught in the trap that haunts the notion of using language to deconstruct language—the idea of naming the horror of naming. And so Delese, Mary, and I jump in, cognizant of the dangers, yet determined to express something of our own journeys inward, encouraged by the words of others who have traveled roads along which we might never venture. It's a time-honored educational tradition to harness the power of literature in an attempt to disturb (dismantle? disgrace?) carefully shaped perceptions. When the writers one encounters are significantly Other, the potential power of the journey intensifies. Subsequent to our engagement with J. M. Coetzee's complex and moving novel *Disgrace* (1999), we were pleased to learn that he had received the 2003 Nobel Prize in Literature. He was described as an author who "in innumerable guises portrays the surprising involvement of the outsider." His guises, we agree, allowed us to journey inward toward a deeper understanding of oppression within close relationships and between cultures that share territory that is stained with blood.

As I write this introduction, the faces of the students currently enrolled in my doctoral foundations of education class are fresh in my mind. Some are eager, some incredulous, some intensely resistant to the readings of the semester. Just as Mary's students struggle with the language of stereotyping, mine struggle with theoretical perspectives grounded in worlds they can barely bring into focus. Their struggle strengthens my resolve to talk personally and passionately with them, searching for the balance between urging us all to struggle as best we can and imposing an experience that might be interpreted as yet another (and therefore easily dismissed) required conversation. Words are the dominant currency of our time together. Can we turn them in ways that will unsettle our thinking and living? If we are to write under erasure, can we also speak in ways that will allow the words to enlighten but not to reify? Does the "postmodern classroom" Mary names exist? There are plenty of world views being espoused—out there. Can we accept the call to journey inward, the challenge to be silent and to listen to the voices of others whose stories have the power to disrupt the words we were about to speak?

Mary sets the stage by introducing us to the voices of postcolonial writers whose fictions disrupt categories and supposed truth-telling. She leaves no doubt that the power of language is ever with us. The authors she highlights provide examples of how they meet "lofty lingo" with silence or with tangible, visible resistance. Disruption and the separation between worlds, within worlds, between people, within people call into question the stability of colonizing language and reason. Leaning on the defiance of Stanley in Brink's novel to the pragmatism of Coetzee's Lucy, she helps us remain in that place that resists complacency while urging self-examination. These authors, whether speaking their own lives (Fugard) or speaking through the life of a character (Gordimer), call us to wakefulness and invite us to deconstruct, lest the taken-for-granted remain "taken as granite."

Evolutionary visions of grace are woven through Delese's examination of lived experiences brought to us by Coetzee's *Disgrace*. The central character, David Lurie, moves haltingly from firm ground and a position of relative power to a new location where he is unexpectedly unnecessary to the lives and worlds of Others. Along the way, Delese helps us examine the difficult dynamics of redemption, and grace, ending with a sense of just how mighty the forces of grace can be to decenter our assumptions about disgrace. She helps us see disgrace as a social construction that can become a place of refuge. If the social hierarchy disintegrates, disgrace can no longer be a place to hide; one must come to grips with life, whatever it has become.

Delese helps us see Lurie's evolution from one clutching his patriarchal right to desire, to one hanging on to disgrace as a last hiding place. In the end it is the women in his life who call him to humility and "minding." Perhaps these are destinations we might struggle toward on our journeys with students.

Like Delese, I became inextricably connected to Coetzee's main character. Early on I realized that as life painfully peeled the layers of his life away, I was strangely aware that my own lived experience has been characterized by a peeling away of the layers. If I dare, I can view the world through his lens, understanding, if I allow it, that the right to hold the camera is gradually being

wrested from his hands and from mine. The brutality of the events of his journey hammer at me as I gradually realize that it may require brutal experiences
for each and all of us who have been schooled in the language of rationaliza-
tion to begin to awaken. Indeed, we may be entering the most brutal of chapters in a world that is newly configured by the rhetoric of patriotism. To journey with Lurie is to see the "rational" view flipped on its head.

Like Lurie, we and our students may be tempted to flee when faced with
the difficulty of new language, a new cacophony of voices—unfamiliar and,
though willfully nonconsolidated, newly powerful. But this chapter calls us to
return again and again—not to remain in a place of disgrace, but to move
toward a clearer understanding of our relation to those whose multiple voices
are beginning to question the intention of those who name.

MADE OF OTHERS' WORDS: LANGUAGE'S
DISGRACE IN POSTCOLONIAL AFRICAN WRITING

Mary

I'm in words, made of words, others' words.
—Samuel Beckett, *The Unnamable*

In the beginning was the Word.
—Gospel According to St. John

The World Conference against Racism, eighteen years in the making, chose a
place—Durban, South Africa—where even now "you see two nations in one
area" (Mokhara, in Nessman, p. 10A). That, indeed, is the problem that
Nadine Gordimer, André Brink, Athol Fugard, and J. M. Coetzee address in
their fiction and drama. Politicians and diplomats use what Rosa Burger, in
Nadine Gordimer's *Burger's Daughter*, calls "the long words" (1984, p. 194).
She refers to First World words uttered during apartheid to justify colonialism. What African writers emphasize is that the colonial language of most
use, even today, comes from a history and tradition embedded in European
thought. As we know, Eurocentric thinking is logical. Language is logos: classification, dichotomy, abstraction. It is what some people eventually come to
believe as a way of life, an absolute, a metanarrative: immutable, fundamental,
preconditional. Such is what one character in André Brink's novel *A Dry
White Season* calls the "spell of the Abstract" that allowed the emergence of
phenomena like Hitler or apartheid, the false ideals known as Manifest Destiny or The American Dream, or the frantic backtracking of Trent Lott trying to pretend he is not a racist.[1] Lofty lingo is what Bill Pinar calls "racial-
ized fantasies of civilization, religion, and manly conquest" (2000, p. 273).
"And what has all your history taught you?" asks Stanley in Brink's novel.

"Fuck-all," he says. "Because you *lanies* keep thinking history is made right here where you are and noplace else. Why don't you come with me one day, I'll show you what history really looks like. Bare-arsed history" (Brink, p. 86).

The point about language's stranglehold on history, culture and identity has been made, of course, in theoretical and scientific writings as well in fiction. Franz Fanon, in his groundbreaking treatise on South Africa, observed, "the colonial world is a world cut in two" (1963, p. 52). And Sartre, in his preface to Fanon's book, remarked that Europeans would "do well to read Fanon" (p. 21), observing that apartheid not only dehumanizes by violence and imprisonment but also by substituting European language for African language, thereby wiping out tradition (p. 15). The first systematic defense of apartheid theory, 1945–1948, was elaborated in a series of widely read books by one Geoff Cronje, a sociology professor of Pretoria University, who based his purity and separation theory on the Bible, claiming that it was God's injunction to respect the diversity of nations, meaning the purity of the white race (Deb, 1995, p. 174). Cronje further did a "study" of South African literature, concluding its inferiority because of the nonabstract way in which Africans perceived the world. One response to such scientism is aptly put by Trinh-minh ha: "Trying to find the other by defining otherness or by explaining the other through laws and generalities is, as Zen says, like beating the moon with a pole or scratching an itchy foot from the outside of a shoe" (1989, p. 75).

Another response is offered by Ben-Du Toit, a white schoolteacher in suburban Johannesburg and the protagonist of Brink's aforementioned novel. Ben is jolted out of a life comforted by the belief in a fairminded South African government when a black friend is arrested and then supposedly commits suicide. Investigating the incident draws Ben farther and farther away from his security and into a world about which he knows nothing. Brink offers several pages of some of the clearest writing I have seen on what constitutes white privilege:

> From a very early age one accepts, or believes, or is told, that certain things exist in a certain manner. For example: that society is based on order, on reason, on justice. . . . I've always taken "my own people" so much for granted that I now have to start thinking from scratch. It has never been a problem to me before. "My own people" have always been around me and with me. . . . People speaking my language, taking the name of my God on their lips, sharing my history. That history which Gie calls "the History of European Civilization in South Africa." . . . And then there were the "others." The Jewish shopkeeper, the English chemist. . . . And the blacks. . . . But it remained a matter of "us" and "them." It was a good and comfortable division. . . . If it hadn't been ordained explicitly in the Scriptures, then certainly it was implied by the variegated creation of an omniscient Father, and it didn't behoove us to interfere with His handiwork. . . . His ways by bringing forth impossible hybrids. That was the way it had always been. (160, p. 162)

Hybrids. The variegated creation. Not high breeds. My animal family are hybrids. So too my flowers. I am a hybrid. And now my classes are hybrids, students from all over the world. Such a different teaching situation from those classes I taught in blond California or West Bank New Orleans, in Algiers parish, where the world "parochial" takes on literal meaning. But now my white students from Cincinnati talk with my black students from Togo, and soon we are examining exactly what my white students had always taken for granted: their privilege. I think particularly of the class discussion concerning Nadine Gordimer's "Town and Country Lovers," which once again forefronts the two Africas, one of white privilege and one of the townships.

The story concerns an Austrian geologist—a prospector—who comes to South Africa to mine its rich resources of gold, copper, platinum, uranium, flesh. He gets involved with a black cashier in the local grocery store; one thing leading to another, they become lovers until one day the police arrest them for contravening the Immorality Act, the backbone of the apartheid laws against interracial relations. I made particular point in teaching this story to ask the students to find examples of Dr. von Leinsdorf's stereotypical thinking, carefully laced inside the sentences of Nadine Gordimer's prose. I wanted to emphasize that racism depends on an "us" versus "them" mentality that places "them" in broad, sweeping categories (stereotypes) of lesser value than those accorded "us." I also wanted to emphasize that racist language can be extremely subtle, sometimes overlooked or ignored because so seemingly innocuous ("Some of my best friends are black"; "I don't see color, I just see people"). Other formulations equate racism with the pride of heritage ("I voted for Strom Thurmond and I'm proud of it"). Quite a few of my white students just didn't get it. Not even when we reread the text for lines like this, reflective of the Austrian geologist's thinking: "These young coloured girls are usually pretty unhelpful, taking money and punching their machines in a manner that asserts with the time-serving obstinacy or the half-literate the limit of any responsibility towards customers" (Gordimer, 2003, p. 367). What is his attitude, his assumption here, I prod. Or this line: "It was difficult to know how to treat these people, in this country" (p. 368) Or this line: "He laughed, instructive: . . . In my country we drink only real coffee, fresh, from the beans" (p. 368). Or his description of her face: "She had a little yokel's, peasant's (he thought of it) gap between her two front teeth when she smiled that he didn't much like. . . . He said, watching her sew, 'You're a good girl'" (p. 369).

Gordimer, in this story, skillfully shows how racism and sexism are connected. Both are attitudinal assumptions that Europeans are higher on the scale of humanity, and are "pure." The purity fantasy is, of course, racism's first line of defense. What astonished me in my classes was the extent to which some of my white students could not get off their defensive positions. They simply accepted von Leinsdorf's thoughts and descriptions as "natural" "given the circumstance." Loaded word, that—"natural"—and transparent phrase, that—"given the circumstance." Most of my black students understood what language was hiding. Some smiled but refused to speak. Others offered personal examples of how situations like those faced by the country lover were also faced by them. And they instructed the class and me in even more subtle examples from the text of the kind of arrogance that accompanies the racist mindset. So indoctrinated are these stereotypes, as if they are ordained, that one particular white student, coming back to the text for the third time, shook his head in disbelief. "I don't see any stereotyping here," he announced—proudly, I thought.

Perhaps I should have shown George (I'll call him) this remarkable passage in Brink's novel that says in plain talk what whites are often completely unaware of—their privileged position in social contexts:

> I am white. And because I am white I am born into a state of privilege. Even if I fight the system that has reduced us to this I remain white, and favoured by the very circumstances I abhor. Even if I am hated, and ostracized, and persecuted and in the end destroyed, nothing can make me black. (p. 304)

Ironically, I think my student could have grown up when I did, during the era when America was touted as the "melting pot." We all were to simmer together in this stew of national identity. But as Henry Giroux (1994) points out, the problem of nationalism is its appeal to a cultural uniformity that removes difference. Not only that, the appeal to one nation indivisible operates to keep the stereotypes in place and whites in power. Whites like my student or, more dangerously, like the former majority leader of the United States Senate, have immersed themselves in what Martha calls the fictions of their lives. When different identities are ignored, overlooked, or invisibled, then communities become frozen, or gated (the same thing), and landscapes lack nuance.

The psychosocial dimension of language is a major issue in Athol Fugard's *"Master Harold"... and the Boys*. Fugard himself was the son of a mother who was an Afrikaner and a father of English descent, thus representing two different white communities in South Africa. The play immediately indicates racial divide with the words "boys"—two older black servants—and "master"—young white Harold. We learn that Harold, or Hally as he is called (a nickname that points to his youth and naiveté), hates his father, a drunk and a cripple; Sam, the older of the two black men, is his father substitute. When a child, Hally would go into the cramped servant quarters and play games with the two men. Hally still spars with them after school and, on occasion, the young "master" teaches the older "boys" geography lessons: "Gold in the Transvaal, mealies in the Free State, sugar in Natal, and grapes in the Cape" (2003, p. 564). What lies beneath the lesson is the lure to Africa of racist colonists like Hally's father—a point the young master seems not to recognize.

The young master also seems not to recognize his own relocated desire for the black older man as mentor, father, playmate, lover. But Sam rejects all such projections and instead tries to get Hally to have compassion for his father. Hally will have none of it: "What you are trying to do is meddle in something you know nothing about. All that concerns you in here, Sam, is to try and do what you get paid for. . . . You're only a servant in here, and don't forget it" (p. 582). As Sam stands his ground, Hally reaches for the only strength he has: language. "Why don't you also start calling me Master Harold" (p. 583). And then he brings the situation to a head by taunting Sam with a joke he and his father share: "'It's not fair, is it, Hally.' Then I have to ask, 'What, chum?' And then he says, 'A nigger's arse' and we both have a good laugh'" (p. 584).

The climax comes when Sam calls Hally's bluff: "It's me you're after. You should just have said 'Sam's arse' . . . because that's the one you're trying to kick. Anyway, how do you know it's not fair? You've never seen it. Do you want to? *(He drops his trousers and underpants and presents his backside for Hally's inspection)*" (p. 584). What Hally tried to do was "put Sam in his place" by symbolically castrating him. Instead, Sam, by literalizing the joke, refuses to be phallicly identified with white male privilege.

Fugard raises issues about the gender of racial politics (Pinar, 2000). In the wake of sublimated desire churns the flotsam of disavowal and racism (Pinar, p. 1103). Language, white Eurocentric language, keeps the disavowals going by using terms like Master and jokes about "a nigger's arse." Language, Fugard implies, is the skirt behind which homosocial, racist truths can hide. Who really wants to be dominated here? Why is desire so dangerous? And what, at bottom, is the racist's fear?

Fugard's play is taken from an actual incident in his own life. The character of Hally is, as one reviewer wrote, a "ruthlessly honest portrait of the playwright as a young man" (Rich, 1999, p. 640). If, as the reviewer claimed, the play forces viewers to confront their own capacity for cruelty, then that would indeed be a huge move in the process of "unself-knowing" (Pinar, 2000, p. 856). I think many of the novels about postcolonial Africa written by whites depict protagonists struggling with their unconscious, and this, it seems to me, is the brave and wonderful thing these writers offer. For there can be no movement on the social front if there is no movement on the psychic front.

Ben's daughter Linda, in Brink's novel, expresses her struggle with this point:

Dorothy was someone I thought I knew; she'd helped Dad to bring me up; she lived with me in the same house every day of my life. You know, it felt like the first time I'd ever really looked right into someone else's life [when she went to Dorothy's home]. . . . It wasn't the poverty as such: one knows about poverty, one reads the newspapers, one isn't blind, one even has a "social conscience." As if for the first time, I made the discovery that other lives existed. And worst of all was the feeling that *I knew just as little about my own life as about theirs* [italics added]. (p. 130)

What Ben and his daughter Linda reveal to us is their struggle to live as decent human beings able to see injustice as it really is and to work for change. But their seeing comes only as they walk in others' shoes and visit the tin shacks and see to what extent the colonial system has displaced blacks both physically and psychically, taking them away, as one writer put it "from ourselves to other selves, from our world to other worlds" (Thiong'o, 1995, p. 288). This seeing then gives Ben and his daughter the "anxious knowledge" (Britzman, 1998) about their own ignorance, as if, suddenly, they have come to realize that there is another side of the moon and that people have landed there. This knowledge forces them to take the next step: to see through the hypocrisy of the noble-sounding words they had grown up with—"authority," "law," "reason"—and to admit that "truth" means to reject the notion of "justice." What is justice if it incarcerates the innocent, murders the guiltless, legitimates discrimination, instantiates policy? When attitudes become policy, as in apartheid Africa, the issue of racism becomes ever more problematic (Morris, 2001b). Ultimately the issue forces understanding of what Braj B. Kachru says: "The English language is a tool of power, domination, and elitist identity, and of communication across continents" (1995, p. 291). As Ben and Linda each begin to question language, each does the far more scary interrogation into that other self, the self within.

Nadine Gordimer (1984) examines the unexamined life of an elitist daughter of a social reformer, in *Burger's Daughter*. As the title indicates Rosa Burger is known only through her father, who died a martyr's death fighting against apartheid by espousing Marxist solutions. "I lived in my father's presence without knowing its meaning," she says (p. 82). It is as if she occupies a place in which something has occurred of which she knows nothing. She, too, is a Marxist, attends rallies, supports the cause, gives interviews about her father, abhors bourgeois concerns. But always she lives in the shadow of the great man who taught her how to act so well that her second nature has become her first.

Gordimer shows the irony of Rosa Burger's existence: it is her own mother tongue, spoken by her father, that keeps her from herself. Deleuze says there is no mother tongue, "only a power taken over by a dominant language within a political multiplicity" (Deleuze & Guattari, 1988, p. 7). Rosa, I suggest, has been "taken over" by the powerful influence of her father's speeches. And, like the "political multiplicity" of Africa, she too has been colonized by the patriarchy, with its phallologocentrism.

In one scene, Rosa examines a medieval painting of a lady and a unicorn. The passage serves, I think, as Gordimer's critique of the art/life opposition inherent in European painting and writing, and representative of Rosa's stunted inner life:

On an azure island of a thousand flowers the Lady is holding a mirror in which the unicorn with his forelegs on the folded-back red velvet of her dress's lining sees a tiny image of himself. But the oval of the mirror cuts off the image just at the level at which the horn rises from his head. . . . An old and lovely world, gardens and gentle beauties among gentle beasts. Such harmony and sensual peace in the age of the thumbscrew and dungeon. (Gordimer, pp. 340, 341)

Rosa can't get enough of this painting. She gazes and gazes at it. On one level it represents reified perfection, the sort of classicism that colonialism sought to perpetuate. But on another level the painting mocks that which it purports to portray. What so fascinates Rosa, I suggest, is the painting's doubling and tripling of realities: complexities within the frame. This contrast to her mode of being draws her into the heart of the painting without her knowing quite what it is that compels. For, while the unicorn is classically a symbol of purity, its horn is cut off in the reflection, its sexual power truncated. And while the still-life garden seems paradisial, it is ruptured by the incongruity of overt harmony and covert violence. Rosa's fascination offers a glimmering into her own passive resistance to full conscious awareness; until now, she has been able to see only her father's image in her mirror: a reflection that, like herself, like South Africa, is cut in two.

By focusing on the daughter of a Marxist hero, Gordimer problematizes the notion of Rosa's father's righteous cause. After all, Rosa's world is peopled with people of good intention. They keep up the fight against apartheid by holding meetings, visiting prisoners, speaking out, agitating; they discredit their Boer ancestors as well as the standards of Western civilization. But throughout all the sloganeering, Rosa remains a half-person, as if she herself has had her identity "narrated" by her father's words. She smiles with her father's smile. She adopts a pattern of evasion, detachment, and deviousness, changing the subject whenever questioned by her collective about her personal thoughts or feelings. "For me to be free," she says, "is never to be free of the survival cunning of concealment" (p. 142).

And then Rosa has a terrible-wonderful thing happen to her. She receives a phone call in the middle of the night from her long lost childhood friend, a *kafferjie* named Baasie whom once she called her "brother." The night before the two had, by chance, attended the same party in London, where Rosa now was visiting. The night caller needed to express his disgust at Rosa's willingness to talk so publicly about her father at the party:

Everyone in the world must be told what a great hero he was and how much he suffered for the blacks. Everyone must cry over him and show his life on television and write in the papers. Listen, there are dozens of our fathers sick and dying like dogs, kicked out of the locations when they can't work any more. Getting old and dying in prison. Killed in prison. It's nothing. I know plenty blacks like Burger. It's nothing to us, we must be used to it. . . . Whatever you whites touch, it's takeover. He was my father. Even when we get free they'll want us to remember to thank Lionel Burger. (pp. 320, 321)

The telephone call wakes Rosa up, finally, from her long slumber in unconsciousness. Both her "brother" and she had been diminished by the father's heroism. She did not know this consciously until her "brother" literally woke her up. The dismantling of the father, together with the rage of the caller, signals that the revolution has entered a new speaking place. The "brother" has asserted himself with new words to Rosa's ears, words that do not speak Marxist white talk. It is significant, too, that the" brother" has changed his name so as to rid himself of his white "father." "I'm not 'Baasie,' I'm Zwelinzima Vulindlela" (p. 318). By Zwelinzima's speaking to Rosa about the privilege of her white father's death—that which afforded Burger martyrdom, legacy, a name for history; that which afforded her respect, honor, a name for reporters—he asserts a different speaking place for himself. Actually, he becomes a true brother, freeing both himself and Rosa from the white patriarch's words. As Jeremy Cronin puts it, "the achievement of liberation will inevitably also be a major linguistic event" (p. 11).

So what can be done in a continent composed of so many traditions and languages? Not only are there Swahili, Sulu, Yoruba, Arabic, Griqua, Amharic, and other African languages; there are also Afrikaans, English, and creolized slang, as well as other cultures like Khoi Greek, Jewish, and Portuguese. Enter a "motley space," as Ralph Pordzik (2001, p. 181) terms it or a "pan-colonial society" as Adebayo Williams calls it (1999, p. 8). Could this societal space offer a possibility for agency and change? Or is such thinking "a Sisyphean venture"? (Williams, 2000, p. 179). Perhaps what had been, under the social-symbolic system inherent in the colonial language, a freezing of movement and expression now can open into a new "disarticulation" (Barnard, 2001). Perhaps the sheer materiality of noise can dissolve the univocal voice of apartheid South Africa. The new poetry that emerges in the new speaking places seems now to be characterized by a stumbling, exploding, grinding, stuttering: language of sound, not sign. This "jerking talk" (Barnard, p. 164) would seem to make new spaces from within a discourse that had denied space. There is, in much new poetry of South Africa, a sense of renewal and reversal because meaning is produced outside the English sentence in other sound forms. The poet Jeremy Cronin exclaims, "let flesh be made of words" (1987, p. 52).

Something of the flesh of words can be felt in the writing of novelist and essayist Toni Morrison. I recall teaching her *The Bluest Eye* as an oral exercise. The text seemed to demand being heard. Otherwise, students would miss the sing-song of the characters' voices as they play back and forth with one another, even in the midst of poverty or despair. What Robin Small-McCarthy calls Morrison's "transmodal discourse" offers multiple ways to "sound" African American experience, everything from literary improvisation and call-and-response patterns to nonlinear narrative shifts and dissonant characterizations (1999, p. 171). These new sound forms of expression are what Homi Bhabha refers to as an "an enactive enunciatory site that opens up possibilities for other . . . narrative spaces" (p. 178). These open spaces seem free from polarities and totalities, employing music, drumbeat, or ritual for another instance: a new "cultural mode of articulation" (West, 1988, p. 281). Nothing is meant to be coherent. Rather, the language of resistance by black artists is energetically fractured, multiple, as if "being pieced together from scraps of random, irreverent words—some of hybrid colonial history" (Cronin, in Barnard, p. 167). In sounding out identity, the struggle for decolonization takes on shape and space in the wide open theater of the mouth.

If not all postcolonial writing is celebratory, it does complexify Eurocentric conceptions of heroism and history, as the works by white writers like Nadine Gordimer, Athol Fugard, and André Brink demonstrate. In taking that step, these writers offer something unique, particularly to white educators. Each of the cited works transforms our sense of what it is to live, to be, in other spaces. As Homi Bhabha puts it, "It is from those who have suffered the sentence of history—subjugation, domination, Diaspora, displacement—that we learn our most enduring lessons for living and thinking" (1994, p. 172). Where we readers of these fictions find ourselves is in a place of disjunction, displacement, and disorientation. Another "dis" underlies J. M Coetzee's novel *Disgrace*, suggesting that not only place but grace is hidden in the new postcolonial moment. Can we learn, live, and think in the moment? As I offer final comments, I need to caution myself against generalizing the contingencies of local circumstances. But with the help of Homi Bhabha, I see these writers urging the need to "grasp the hybrid moment outside the sentence" (1994, p. 178).

J. M. Coetzee shares with Nadine Gordimer the distinction of being the second South African to win the Nobel Prize for Literature. Commenting on Coetzee, the Nobel committee described him as "a scrupulous doubter, ruthless in his criticism of the cruel rationalism and cosmetic morality of western civilization." *Disgrace* defies classification, just as the writer himself is uncomfortable with either/ors—a form of thinking that gives rationalism its prime place in the cruelties of Western thought. Rather, I consider his purpose similar to that of the ancient alchemists, who saw their project of transforming lead into gold as an *opus contra naturam*, a work against nature. Salvation, if that can be the word, comes to his characters through a downward spiraling: in the case of *Disgrace*, through thoroughgoing humiliation.

Coetzee's protagonist thus enters the hybrid moment of a "post" era and takes us to the brink of an emergent knowledge.

Professor David Lurie is filled with desire but lacks passion. "Desire is a burden we could well do without," he says (Coetzee, 1999, p. 90). Because of this burden he cannot rid himself of, he is disgraced when an affair costs him his academic position and forces him into exile to live with his lesbian daughter on her small farm. But, like Camus's "stranger," Lurie exists on the outskirts of all social norms. In that sense he is the perfect ex-centric to deal with the indeterminacies that face him and his daughter Lucy. Living outside the Englishness of the city, his country life is surrounded by menace and terror: Lurie's daughter is gang-raped, one of the rapists being the son of her yard man. She refuses to report him and insists on marrying her rapist's father, a polygamist. The situation defies English logic. But that seems to be Coetzee's point. He forces us to rethink the profound limitations of liberal thought. Rather, cultural identity is constructed through a process of alterity, with no possibility for assimilating. Lurie's daughter will not be sleeping with her yardman-husband but will be engaging in a swap: "Petrus [the husband] is not offering me a church wedding followed by a honeymoon on the Wild Coast. He is offering an alliance, a deal. I contribute the land, in return for which I am allowed to creep under his wing. Otherwise, he wants to remind me, I am without protection, I am fair game" (p. 203). Lucy knows the full extent of her limitations. While the situation for her is humiliating, she observes, "But perhaps that is a good point to start from again. Perhaps that is what I must learn to accept. To start at ground level" (p. 205).

The unflinching narrative Coetzee writes gives an entirely new idea of ground level culture. As Homi Bhabha says, "culture becomes . . . an uncomfortable, disturbing practice of survival" (1994, p. 175). It is the white woman who accepts her defeat; it is the white woman's father who sees his future grandson not as his grandson but as a child of the earth. These are what Delese calls the simple truths that come from watching more carefully the circumferences of one's world. Coetzee thereby changes the subject positions, providing, in Homi Bhabha's words, "a process by which objectified others may be turned into subjects of their history and experience" (p. 178).

The implications of postcolonial writing for the postmodern classroom are several. We are in the territory of emergent knowledge. The project is basically one of deconstruction. Derrida reminds us that deconstruction "has nothing to do with destruction" but rather involves "being alert to the implications, to the historical sedimentation of the language we use" (1972, p. 231). What may appear objective, universally valid, and consensual needs to be demystified. Meanings, after all, are produced and identities are narrated in what may seem to be perfectly logical ways (Giroux, 1994). But unless we learn to recognize the exclusions from the discussion, we will be blinded by our own privilege. As Noel Gough writes:

> The particular ways in which we give meaning to ourselves, others and the
> world may be formulated through discourses of which we are largely unaware

or which are taken for granted. Novelists like Coetzee give these discourses substance and pattern and help us not only to perceive the stories and mythologies that frame our social interactions, but also to recognize and deploy their potentials for renewal, metamorphosis, and reinvention. (2001, p. 110)

The project involves more than finding the gaps. As the disgrace of Senator Lott's words reveals, sometimes what is taken for granted will remain forever taken, in granite. Perception is not always possible, even when multiple examples are brought to attention. The postmodern project is fraught, since the position of privilege is mighty, it is comfortable, and it can lead to the highest chambers of our land. So the project requires listening, as well perceiving. The new languages emerging from the African postcolonial period are less noun-centered, more verb-oriented, to suggest both movement and constraint so common to the African experience. Perhaps as the ear is attuned to the "jerking talk" (Barnard, 2001) of new voices, a new space can open up for a new listening.

Africa, in the postapartheid age, is clearly in transition. Nadine Gordimer thinks it is a new world for the displaced and denied and dishonored (Brown, 2001, p. 496). Coetzee thinks that the new postapartheid government is not the opposite of the old, not better. This is no time for sentimentalisms but for a clear eye into disruptions, debasements, and disgraces. For being so unsentimental about South Africa's new rulers, Coetzee has been criticized. He answers equivocally, "I am a writer, a trader in fictions. . . . I maintain beliefs only provisionally: fixed beliefs would stand in my way" (Freemantle, 2003). Africa's transition opens up a space for talking or thinking, or perhaps drumming or dancing, so as to create a scaffold for that which has been left void. Perhaps. The transition puts in question fixed belief, as demonstrated by the conferees at the Durban international meeting on racism. They hurled slogans at one another, or boycotted attendance, leaving, in the wake of their disagreements, renewed racial and religious hatred worldwide. In the United States as in Africa there is a desperate struggle of values and resentment, more desperate now than I could have imagined when I began this essay. Ending this essay more than a year after the 9/11 attacks and an hour after the Lott debacle, I am realizing that, like Beckett's Unnamable, "you must say words, as long as there are any" (1958, p. 414), but the words you say are loaded.

AMAZING (DIS)GRACE

Delese

Redemption can be corny, of course, but so can despair.
—Ravitch (2001, p. 151)

I picked up J. M. Coetzee's *Disgrace* after a friend told me I would be terribly disturbed by it. The book is the story of fifty-two-year-old David Lurie, a white academic who loses his teaching position after having an affair with Melanie, a female student in one of his classes. He leaves postapartheid Cape Town to live with his daughter Lucy, a woman in her mid-twenties who lives in the Eastern Cape where she owns a small farm and supports herself by growing and selling produce and flowers and by kenneling dogs. But the deceptively quiet life in the country is broken when two men and a young boy, all black, attack Lucy and David in her house, gang raping Lucy and setting fire to David, killing the dogs, and robbing them.

David's public disgrace refers to losing his academic position. He is a disgraceful man because of his actions, but also seems to be without grace long before the story opens. We learn on the first page that he thought he had "solved the problem of sex rather well" by visiting a sex worker for ninety minutes a week, but his pathetic harassment of a female student indicates how little he had "solved." He tells her, with astonishing self-absorption and manipulation wielded by his power, that "a woman's beauty does not belong to her alone. It is part of the bounty she brings into the world. She has a duty to share it" (Coetzee, p. 16). A few days later, nothing could stop him on his living room floor, even her lack of response: "She does not resist. All she does is avert herself: avert her lips, avert her eyes. . . . Not rape, not quite that, but undesired nevertheless, undesired to the core" (p. 25). When the university catches wind of his behavior, he sits before a committee of his peers but refuses to act penitent. "I became a servant of Eros" (p. 52), he says. He wasn't much better with his explanation to Lucy later in the book when she asks him to tell her his "side": "My case rests on the rights of desire," he says. "It was a god who acted through me" (p. 89).

I read on, repulsed yet intrigued with this character, this caricature of unbridled male libido, this abuse of power as a male/teacher. He is grotesque in his arrogance and contempt for women even as he uses them, unconcerned with how they experience him. It is as though apartheid-ways of thinking about domination, superiority, and separateness frame his view of women, too. Indeed apartheid and sex were inextricably linked by the Immorality Amendment Act Number 23 of 1957, which prohibited "unlawful carnal intercourse . . . between a white person on the one hand and an African, Indian or Coloured on the other" (Omond, 1985). David's "carnal" behavior steps over the divide even as his condescension toward women does not.

Grace: from the Latin *gratia*, pleasing quality, favor, good will.

Everything changes after Lucy is raped. When she reports the robbery but not the rape to the police, David listens without interruption with images and chants from his childhood coming back "to point a jeering finger . . . [at] Lucy's secret; his disgrace" (Coetzee, p. 109). Another disgrace added to his behavior with a student: He was unable to help his daughter as she was being raped, just as he was "unable" to help himself as he was forcing himself on Melanie. Were his daughter's attackers also carrying the "burden" of desire David could not rid himself of when he had sex with a student who did not want him? Of course they were not, David would say. He was an intellectual, a white intellectual, a student of Byron and opera.

The emotional damage Lucy suffers is severe, but she is unwilling to communicate with her father, telling him he is incapable of understanding what she has been through and what her attitude is toward the event and her attackers. She's right, David thinks, but he does understand one angle of the event. "If he concentrates, if he loses himself, [he can] be there, be the men, inhabit them, fill them with the ghost of himself. The question is, does he have it in him to be the woman?" No, David cannot understand why she does not mention the rape to the police, or confront her neighbor and farm assistant Petrus, who seems somehow an accessory to the attack. As Lucy sinks silently into a depression, David begins to spend more time with Bev Shaw, Lucy's friend who is a kind of lay vet, helping her put down sick and unwanted farm animals and pets.

I almost began to feel some sympathy for David at this point, some kind of parental bond we feel in the protective love we have for our children, I suppose. That is, until he sleeps with Bev, all the while noting what an unlikely sexual partner she was for him, this "dumpy, bustling little woman with black freckles, close-cropped, wiry hair, and no neck . . . who make[s] no effort to be attractive" (p. 72). When it is over, he chides himself to stop calling her "poor Bev Shaw," for "if she is poor, he is bankrupt" (p. 150). Even though Bev initiated the sexual relationship, David is a cool, perfunctory participant: "He does his duty. Without passion but without distaste either. So that in the end Bev Shaw can feel pleased with herself. . . . He, David Lurie, has been succoured, as a man is succoured by a woman" (p. 150). His condescension toward Bev becomes another contemptible moment in his twisted attitude and behavior toward women.

Grace: a sense of what is right and proper; decency.

David Lurie, once quite handsome, an intellectual, a scholar of Romantic poetry, author of books on opera, Eros, and Wordsworth, is now an unpaid worker at an animal shelter. Not just any worker, he is the one in charge of disposing the remains of the animals Bev euthanizes. Each morning he drives a loaded truck to a hospital incinerator where he throws the black bags into the fire. But somehow this act has turned into something more than mere disposal of soulless animals:

> It would be simpler to cart the bags to the incinerator immediately after the
> session and leave them there for the incinerator crew to dispose of. But that

would mean leaving them on the dump with the rest of the weekend's scourings: with waste from the hospital wards, carrion scooped up at the roadside, malodorous refuse from the tannery—a mixture both casual and terrible. He is not prepared to inflict such dishonour upon them. (p. 144)

How can this be the man who, only months before had so "casually and terribly" violated a student, now worries that already dead animals are "dishonoured" if he personally doesn't handle this final act?

I am not seduced, even if I do acknowledge that there may be a small place in David's heart that is soft and tender and compassionate. Even he is confused with his feelings; until now he had been "more or less" indifferent to animals. Now he grieves for the animals he helps to kill, fetching them from their cages and holding them while Bev injects them. He believes the dogs know what is going on: "They flatten their ears, they droop their tails, as if they too feel the disgrace of dying" (p. 143). How is their death a disgrace, I wonder? Why has Coetzee used this word here, too? David's disgrace, on the other hand, is apparent and deserved. Do the animals' deaths reflect humans' careless, disgraceful treatment of them, these creatures who co-inhabit the earth with us?

Grace: mercy; clemency.

After Lucy is raped David somehow begins to realize that his student Melanie Issacs has a father who, like him, must feel pain for his daughter and anger toward her attacker. David arrives unannounced at the school where Mr. Isaacs is an administrator, offering "his side" of the story that Mr. Issacs never requested. David tells him that his relationship with his daughter was not premeditated but began as an "adventure" until something unexpected happened and she struck up a "fire" in him. Still arrogant, he is shockingly clueless as to the effect such a disclosure would have on the father of the young woman he had raped. Nonetheless, Issacs returns the shock by inviting him to dinner, which turns into a painfully awkward encounter with the rest of the family, minus Melanie, that includes her mother and sister younger Desiree. "Desiree, the desired one," David thinks as he watches her closely, intimately, even in her prim school uniform. Still a "servant of Eros," he gazes on her body and thinks, "Fruit of the same tree, down probably to the most intimate detail. . . . The two of them in the same bed: an experience fit for a king" (p. 164). Even during this apparent gesture of atonement in Melanie's parents' home, his desire is incorrigible.

Just as he is getting ready to leave, he once again brings up the subject of Melanie to her father, this time apologizing . . . sort of: "I am sorry for what I took your daughter through. . . . I apologize for the grief I have caused you and Mrs. Isaacs. I ask for your pardon" (p. 171). Isaacs accepts his apology, but turns it back on him by asking what he was going to do now that he was sorry, and if he knew what God had in mind for him. Explaining that he was not a believer, David nonetheless offers the following response:

> In my own terms, I am being punished for what happened between myself and your daughter. I am sunk into a state of disgrace from which it will not be easy to lift myself. It is not a punishment I have refused. I do not murmur against it. On the contrary, I am living it out from day to day, trying to accept disgrace as my state of being. Is it enough for God, do you think, that I live in disgrace without term? (p. 172)

Before he leaves, he seeks out Melanie's mother and her younger sister, gets to his knees and touches his forehead to the floor. "*Is that enough?* he thinks. *Will that do? If not, what more?*" (p. 173).

I am appalled, again, probably too unyielding in my own beliefs, hypercritical of this apology. No, it isn't enough that he apologize to her family for the grief he caused them all, and no, it isn't enough that he live in disgrace. I have become the committee at the university: I want contriteness for his crime against a young woman, not remorse that he wasn't lyrical enough.

Grace: a divine or cosmic influence on humans making them kind, loving, and forgiving.

All the while the action of the story is occurring—the crimes and relationships between fathers and daughters, blacks and whites, humans and animals—I almost missed the quiet, honest, organic integrity moving the novel along, mostly by Lucy. Her life and beliefs are reflected by the grace of living her life as the practice of survival. "This is the only life there is," she tells her father, "which we share with animals. . . . That's the example I try to follow. To share some of our human privilege with the beasts. I don't want to come back in another existence as a dog or a pig and have to live as dogs or pigs live under us" (p. 74). When she decides to turn over her land to Petrus and marry him in return for her safety, David cannot believe it. "How humiliating," he says finally. "Such high hopes, and to end like this." Her reply:

> Yes, I agree, it is humiliating. But perhaps that is a good point to start from again. Perhaps that is what I must learn to accept. To start at ground level. With nothing. Not with nothing but. With nothing. No cards, no weapons, no property, no rights, no dignity. (p. 205)

"Like a dog," David answers, to which she said, "Yes, like a dog" (p. 205).

By the end of the novel, David is similarly contemplating such simple truths, most of them arising from his work with animals. He has also come to believe that "the enormous violations of South African history can be met only with absurdly small acts of recompense" (Merkin, 1999, p. 111). He has learned this from watching Lucy as she tries to live with humility, patience, and tolerance of her black neighbors, even those who hurt her; he has learned this from watching Bev as she cares for cast-off animals, treating them with tender respect even as she injects them. "You don't mind?" David asks Bev about injecting the animals. "I do mind," she answers. "I mind deeply. I wouldn't want someone doing it for me who didn't mind. Would you?" (Coetzee, p. 85). So David comes to mind, and in minding, he moves slowly toward grace in that realm and in his relationship with Lucy and his not-yet-born grandchild, this child of "mixed" blood that represents a breakdown of one of the key elements of apartheid: "keeping things apart at every level: sexual, social, conceptual" (Ravitch, p. 149). As Michael Gorra wrote in his review of the novel, Coetzee "makes us understand but not sympathize with David's intellectual arrogance and incorrigible desire" (1999, p. 7). And now, as I put the book down, I can't help it: I begin to sympathize, too, and moments of grace begin to appear everywhere.

DISGRACE: A PLACE TO BEGIN ANEW

Martha

Is it true, then, that we must delve into the psyche, if we are to create movement on the social front? It's a lot to ponder. In the Western world, critical theorists, socialist feminists, poststructural analysts, educational anarchists, proponents of democratic classrooms—those who scoff at the impossibility of such an ideal—pour words onto the page with the intent of moving society forward. I show up each day, in part, because I believe doing nothing not only results in stasis but in atrophy—the fragile strands of hope woven through my days must be tethered lest they float away on the weakest of breezes. But there are always dangers lurking beneath the surface. When you're white and employed by the academy, no one asks if you're encouraging movement on the psychic front. And it's easy to feign empathy.

Professor David Lurie of Coetzee's *Disgrace* journeys inward. Against his will, perhaps. But the journey is decidedly interior. Along the way, I am captured by his point of view. Initially, he claims self-knowledge. Knows "his temperament." Makes moral and ethical judgments based on those perceptions. When your choices are real, your position relatively secure, your privilege in place, your skin, your language, your degrees steadily paving the way for you, judgments come easily. I begin to journey with Lurie as his life spins out of control. Alternately taking his view (not difficult, given our common life positioning) and loathing his choices (not difficult, given our gender disconnect), pulled in by the bizarre circumstances that force Lurie into a process that might best be described as incremental decentering. His daughter finally sums him up. "You behave as if everything I do is part of the story of your life. You are the main character" (p. 198). She is exhausted by his expectations, his confusion, his lived experiences continually impinging on her own during an unbelievably difficult time. Like Delese, I find Lurie despicable—yet intriguing. And as I am batted about, shifting my positionality unexpectedly—now Lurie, now not—I, too, am forced to decenter.

Here's the black man, Petrus, complicating things by refusing to be predictable. There was a time when apartheid guaranteed certain simplicities. Us and them. But Petrus refuses the stereotype, nor will he succumb to Lurie's attempts to deconstruct his being. First, Lurie hopes to accept him, even be his friend—never expecting that this black man will transgress the boundaries of his expectations in ways that will rattle the core of the scholar-dreamer's being. And how could Lurie have guessed that his own daughter would enter the dance with this boundary breaker? In so doing, she defies his multiple attempts to take in her chosen life without dismantling his own.

Disgrace. First Lurie seems liberated in some way by his unwillingness to move beyond his admission of guilt. Guilty as charged. But sorry? Disgraced? Disgrace, he asserts, can only be externally imposed. He will not get emotional about this. Certainly not in public. He'll leave the moral rectitude to his accusers. His first glimpse of the difficulty of such tidy compartmentalization occurs when his weekly sexual liaison (purchased, therefore somehow justified) turns up unexpectedly outside the boundaries of their clandestine meetings—with children. Where there are children there is likely to be a husband, he thinks with a shudder. As if this were not messy enough, he lures a young student into his lair. Confused by what he considers the curse of desire, he seems almost to be seeking conviction with his foolhardy behavior. But when conviction comes, it is only the conviction of others since he stalwartly refuses self-indictment. There's a process here. And it feels entirely too familiar. For Lurie, it may be a tug-of-war between believing his life is "handled" and crying out for a dismantling of his charade. For me, there is tension between living the life I've been given without scratching the surface of my privilege too deeply, yet aching to do something that matters. Really matters.

Suddenly, against his will (or is it?), Lurie is plunged into experiences that inescapably lead to psychic movement. His world is no longer his. The ground beneath his feet has shifted. Not just horizontal adjustments. Upheaval. After the dreadful attack, seeming near death, he resists depending on others, despite his obvious need. Unable to pull himself from the charitably provided bath, he slips back in, as if the baptism has begun. He must be lifted, like a babe, the grace of others surrounding him when he is bereft of resources. Desperately he attempts to shift his thinking toward Lucy. She will need him. He must watch over her. See her through. She will have none of it. Not immediately following the beginning of their new existence. Not as their changed lives unfold. And so, without his even realizing it, Lurie has been thrust through the narrow aperture of his camera lens, leaving behind the world he has been privileged to view, to analyze, to name. He's in the picture now, no longer able to "call the shots."

Lurie and Petrus. The postattack ironies of their relationship serve as signposts for the psychic journey Coetzee's writing demands of Lurie—and me. In the beginning, it is Lurie who is privately making decisions and judgments about Petrus and his world. At first, Petrus had hardly been worth contemplating—an unexpected and puzzling addendum to his daughter's strange life. Even after the horror of the heinous attack Lurie considers the possibility of liking Petrus, of feeling some sensitivity toward the tragedies of his past, whatever they may be. He assumes the position of the understanding academic, musing over the insufficiencies of the English language when used to tell the "truth of South Africa" (p. 117). Yet, the upheaval has happened, despite Lurie's inability to take in its magnitude. He toys mentally with the "new world they live in, he and Lucy and Petrus" (p. 117). Yet as he contemplates their lives and this new world, he is aware that he is being pulled into the center of a whirlwind of experience that will nearly erase the sense of control that has allowed him to consider, to analyze, to name. He will fight it. The vestiges of privilege die hard.

I'm drawn inward myself. Theory has upset my world. Theory and the stories of poverty, disadvantage, and disease in the United States. I've seen my privilege reflected in the arduous challenges faced by homeless women (Liebow, 1995) and it is not a pretty sight. I attempt to help others awaken and join in the consciousness-raising process. Planning conferences about diversity awareness, encouraging my students to "rethink whiteness." Reading the lives of innercity children and their mothers and grandmothers in Kozol's *Amazing Grace* (1995). All the while remaining at the center of my universe, viewing, analyzing, naming. While the world shifts beneath my feet. I know it's happening. Like Lurie, I can mouth the words of a world in transition. Talk about the insufficiencies of mainstream curriculum and the English language to describe the tangle left from more than five centuries of colonialism. But I am still holding the camera. Like Lurie, I sense something on the horizon that is more than I can imagine. It is one thing to purport to be sensitive when the ground is still under one's feet, quite another to face a world unknown and unnamable.

It isn't long before Lurie, nonetheless, works to stifle his fury as a father whose daughter has been *violated* (italics in text). Eventually, as he attempts to make sense of the onslaught of emotions (for, miraculously, he still feels in charge of his journey), he finds himself revisiting the father of the young girl *he* violated in his former life. Spiritual imagery abounds. They break bread: Lurie, this man, his wife, and their daughter, the younger sister of the object of his indecent tryst. And Lurie brings wine. An intimation, perhaps, that some part of him wills this encounter to be a cleansing confessional. In the end, Isaacs, the wronged father, introduces God into the conversation. How did Lurie get to this place, he asks? Indeed, this may be the most important question of all. Is this visit part of the whirlwind whose vortex has now taken complete control of his life? Must such a centrifugal shock happen to each of us if we are to experience cleansing? And is the cleansing about getting past the past? Isaacs doesn't see it that way. The only way out of disgrace, if this is truly where the whirlwind is leading, is through life. Life informed by the past. Daily, difficult, life. We may stoop, we may bend to the floor, genuflect and name our desperate condition. But when we rise, life is waiting. And Isaacs wants to know what Lurie will do now. Lurie, still grasping for some sense of control, hopes to live out his life in disgrace. Not satisfied with the answer, Isaacs intimates that neither the visit nor Lurie's journey is of his own making. "The path you are on is one that God has ordained for you. It is not for us to interfere" (Coetzee, p. 174). Not for *us*. Not for Isaacs *or for Lurie*. The journey is his, and yet it is not. The last vestiges of control are being wrested from his loosening fists.

Unaware of the changes gradually overtaking his perspective, Lurie returns to his past. He visits his old office, collects his accumulated mail. Dines with his ex-wife. Tries to revisit Melanie, the student he wronged, but is forcefully kept away by the strange young man who has stood between them before. "Find yourself another life, prof. Believe me" (p. 194). His attempts to move back toward the experiences that had numbed his emotions and helped him avoid the journey inward are a splendid disaster. Even a pay-per-visit sexual encounter fails him. And so he returns to the place that will allow him to continue to journey inward. To Lucy's world. He is no longer in charge of the view, no longer analyzing and naming. Stripped of virtually all of his props, he clings to the opera that has played in his soul for so long. Perhaps it will rescue him. And, in a way, it does.

While continuing on with his duties as a "dog-man," he fiddles and plays out the opera in his mind. He is Byron, who, despite his demise, is the object of Theresa's desire in the drama. She tries to pull him back from death to the life she imagines. Yet Byron will not be seduced. He is where he must be. As is Lurie. Life moves along, a lesson in letting go. The journey inward seems almost complete. Or, if not complete, accepted. Now Lurie is finally privileged to glance through the lens of the camera once more. Gazing at his daughter from a distance as she "bends over [her flowers] clipping or pruning or tying," her dog dozing beside her, he sees a world he no longer owns. And it is beyond beautiful. The pastoral description leaves even the most jaded reader breathless. Pastoral, not perfect. A place where life happens and people adjust.

The child incubating in Lucy's body will at once represent this new world he no longer owns and make him a grandfather. In this peaceful moment, he contemplates the possibilities of beginning again, of learning new virtues. In the end, on a Sunday, day of resurrection, Lurie parts with the final being that seems to have a hold on him. A helpless dog who has loved his music. He "gives him up." And with that one act, he seems to have accepted the grace that might come to us if we will journey inward.

Will the result of the psychic movement be an open door for social change? Can we proceed as if there is a chance to make a better world? My students want to know. I want to know. The vestiges of privilege (for knowing and certainty are the currency of privilege) die hard. My only certainty for now is that the journey inward is requisite to answering the siren call from Coetzee and others who seem to understand the conflict between positioning oneself as viewer, analyzer, namer, while considering the difficulties of the lives of the "other." Even Kozol (1995) has refocused his quest for understanding.

> When I look for hope these days, I tend to look less often to external signs of progress such as housing reconstructions—which can be too rapidly arrested and reversed by shifts in public policy—than to the words and prayers of so many of their mothers and grandmothers. It is, above all, the very young whose luminous capacity for tenderness and love and a transcendent sense of faith in human decency give me reason for hope. (p. xv)

Still, in Kozol's next paragraph, he refers readers to the listing of advocacy groups included in his book. For as Isaacs reminded Lurie, there's still life to live and we cannot hide in disgrace. Perhaps if we will abandon grand theorizing, relinquish the privilege that accompanies deconstruction as well as naming, immerse ourselves in Coetzee's fiction, in the fictions of our own lives, we will be able to view without imposition, the possibilities before us. Giving up control of the journey may lead to the greatest hope of all: the chance to live with grace.

FOUR

Distance

INTRODUCTION

Martha

THE OFFERINGS IN THIS chapter unearth the complexities that can be associated with one seemingly simple term: distance. Perhaps more than any of the topics we've engaged, distance begs us to think visually, to identify the movement that is possible in each of our life experiences. Distances in space and time, distances between people, and distances between who we appear to be and the person who lies deep within. Distances between who we are and who we might become. I am struck by the expansiveness of the terrain of this chapter. It reminds me of the "wideness" Mary notes in Eve Sedgwick's writing. Although the adjectives used in the titles—shrinking, embracing, and troubling—seem to contradict, each piece grapples with blurring the categorical lines drawn by families, communities, institutions, and governments. And each does so by dancing with the concept of distance in particular ways.

The lines others make for us, lines between self and other, between past and present, between patient and doctor, between our outer and inner worlds are more readily held in place when we are immersed in the ideology of individualism. The binary of distance/intimacy holds fast. Intimacy, relegated to the private sphere, allows distance to shape public sphere relationships and responsibilities. In this scenario, distance, and its companions individualism, reason, ambition, and competition, provides privilege to those empowered in the public sphere. They learn to draw lines, to create a safe space for themselves, to keep others at arm's length. The popular expression "go the distance" includes no inclination to "bridge the gaps" that gape in the social fabric.

And so, Delese urges us to shrink distance. To draw on literature and imagination to develop a rich heritage of possible stories, possible emotions, possible lives. We can, she shows us, move from our particular circumstances to the abstract and then return to a different particular instance and be more able in that moment to know the other as fully human. In a world of white coats and expertise, stories become essential. Reading stories of genuine emotion given to us through literature provides confirmation of her assertions.

Mary, on the other hand, is adamant about the importance of seeking out distance intentionally. It may take a considerable dose of distance, both from daytime activities and nighttime revelations, to develop skepticism, a resistance to well-learned mores and moods that seduce us back to "normalcy." The list of "disses" she identifies within distance is complex and reminds us that the work of remaining undefined, the challenges of seeing the world as changing and unknowable, is immense. If we will stay there, in the spaces created by distance, however, we may be led out, eventually, toward new expressions of self, new opportunities, new and exciting possibilities.

It is, then, a troubling concept, this distance. I trouble it in three ways by examining the distances between past moments and present realities, the distances between individuals, particularly the inhabitants of my classrooms, and the distances between what we believe and what we decide to do. Each moment can be accepted as it seems to be or it can be highlighted intentionally, shifting the beam of light first here, then there, in search of the unexpected, the telling. In each of these chapters, the intent is the same. To break down the barriers of privilege and protection. To shake off the drowsy acceptance that allows us to move along without noticing the essential detail that emerges when we pay attention to distance.

SHRINKING DISTANCE

Delese

> The secret of seeing is to sail on solar wind. Hone and spread your spirit till you yourself are a sail, whetted, translucent, broadside to the merest puff.
>
> —Annie Dillard, *Pilgrim at Tincker Creek*

Distance involves space—the road between here and there, the heavy air between persons sitting in the same room, the minutes between now and then, the airborne messages in flight between sender and receiver. I grew up with an acute sense of distance, daughter of two transplanted, farm-grown parents whose attachment to the earth and its cultivation, to the ebb and flow of seasons, to the work of hands and machines, and to the beauty of both solitary and communal work was coded in their children's DNA. Each July when I—urban dweller fifty-one weeks a year—draw near to the Missouri farm that delivered three generations of Wears, the distance vanishes behind me and I fall into the beauty of the endless fields of corn and wheat, the dust billowing behind me in the narrow dirt road, the hum of a tractor. A man waves to me from a field as I drive by; he has no idea who I am but he instinctively waves because I am worthy of a wave. I smile and wave back: I become my Missouri farm self and remember that here I believe "that there is a universal element in the human condition, something alchemical, and it's nearly visible, it radiates off people in waves, and you can see it everywhere, all the time" (Kimmel, 2002, p. 13). To think this way, to become my farm self, I leave my urban self behind, literally in this case, traversing miles across Rand McNally's green Ohio, through pink Indiana and yellow Illinois, into blue Missouri.

But I can become my Missouri farm self without going to the farm when I imagine the farm.

> I keep my tale as wide open as I can.
> —Nancy Mairs, *Voice Lessons*

Okay, so I have a frame of reference when I imagine the farm—I've been there dozens of time, I've driven the same route, I know the sights and smells and sounds. These images are tethered to the "real" thing. But what about that man in the field? I can imagine so much more about his possible life (undoubtedly a farmer, the occupation I've just given him), this man who waved to me as I passed: the kind of house he lives in, what his wife looks like, how he talks to his dog, what he does upon rising. My imaginings arise from narrative snapshots I've accumulated over a lifetime—real people I've known right there in Prairie Home, plus characters from movies or novels, persons from newspaper articles, faces on the 11 o'clock news. And when I engage in the act of imagination, culling from all those random memories and strings of associations, I close the distance between myself and that farmer as he changes from a static, one-dimensional image to someone fully fleshed out, someone's father, someone's husband . . . someone with a *story*.

It doesn't matter if the story is true. All the details I imagine for this man are most likely not true. He may not even be a farmer but is, rather, some government functionary from Jefferson City testing the soil. The point is, through imaging this man's life, I give him more attention. The story I make up offers possibilities that the physical world might deny. Stories provide the "sensual experience of another world" (Nafisi, 2003, p. 110). Entering other worlds involves distance—collapsing it, shrinking it, ignoring it. That is, if we stay put in our own worlds, we are unable to enter the life world of someone else, real or fictional.

Collapsing worlds is my challenge as a teacher.

> Literature is the lie that tells the truth, that shows us human
> beings in pain and makes us love them, and does so in a spirit of
> honest revelation.
>
> —Dorothy Allison, *Skin*

Sometimes I hesitate to disclose what I believe about reading and the power of literature. It seems quaintly modernist, grounded in some vaguely humanist project, decidedly unhip in its focus on the printed word in a world saturated with visual images on split screens, a matrix reloaded with everything except novels. Susan Sontag describes this culture as one "whose most intelligible, persuasive values are drawn from the entertainment industries" (2001, p. 273). Jonathan Franzen is even more cynical and describes the "powerful narcotics technology offers in the form of TV, pop culture, and endless gadgetry," a culture where soon the "old generation of readers has gotten tired and no new generation has taken its place" (2002, pp. 203–204). Still, Sontag gives me the go-ahead to make my case for the novel, poetry, and other literary forms. All the technoentertainment that transforms seeing and experiencing and knowing

> do not make me care less about Aristotle and Shakespeare. I was—I am—
> for a pluralistic, polymorphous culture. No hierarchy, then? Certainly there's
> hierarchy. If I had to choose between the Doors and Dostoyevsky, then—of
> course—I'd choose Dostoyevsky. But do I have to choose? (2001, p. 270)

Out in the world I do not choose one over the other, but in my classes I do with hope that my students will remember that a polymorphous culture includes literature, and that literature is an amazing source of images, values, and meanings. In my medical school classes I choose stories I hope will collapse the distance between doctors and patients. We see better—more details, more nuance, more subtlety—when things are close up.

Ironies in medical education are ubiquitous, but the one that prevails is this: A patient walks into an examining room, removes all her clothes, and has a total stranger—the doctor—touch, probe, and peer into her body with little more than a perfunctory exchange of words beforehand. A surgeon cuts open a human body, an obstetrician guides a baby exiting her mother's womb, an oncologist pushes chemicals through the blood of a very sick person—yet the possibility always exists that these doctors know very little about the lives their patients live outside of medical settings, lives that have a profound influence on how those patients' health and illness will proceed. In spite of the deep physicality of the doctor-patient relationship, patients often remain at great distance from their doctors.

Would more knowledge about patients' lives lead to better doctoring? You bet it would, but to gain such knowledge firsthand of each and every patient is not possible. But it is possible for doctors to develop a profuse, complex, evolving bank of images to draw upon as they care for patients, a compendium of stories of sickness, recovery, coping, fear, uncertainty, and joy that increases empathy and understanding with each entry, bringing them closer to their patients. Nussbaum (1997) describes it this way:

> To be deprived of stories is to be deprived, as well, of certain ways of view-ing other people. For the insides of people, like the insides of stars, are not open to view. They must be wondered about. And the conclusion that this set of limbs in front of me has emotions and feelings and thoughts of the sort I attribute to myself will not be reached without the training of the imagi-nation that storytelling promotes. (p. 89)

A woman arrives at the doctor's office for an appointment where she will learn the results of the needle biopsy done on her breast. She waits—"nobody, not even a lover, waits as intensely"—for the doctor to come into the examin-ing room, feigning calm but utterly terrified (Broyard, 1992, p. 22). The doc-tor walks in, his head in a chart, and greets her warmly but gets down to busi-ness. What if, just for a moment, he were to retrieve an image, the story of a woman facing this exact moment? In his image bank, he might remember Ali-cia Ostriker's (1999) intelligent, frankly uncensored account of her experience with breast cancer, particularly her reading of hospital rituals on her way to surgery and her need for self-control:

> Horizontal on the stretcher pushed by an orderly—why a stretcher? Why can't I walk? Or sit with dignity in a wheelchair? Why can't the anesthesiol-ogist who has just given me the explanatory talk push me? Is maximal humiliation the intention? I watch ceilings and corridors slide endlessly by, recalling how often I have seen others in this sad position. (p. 189)

What if he were to remember the ferocious courage, honesty, and anger in Audre Lorde's *The Cancer Journals* (1980) when he looked into eyes of the patient before him, wondering if she would respond to her diagnosis and forthcoming surgery with the same anguish Lorde described:

> I want to write of the pain I am feeling right now, of the lukewarm tears that will not stop coming into my eyes—for what? For my lost breast? For the lost me? And which me was that again anyway? For the death I don't know to postpone? Or to meet elegantly? . . . I'm so tired of all this. I want to be the person I used to be, the real me. I feel sometimes that it's all a dream and surely I'm about to wake up now. (pp. 24–25)

Conjuring up those images has the potential to reduce the distance between that doctor and his patient, invoking what Nussbaum calls "the habits of wonder" promoted by stories that "define the other person as spacious and deep, with qualitative differences from oneself and hidden places worthy of respect" (1997, p. 90). Conjuring up those images, even for one moment, may remind that doctor to wonder and care about what his patient will do with the information he is about to give her.

Often what patients do about their illnesses confounds and angers doctors because such actions are not what doctors advise. Stories show why humans act as they do when readers can see how "circumstances shape not only people's possibilities for action, but also their aspirations and desires, hopes and fears" (Nussbaum, p. 88). Safiya Henderson-Holmes's "Snapshots of Grace" (1990) is the story of a woman whose breasts were such a profound part of her identity that she waited a year in denial after a bad biopsy report to see a doctor. Each snapshot is an image of Grace in relation to her breasts—as a young girl looking at herself in her mother's bedroom mirror, "her blouse is above her chest, two perfectly round, perfectly mahogany-brown circles stare at her" (pp. 331–32). In another snapshot we find her asking, "Mama, am I gonna have real big titties like you and Mrs. Warren?" In one snapshot with her girlfriends they worry about having imperfect breasts, wondering "how would we get a husband then?" As she matures she receives many messages about her large breasts, all positive, and she is not immune from such affirmation. What is she to do with the news of a suspicious mass in her breast?

But then, not all women have such attachments to this part of their body—or their lover's body. Barbara Rosenblum (1991) describes the profound changes in her body and the responses of her lover Sandy to those changes, sounding much like Audre Lorde who believed that "a lifetime of loving women had taught me that when women love each other, physical change does not alter that love" (p. 56). While losing her breast did alter her body image, Barbara "never felt a diminishment of [her] femininity" because her breasts had never been the focus of her womanness (p. 138). She writes:

> I'm very lucky. Sandy has been exceptionally steadfast and easy about the changes in my body. She did not compel me to pay attention to her needs, her anxieties, her worries. She never made me feel inadequate or freakish. Her face never revealed shock or terror. She was easy with my scar, touching it delicately. . . . She was always softly, gently there, through everything. (1991, p. 138)

What might these images mean to doctors? I think that the more images they have, the more they are likely to wonder about their patients and the meanings patients' various illnesses have in lives lived outside of examining rooms. I think they are more likely to be compassionate: L. *com-*, together + *pati*, to suffer. Nussbaum believes that serious engagement with literature, reading with an open heart and mind, with wonder, can move readers again and again toward such compassion. This is possible because "the artistic form"—here, literature—"makes its spectator perceive, for a time, the invisible people of their world" (p. 91). Wayne Booth takes this proposition even further:

> Perhaps we all underestimate the extent to which we absorb the values of what we read. And even when we do not retain them, the fact remains that insofar as the fiction has *worked* for us, we have lived with its values for the duration: we have been *that kind of person* for at least as long as we remained in the presence of the work. (1988, p. 41)

It has amazing implications for the distance between doctors and patients, these doctors who have "known" Alicia Ostriker, Grace, Audre Lorde, and Barbara Rosenblum.

> "Real life" is lived *in* images derived in part from stories.
> —Wayne Booth, *An Ethics of Fiction*

As I round the last curve on Hazel Dell Farm Road, I see the farm come into view—the house sitting in a grove of trees, the ramshackle buildings full of tractors and mowers, my dad's truck, the black speck in the front yard I know will turn into Jake the dog. The front door opens and out walks my mother who has undoubtedly been watching the road for the last hour. I smile as a lump grows in my throat, amazed and proud of this seventy-seven-year-old woman who stays alone on the prairie, miles from the nearest house, even farther from the nearest town. I can't help it, I didn't will these lines into my mind, they just appeared—a Denise Levertov poem. Something about the solo figure of Mom walking out the house evokes an image from "A Woman Alone"—an older woman, without the dailiness of family, is finally about to live without "worrying/that it's late, dinner at midnight, her time/spent without counting the change" (1975, p. 16). Most important—and what I love about this image—is that she lives with a kind of "sober euphoria," believes in her future as an old woman, "seamed and brown," and is finally able to say "without shame or deceit/O blessed solitude" (p. 17).

Saying these words out loud as the distance between us shrinks, I feel even closer to my mother.

EMBRACING THE DIS STANCES

Mary

> Life has been called a series of habits disturbed by a few thoughts.
> —George Will

In Greek and Roman mythology, the Underworld is a far more complex and interesting notion than the Christian idea of Hell. This is partly because of the attributes given the rulers of these underground regions: Hades for the Greeks, Pluto (also known as Wealth-Giver) for the Romans. For both mythologies the hidden gods who rule the underworld proffer deeper meaning to things, revealing hidden or not-normally perceived aspects of upperworld activity. According to Neoplatonic fantasies, the richness of Pluto's realm was granted an especially exotic otherness that makes orthodox Christian teaching seem "maidenly pure . . . woodwashed and bare" (Hillman, 1975, p. 206).

Were it not for departures from earthbound belief systems, there would be no new birthings of thought. Departures allow for distance, and distance can occasion understanding when habits are disturbed. The many disses of distance are the occasion of this chapter—and how many disses there are! Disillusionment, disorder, discontent, discreditation, disorientation: these are just some dis-stances.

To be disillusioned is to shed one's illusions, becoming a little less naive. Disorder helps to give the lie to order. Discontent arises from civilization. Discreditation is what academic committees fear most. Disorientation might plunge one away from one's moorings. So what does it mean to *cultivate* distance, as I am suggesting? Is the detached or impartial view desirable, possible, achievable? Borrowing Amanda Anderson's (2001) phrase "the powers of distance," a dis-stance focuses attention on forms of control, domination, or management that reduce us into woodwashed human beings. As Oscar Wilde remarked pointedly, "I consider that for man of culture to accept the standard of his age is a form of the grossest immorality" (1993, p. 57). In the spirit of disagreeing with standards, I will focus on the dis-stances of displacement, distrust, and disidentity as these give meaning its edge and being its worth.

We experience displacement every night, of course, when we dream. The ancient Egyptian word for dream derived from the verb "to awaken" (Coxhead and Hiller, n.d., p. 20). Paradoxically, when we go the great distance into the dream world in sleep, we are awakening to some deep, primal, ancient knowing about ourselves which speaks from a different place in a symbolic language alien to conscious thinking. We are, as myth would put it, returned. As Freud puts it, we are displaced. Dreams reveal secrets hidden in large houses with many rooms, doors, and stairwells. The quest to unearth the secrets confuses us with shifting narrative voices, humor, perversion, violence, all of which partake of basic anxieties the dreamer might have about gender, class, or identity relations (Young, 1993, pp. 213–15). For James Hillman, dreams have an other world or underworld quality: "The deformative, transformative work in dreams constructs the House of Hades. . . . Each dream builds upon that house. Each dream is practice in entering the underworld" (1979, p. 133). Hillman also says that dreams that have their home in the underworld must become anti-Christian. Since so much Christian teaching is based on a literal reading of the Bible (Fundamentalist notion: homosexuality is a sin, like adultery or murder), I personally prefer Hades to Hell.

The displacement of the day world by the night world of dream takes one far away from everydayness. Usually, the main problem with everydayness is its concern with normal problems requiring normative solutions. Difficulties are understood literally, often with a petty peevishness. Partly because of their placement outside the norm, however, dreams offer a fresh point of view (Moore, 1992, p. 292). Sometimes the dream might have the sense of undercutting basic habits. Since one function of the dream is to disturb dearly held beliefs, one could do worse than be a listener of dreams.

Alan Block (1997) correlates dreaming with lostness: "the subjective self is immersed wholly in the dream. In a sense there is a quality of lostness about this immersion" (p. 62). Being lost is not a bad thing at all, especially, as Alan argues, if space is subsequently provided for reflection upon the lost experience. Alan refers to dayworld reflection as needing a "holding environment" (pp. 63, 67, 76), "framed space," or "gap" (p. 71), wherein the objects of the dream world may be collected anew and considered. Little is available in the workworld of school or business for such location, but allowing for places away from everydayness, perhaps inside every day, is a practice that can only be helpful for the construction of knowledge. There are, in this "oscillation between immersion and separation" (p. 75), two stances of distance: one that immerses the dreamer into the other world of dream and another that allows the dreamer pause to think about the immersion. Both are dis-stances from daily living.

It was through the practice of dream journaling that I was able to get distance from the chaos of my day world by reflecting on the images in my dream world mirroring back to me my own bizarre behaviors. A pattern emerged in my dreams that allowed me to see what I had been doing. All those costumes, masks, and layers and layers of clothes in my dreams were pointing me, insistently, absurdly, embarrassingly, to my wearing a false identity. Knowing the power of oscillating between the dream and the journal, I have incorporated journaling in my classes with the hope of allowing the displacements of thought or dream to find new locations for student understanding.

Another power of distance can be found in withholding trust from sources that pose as authentic, believable, fact-finding authorities. A stance of distrust serves as a way of critiquing, for instance, public statements by those who see themselves as the purveyors of truth, justice, morality, and hope because of the trust "vested" in them. I suppose things have been falling apart for every era, not just ours or Yeats's. Certain it is that the center is not holding now as America takes on its war with terror. Information given to the public turns out to be disinformation about the justifications, cost, duration, difficulties, and casualties of occupying Iraq (a country that did not attack us nor have WMD nor have proven contact with Al Quaida). Informed sources knew of the problems with administration plans for war in the early nineties, but the administration did not heed those dissenting sources then or now. While political satire has never been strong in this country, a healthy distrust can disillusion us from thinking that what our leaders say is always in our best interest. A postmodern mindset would seem ready to distrust metanarratives that sweep enemies into the camp of Evil and us in the camp of Good; that American forces will "liberate" the Iraqis; or, more improbably, that God (in whom we trust) is on our side. To believe in hope for better tomorrows "imprisons us," Peter Taubman writes, "in overdetermined scripts or fantasies" (2000, p. 27).

Indeed, altruistic motives require a dis-stance, as Anna Freud observed. She wondered "whether there is such a thing as a genuinely altruistic relation to one's fellowmen, in which the gratification of one's own instinct plays no part at all, even in some displaced and sublimated form" (in Coles, 1986, p. 183). President Bush's frequent use of the word "believe" and his references to prayer and God are occasions for distrust (where is the separation of church from state?) since the most powerful man in the world seems to be in the grip of his own Christian belief system at the expense of external information systems with differing points of view. Is the former alcoholic George Bush leading the country on a twelve-step program?

Alcoholics Anonymous depends on their members' surrender to a Higher Power, described in the Big Book as the "Father of Light who presides over us all" (Wilson, 1939, p. 14). Sin, alcohol and the devil are on one side—that of a "perverse soul sickness" (Wilson 1953, p. 44)—and redemption, purity, and recovery are on the other side. If the AA plan is followed closely, salvation will remove the defects of character and the dangers of "excitement, fear, anger, worry, self pity [and] foolish decisions" (Wilson, 1939, p. 88). As Joseph Landry said of his experience, "Every AA meeting is an archetypal reenactment of the Christian drama of the sinner's battle with Satan (the disease), the eternal battle of the light forces over the dark" (1995, 11). With all his talk of good over evil, Bush seems bedazzled by his own Christian stance—especially as a saved alcoholic. His conviction in his personal beliefs, coming out of his past experience with alcohol, is no doubt sincere. But belief in an age of terror is what may have led to false justifying claims for war. A recent Doonesbury cartoon makes this point. Frame two reads: "Bush is so pathologically 'certain' about everything." Frame three in silhouette: "He feels no need to revise what he wants to believe about Saddam to conform with reality" (Trudeau, 2003, p. 7A).

It may be disillusioning to adopt a stance of distrust in government but such is my urging. The public would be dupes not to express fear, worry, and anger at an administration that sees itself as acting in accord with a Higher Power. Fear, worry, and anger are at the heart of political energy and activity.

Who better to speak on behalf of the public than the public intellectual, those of us who work in schools and universities? We should be prodded to take on the stance of distruster. This is a matter of "detaching the power of truth from the forms of hegemony . . . within which it operates" (Foucault, 1980, p. 133). Perhaps this is also a position for those of us who hear underworld rumbles in our nightly visits to Pluto's realm. But wait! I forget that my colleagues do not get tenure if they are perceived as too political. And I forget that in my college we are disciplined if we discuss matters not strictly pertaining to our syllabus, like the war!

A final stance of the distancing strategy, as I am seeing it, may be located in acknowledging our disidentities. The process by which one sheds the skins of labels or roles is a liberating rebirth. I should know. I was so firmly fixed in my identity as white het girl that I think I blanked out half of my younger years. I grew up privileged. I grew up in the center. And what a place of nonunderstanding that is! Looking at a photo of me taken when I was twelve, I see a contented child. I had just been elected an officer of my class, the only girl. Of course, I was secretary. I recorded the notes of my fifties era well; for, like many of my fellows I believed what I was told about my culture: Russia was bad, America was good, and my destiny was marriage. We were a contented lot, unaware of Oscar Wilde's epigram: "Discontent is the first step in the progress of a man or a nation" (1960, p. 128). I think that as I began listening more to my dreams, I became dislodged from my firm positioning. The dreams disoriented me, and in this disorientation I found myself shifting thought; things weren't as certain as I was told. There were ideas and life opportunities that lay beyond the compass of my circumscribed identity, nuances that came seeping up to me in dreams.

The feminist movement in the sixties and the queer movement of the nineties have helped many of us achieve the power of distance from the demands of normalcy. The absolute relevance of queer education is expressed by Marla Morris in her jaunty article "Dante's left foot kicks queer theory into gear":

> Queer theory might seem completely irrelevant to education, but it isn't. Consciousness-raising about this new field might help teachers better educate their students about the complexities of identities. Perhaps queer theorists might help foster understanding and even empathy toward those who have been labeled in damaging, violent ways. (2000, p. 27)

While the damage of labels is needed for understanding and empathizing with those already considered outside the norm, such understanding is needed, as well, for those who don't know all options in this life are open; for those who don' t realize that "normal" is a social construction (mainly of religious institutions). Everything in the fifties in my part of the privileged world was normalized. I didn't question what "natural" was. Perhaps I should have been influenced by Shakespeare at an earlier age to see what Harold Bloom means when he writes, " Shakespeare's mastery of ironic distancing is one of the poet-dramatist's central gifts, creating a pragmatic skepticism in regard to all questions of 'natural' value" (1998, p. 723). Did nature intend only one path for my future: the propagation of my species through marriage? Well, heck yes; the matter was not up for debate. Marla Morris seizes upon the writings of the church fathers to point out the history of thinking about "natural" law, writings that are insistent upon the only one, true, good path for human beings to follow. Citing the thirteenth-century writing of Thomas Aquinas, Marla writes:

> Aquinas stressed that sexuality is an innate, core quality. He said that it is "natural" to be "inclined" to "do good things." One of these good things is engaging in sexual intercourse. But sexual intercourse must be "natural," he wrote. . . . If human beings "act against nature" they act against God. "Thus the natural self is one that acts in accordance with God's laws." This essentialized self, then, must be essentially heterosexual. (1998, pp. 17–18)

Eight centuries after these theological pronouncements we are still under the sway of natural law. But how fortunate for today's youth that Bishop Gene Robinson's amazing election as the first gay bishop in the Episcopal Church sets a new path for the understanding of sexuality, spirituality, the soul, and social justice. But dismaying it is that the Methodist Church did not follow suit, defrocking two lesbian ministers as of this writing. This discrimination against lesbians I term lesbophobia, a worse form of homophobia.

I am interested in a few recent, remarkable writings on disidentity as experienced by queer and possessed human beings. I say "human beings," because the writings of Rafael Campo, Eve Kosofsky Sedgwick, and Oliver Sacks extend understanding of what "human" means to include those of us who do not subscribe to the norm or whose behaviors are not considered "natural."

In *The Desire to Heal*, Rafael Campo distances himself from the anesthetic guise associated with medical doctors. Campo, a homosexual surgeon, wastes no words in shedding the white coat image. He begins, "His erection startled me," and continues, "What could be more natural than that I was there, a witness to another man's ailing body" (1997, p. 13). Here is that word "natural," used now in a totally different context from that of Aquinas's "law." No superorganizing principle intervenes between doctor and patient in this bedside meeting; instead, the writer gives in to his simple, human feeling of empathy. Even so, the doctor-side of Raphael Campo overtakes the human-side, as he admits, "Gradually, I let myself become aware of my stethoscope, my white coat, my cold hands in their latex gloves as they all continuously emitted their signals. The entire milieu . . . seemed to be warning us both of my very great distance" (p. 14).

Throughout the book, Campo writes of his struggles to maintain distance between him and his patients, him and the straight community of med students, him and the God-complexed medical community. He chooses Amherst and Harvard as the straightest, hardest (as it were) environments for medical learning, with the intention of ironing out his homosexuality. His assumed identity as an objective, heterosexual doctor became a goal that would define his success. "I wanted to make a cast to protect myself, to straighten myself out again, to keep me correctly aligned," he says (p. 112). His account is a wide-eyed retrospective of his struggle, all the while with his full knowledge that a society "desperate for homogeneity" (p. 116) was capable of turning him into a monster, "one who killed bloodlessly, silently, with the most surgical of wounds" (p. 113). The series of essays in this book make a resounding point: in his attempt to be what he was not for the sake of profession and social coding, Campo was losing his own humanity. And he concludes with this startling observation: "I have come to appreciate how little one's own sense of identity ultimately seems to matter in the definition of communities" (p. 267).

The medical community's definition can be too clearly seen, interpreted, and understood by the white coat. What a costume that is! Meant to inspire confidence because of its sterility, it serves to distance objectivity from the subjectivities of both wearer and patient. Costumes worn during carnival do the opposite. They serve to bring out the hidden selves beneath the persona. Cubist paintings suggest a similar sense of the multiple self by drawing multiple facets on the surface of the human form. In the Kachina dances of American Indians, costumes and masks allow the dancers to reflect sacred powers released by actions that can be grotesque, outrageous, or humorous (Highwater, 1981, p. 139). These masked behaviors and artifacts are foreign to the Western idea of identity instantiated by the single persona, the one name, the appropriate demeanor. Educational systems rigorously defend singleness when administrators hand down the dress code, require standardized testing, and install the podium. These rituals of costume and prop help keep students lined up on the straight and narrow. We need to find strategies of disidentification. Can we learn to be human again?

Eve Sedgwick writes on positive affect as a structuring fact of identity found, she says, in the preposition *beside*:

> *Beside* is an interesting preposition . . . because there's nothing very dualistic about it. . . . Beside comprises a wide range of desiring, identifying, representing, repelling, paralleling, differentiating, rivaling, leaning, twisting, mimicking, withdrawing, attracting, aggressing, warping, and other relations. (2003, p. 8)

Her sideways celebration gives a wide berth to what it means to be human and culminates in a discussion of the queer-identified performance known as "camp." Camp has usually been seen as parody and "mocking exposure of the elements and assumptions of a dominant culture" (p. 149). Disagreeing with this characterization, Sedgwick sees camp as critical of culture but as acting *beside* culture in a "reparative impulse" to be "additive and accretive" (p. 149). Her descriptive use of language mirrors the sense of amplitude that her vision of camp enjoys:

> the startling, juicy displays of excess erudition, for example; the passionate, often hilarious antiquareanism, the prodigal production of alternative historiographies; the "over"-attachment to fragmentary, marginal, waste or leftover products; the rich, triloquistic experimentation; the disorienting juxtapositions of present with past, and popular with high culture. (p. 150)

Both quotations from her book *Touching feeling* bracket the main discussion almost as if the two sections are "beside" her point. The language is generous, outrageous, ridiculous, startling, delicious. She is having a really good time writing, and although highly theoretical discussions about Victorian writers occupy the central portions of the book, the tone she uses in these front and back portions is fecund, wide. I think wideness is what she intends by her word "beside," since she wants to distance herself from the strident paranoia of much in-your-face cultural criticism.

Oliver Sacks, in wonderfully exuberant accounts of his patients' bizarre behaviors, celebrates the wide range of human possibility he learns as he watches, visits, and lives with (not medicalizes) them. His title, *An Anthropologist on Mars*, gives the clue to his experience with people who are as far away from what is considered normal as to have them seem from outer space. One of his subjects was like the Holy Fool; another was an eidetic artist; another was autistic. All, because they were extra-ordinary, had extraordinary talents, either in art or music or, as in the case of the man with Tourette's, in practicing surgery. With the latter, Sacks is clearly fascinated by the man who couldn't stop touching, vocalizing, and ticking; but who, when in surgery, was the eminent professional with no outward sign of his otherwise usual explosive, guttural, trisyllabic noises and gestures. "Hi, Patty!" was a frequent such vocalization; "Hideous!" another.

Sacks remarks that any disease foists doublenesss on the sufferer, an alien "it" that inhabits the core of one's being (1995, pp. 77, 78). Often this alien "it" overtakes personality to the point that the person seems possessed. But the case of the surgeon is paradoxical, in that the defect is at one and the same time counterbalanced by a high level of skill. And that is the point. "The convulsive or broken motor or speech patterns that may occur in Tourette's can be instantly normalized with incanting or singing. . . . Such identity transformations, reorganizations, occur in us all as we move, in the course of a day, from one role, one persona, to another" (pp. 98–99). What I find so compelling about Sacks's account is how creating and imagining can be at such a distance from what we might expect. Imagination is more strange, more interesting by far, than we can imagine. Further, the "it" that a Touretter tunes into with repeating sounds and rhythms can actually give momentum to the sensation of vitality, even relatedness, between the "I" and the "it." Perhaps what Sacks shows us is that the disidenties of his patients are fundamentally liberating and paradoxically creative.

The dis-stances I have suggested through discussion of displacement, distrust, and disidentity ripple outward into so many other disses. These can help to disturb the status quo and dislodge stodgy thought. To feel the dissonances in our souls is the first hint that something needs to be expressed. The disappointments life throws our way can lead to other, more productive avenues for our talents. The disjointments we feel between ourselves and our culture's norm systems should disabuse us from following low expectations. Each of us is unique, which is to say different, which is to say in the company of the ex-statics:

> take care, do not know me,
> deny me, do not recognise me,
>
> shun me; for this reality
> is infectious—ecstasy.
> H.D., 1983, p. 584

TROUBLING DISTANCE

Martha

Writing/thinking/caring about distance is an important undertaking. For reasons I have found difficult to articulate, it seems to me that understanding distance may be the secret to understanding this dreamlike experience I have anchored myself to for a time, all the while wondering whether the culmination, the grand finale, will be a waking up or a falling asleep. I have struggled with distance mightily for as long as I can remember. In relationships, in metaphysical meanderings, in waking and sleeping moments, in classrooms and airports, in moments of clarity and in times of complete despair. Distance has had a hold on my imagination for years and it's about time I said so.

I live with the notion that I am either here or there—either awake or asleep. Either working or relaxing. Teaching or learning. Even though binaries have been deconstructed (Derrida, 1972; Levi-Strauss, 1972; de Saussere, 1959), they continue to rule. I attend to my current experience as if it were a cohesive, definitive place in time, a clearly demarcated space where I am part of a whole that could become the subject of a painting, a snapshot, a story. As if I know! When, all the while, the part of the scene most worthy of attention is not stable, understandable, tangible, but containing distances (both great and small) that surround and permeate the moment. In any given moment of time, three kinds of distance seem to me to be worth troubling. There are distances between this moment and other moments that have etched themselves into memories waiting to be connected to or challenged by this present flash of existence. Distances between the people who inhabit this bounded landscape. Distances between belief and action. Despite these pervasively present distances that might agitate and warp or distort my view, I struggle to keep the image in focus lest it break apart in uncontrollable ways.

I am here within the scenery. Too much examination, I have been led to believe, can lead to trouble. There exists a suffocating layer, seldom examined, thick and opaque, a weighty part of the atmosphere. In my imagination now I see it as a blanket of haze—with just a hint of translucence that suggests an otherland beyond. The haze wraps around the moments of my life. It's there to keep me focused, always controlling any urge to consider the distances (past moments, interpersonal walls, ethical gaps) that might challenge the normalcy of culturally constructed expectations. The opposite of controlled/focused/efficient behavior—well, there's no stopping the insanity, we're told, once the sunlight is allowed to burn a hole, however small, in this cultural ozone layer.

Lately, I have been searching for the moments etched in my memory that will help me waken more fully in the present. Anthony de Mello's (1992) mantra that spirituality is all about waking up stays with me these days. "Most people, even though they don't know it, are asleep. They're born asleep, they live asleep, they marry in their sleep, they breed children in their sleep, they die in their sleep without ever waking up" (p. 5). I think back to my childhood, trying to distance myself from my current understanding of this journey and I can remember moments that stand stark still against rushing backdrop of time. I remember the coarse texture of my father's pant leg on a Sunday morning as I clung for dear life lest he thrust me against my will into a sea of small bodies being corralled by larger forms—organized activities that frightened me and left me wishing for protection. The smell of the musty basement, the Crayolas, and the perfume that accompanied "Sunday best" is with me still.

Life, I was being made to understand, is all about being born—born into cultural norms. Somehow he peeled my fingers from the harsh wool fabric that was giving me comfort, firmly held my arms at a distance from each other so that they could no longer cling to what was known and I was forced to take a step toward individuality. Who would I be in this room that vibrated with activity and noise? How would I survive? Was this a moment of awakening? The answer depends, I suppose on one's stance. Reflecting now, the clarity of the moment stands in stark relief, calling out to me in a way that signals a warning that I was slipping into a constructed world, rather than a world of my own making. My perceptions would be shaped for me until I would come to accept where what, at that moment, seemed anathema to my own desires would be, after all, the way things were.

And so it began for me. I suspect it began similarly for the students who will share classroom spaces with me this semester. Most of the experiences of life blur into a rather unexceptional tale. I have been socialized to ignore those moments when distance (dissonance?) seems obvious (central?). The memories I have been encouraged to recall are the Norman Rockwell moments—none too controversial. Humorous or sentimental moments, self-deprecating at times, but mostly supportive of who I have been led to believe I am and the narrative I have been encouraged to embrace. Memories that enhance common perceptions. No disruptions, please.

If I lean toward the past, more snapshots emerge. There was the distance, for instance, between me and those black children riding on the school bus, sitting in the classroom with me . . . we were different. There was a vague awareness, also, that the civil rights movement I was hearing about might be connected to that difference. But we didn't talk about those connections. Better to just learn the times tables and play with someone whose story was part of my prescribed narrative. Oddly, no one was pushing me to dive into *that* unknown world in the way that I had been urged into other settings that distanced me from myself.

There are rules, then, unspoken rules about distance. Proceed here but not there. Learn to be like those like me (like who I am learning to be . . .) and beware of differences that might distance me from the world being structured quietly by those who share my space. Learn the dance of my family. Step in time with the music of my community. Sing the camp songs 'round the fire. Practice femininity. Look good at all costs. Smile demurely when someone asks my extremely self-conscious twelve-year-old self if I have a boyfriend yet. *Come on, there's someone you like.* . . . It's all in the handbook, I know. I become so busy constructing the landscape of my life that there is little time to search for cracks in the sidewalk, trees that aren't flourishing, hints that there might be some urban blight threatening my security—distances between the prescription and raw perception. As the rushing backdrop of the scenery continues on, details that contradict the intended whole are pressed underground. I think a thought but don't speak it because I am beginning to know my limits. The insulation that surrounds my developing world, the layer that dims the light just slightly and produces an oddly comforting yet deadening calm, settles a bit more securely around me as I work and play.

Now I face new groups of students in my foundations of education classes. Students who, like me, have learned their social lessons well. And I am faced with a second kind of distance worth examining in any setting. How will I navigate the relationships thrust upon us all by our compulsory attendance at this place and this time? How much distance should I maintain between myself and my students? How much should I encourage them to erase the distances that lie between us? Too little distance and we may lose our ability to think clearly. Too much distance and we'll never challenge each other at all. I am reminded of Anna Quindlen's (2000) insightful reflections on parenting in which she acknowledges that "now I expect that [my children] simply grew into their true selves because they demanded in a thousand ways that I back off and let them be" (p. 86). How much to back off, how much to prod? Parenting and teaching share common ground but they are not the same.

Some of my students are preservice teachers, eager to extend their understanding of how to fill their newly developing role in the community. Others are experienced teachers, seasoned in the rules of the games. All of them, like me, have been maintaining a dreamlike existence. What moments in our lives are worthy of excavation? Is it reasonable to hope that we will be able to dig together for deeper understanding, sifting for those moments worth connecting to the now? In the face of their impending presence, I need, most of all, another kind of distance, some time to reflect about what we will do. The present moments are so filled with information, more than enough to prepare superficial yet time-consuming learning experiences. I need to throw off the prescribed knowledge long enough to search for understanding; the task is daunting. I am lured by Dillard's (1982) pithy adieu as she turns away and begins to create needed distance.

> I have a taste for solitude. . . .
>
> You quit your house and your companions in the tent, saying, "I am just going outside and may be some time." . . . You walk, and one day you enter the spread heart of silence . . . the lightless edge where the slopes of knowledge dwindle, and love for its own sake, lacking some object, begins. (p. 60)

In the silence, will I be able to sustain the eventual exploration of my curricular concerns? What will we investigate, my students and I? How bravely will we examine the distances that exist in our shared space? Between our sheltered lives and the lives of those living in parts of the world (including our own country) that are crumbling in chaos and groaning in pain? Between what we know to be inalienable human rights and what we know of our government's policies? What distances will matter when they inhabit classrooms of their own? I feel a sense of urgency that is tangible. This is dangerous work we are daring to pursue. How much to invite them to demythologize?

A deeply resonant, frighteningly melodious voice plays steadily in my mind, warning of the irreversibility of shaking others in the hope of facilitating a wakeful moment or two. Consciousness-raising takes on a new dimension when I am more than a member of the group. You see, I choose the readings, I control the experience for now. Yes, I intentionally open the space for emotional meandering and I encourage students to introduce other materials, to speak their minds. But I unashamedly shape the questions and responses to their contributions, leading them and, sometimes, inserting a challenge to their view. I bring my politics to the table and frighten them and myself by refusing to think of schooling as an innocuous process of prescribed activities. As I back away from them regularly to catch my breath, I cling to the string of wide-awake moments that continue to pull me from the numbing safety of an uncomfortable, controlling life story. I want these classrooms to be spaces where wide-awake moments are welcome, induced. Not places protected by a blanket of fuzz made thick by unwitting, still-asleep storytellers and purveyors of cultural comfort. No. I am determined to invite them to create a space with me where waking up is preferred to a kind of anesthetizing birth/death.

Distancing myself from the steady hum of academia, from the intermittent stress of promotion requirements and from the faces of my students (sometimes moonlike and naive, sometimes weathered and rigid) is critical. How else to find Dillard's silence or the possibility of what Krall (1994) calls the moments where "past and present mingle and we can see where we have been and imagine what lies beyond" (p. 3). She writes of "ecotones," boundary lands, or, as Anzaldùa (1999) invites us to think of them, "borderlands." Places where the blurring of carefully constructed boundaries can be experienced and nurtured. Krall entices me: "Throughout our lives, we encounter cultural circumstances, changing relationships, and our own growth in these zones of interdigitation of the known and the unknown" (p. 3). I have to separate myself from dailyness (Smith, 1987), from the seemingly urgent. Intentionally create a distance in order to explore the spaces that blur my understanding. The hole in the cultural ozone must be perceived for as the atmosphere thins, I can see on the other side not sky, but otherworlds inhabited by otherlives. Not so distant otherlives but lives that can only be approached by distancing myself from the prescriptions of the narrative handed down to me so carefully.

How strange that as I intentionally stand apart from my students, I find I discover some of the ways of closing the gap between us. But this, I am coming to believe, is the art of teaching/learning. It lies within the choices we make about distance. Which fictions will collapse distance? The fiction that rouses us from sleep, heightens sensitivity to humanity, has a place in my classroom. There is also a place for the stark examination of historical atrocity, cultural genocide, and oppressive standardization of curriculum, a growing abuse. As teacher/learner, I must decide what materials are capable of collapsing unwanted space. And I must consider what I might do with the new knowledge created in the spaces I have nurtured where I have pushed against the cultural ozone layer, challenged the way things are.

This is a third form of distance worth examining here, then. The distance between my growing understanding of the constraints held fast by the cultural dreamworld, and my willingness to commit to social activism. What merit is there in challenging students to question prescriptive educational and social norms without providing a network of supportive colleagues and avenues for positive intervention? How will Freire's (1994) call to praxis find its way into my work? How much energy do I have for coping with the challenges unleashed by demythologizing? How much distance will be forged in my personal relationships if I invest in open-ended activities that can result from collapsing distances in the classroom? My experiences over many years of living in educational settings have been telling. The times I have withheld (distanced?) myself from challenges and students, engaged in supposedly self-protective decision making, that I have been most disillusioned with myself and my work. Leaning into the possibilities is the only answer I know.

All the while I must be on guard. Cultural norms are strong, subverting attempts to understand distance. Teaching/learning is a dangerous business. Clinging to my wide-awake moments, stringing them together in an attempt to deepen my understanding, and developing plans for individual and shared action will not be easy. But moments from my journey will have to sustain me. Whether they are moments of joy or sorrow.

I remember such a moment. I am riding home from the hospital, no baby in tow. How can this be? And yet it is. Nine months and now an empty aching, gnawing pain at the center of my being. The world slides by the moving car. How can those around me be busy with their daily routines? Don't they know? My world is standing still. No movement possible. I am fully awake. Fully aware of the loss. Yet this moment has brought meaning and strength to my daily experiences. My partner and I define our lives around it—before Katie/after Katie. Everything changed. Death wakes me up. Some of my enduring moments shake me to awareness. And connected to that memory are other moments of love and caring, deep connections that could not have been felt any other way. A new understanding of life. A new way of prioritizing.

Do I wish tragedy for my students? For us all? Of course not. Or, perhaps I do. For it is tragedy that erases distance and puts us all on the same mortal page. And it comes to us all. So my wish is not for tragedy but for the willingness to take it in—when it comes to us and when we see it coming to others. To inhale deeply and lean into the experiences of death/life. To slow the pace long enough to learn. Long enough to be changed. What good is life if we are not called at a deep level to overcome the distances that keep us apart, keep us from understanding. No good at all.

And so the loss of Katie is etched in my memory with other glimpses of the wakeful life. Someone told me six months after Katie was gone that she had been unable to talk to me until then. Acknowledging my loss meant such loss could come to her also. We work so hard to keep the blanket tight around our moments. Avoid taking in vulnerability and inequity. Bring them on, I say.

Look squarely at the losses and struggles all around. Weigh circumstances and possibilities carefully before living the next moment—those sequential snapshots of time come only one at a time but they are linked to the past and filled with interpersonal possibilities in the present. It is my privilege to collaborate toward a better future—one where distances are troubled, spaces are created, connections are made and the haze of our cultural conditioning lifts long enough to see beyond the limits I've been given. Breathe in the air we share.

FIVE

Fear

INTRODUCTION

Martha

WE'VE ALL FELT FEAR. We know its ability to isolate, immobilize, demoralize. It circulates quietly among us, inhabiting relationships, classrooms, and countries. Amazingly, we hide our fears—even from those closest to us—perhaps hoping denial will alleviate the terror. Of course, experience tells us our hope is unfounded but we persist, perhaps unable or unwilling to stay with the terrorizing emotion long enough to discover the benefit of leaning into our fears. Each of the contributions to this chapter invite us to tarry a while with the exposure of fear. Tarry long enough to discover the real enemies so powerful that they elicit intense physical and emotional responses. Perhaps we dread confrontation precisely because the sources of our fear are so powerful—the privileges of political might, patriarchal judgment, and heterosexual normativity.

Sometimes fear is a shared experience. The events of September 11, 2001, focused the attention of the world and especially U.S. residents on a single event with collective intensity of unusual proportions. While the immediate impulse is to think of the fear of violence, fear of the Other, fear of vulnerability, staying with the emotion of fear long enough to get past the immediate response and long enough to sort through some of the confusion exposes a more dreadful enemy kept powerful by our isolation from the Other. Political might, fed by the combination of ideological rhetoric and collective fear, rushes us past the opportunity to take in the context, to identify with the Other. How can we introduce conversations in our classrooms that might enlighten us regarding critical shared experiences when those in political power, those who protect their privilege and dominance, drown out less certain voices?

Confusion is not always collective. Sometimes, as in Delese's exploration of fear, it is contained in one person's body, creating physical and emotional havoc. Patriarchal privilege, strengthened when it is located within an institution of privilege, is such a frightful judge of all that falls outside its norms that anyone who threatens the status quo is readily intimidated. The body language and facial expression of disapproval or, worse, the climate of complete indifference to the lived experiences of those who are unknown and deemed unimportant intimidates unselfconsciously and with abandon. Tarrying with Delese's revealing account might prompt us to move toward a more inclusive approach to content and method and might remind us of the importance of advocating for those marginalized by patriarchal privilege.

Mary's words reveal the strength and horror of heterosexist socialization and expectation. How to come to grips with the gradual realization that one's self and one's persona are at odds? Her metaphors of "safe caves" and "security systems" help us realize the seductive pull of "the privileges of heteronormativity." Sometimes we have to stay with confusion for a long time, particularly when the expectations that have been layered onto our exterior for so many years have also been internalized. We begin to see what strength is required to move against such powerful forces. In her willingness to share her "journey bathed in tears" she allows us to discover the nuances that characterize any attempt to "come out" against social norms that privilege the powerful.

Of course there are shortcuts for dealing with fear: sound bytes and frozen images that convince, drugs for getting through the terror of the moment, smiles that belie the pain within. They can still our confusion. But they cannot help us confront the real enemies that retain privilege at the expense of the fearful. This chapter is a call to tarry with our personal fears, our classroom challenges, and our collective terror.

HEART, BE STILL: FEAR OF ACADEMIC PERFORMANCE

Delese

I.

Pray heaven that the inside of my mind may not be exposed.
                    —Virginia Woolf, *To the Lighthouse*

I've told this story so many times, I really don't know what happened anymore. The setting: that ancient hazing ritual called the oral comprehensive exam, taking place in a conference room on the fourth floor of the education building at a large midwestern university. The characters: my committee, comprised of four male professors, all white, ranging in age from thirty- to fifty-something, and me, a thirty-year-old woman/student/mother/wife. The tone: I'm nervous, of course, scared that I don't know enough and can't tell what I know. The plot: here's the way I remember it now, twenty years later.

The examination begins, led by my major professor who had given me no help in preparing for this moment ("You're pretty much fair game"). His quiet arrogance and self-assuredness have always been intimidating, but now I look to him for some reassurance and support. He asks a question I can answer, and I am relieved and grateful. The next examiner, someone not from my area of study—a psychologist, I believe—zooms in on an error I made in my written exam, which I had taken several weeks earlier. I think it had to do with how I used the terms "cognitive mapping" and "cognitive style" in one of the questions he had submitted. I stammer a bit, trying to read his face, which remains impassive. The room begins to take on an embarrassed silence as he repeats and rephrases the question as he watches my face, fear replacing any semblance of confidence I gained through the first question. I struggle more, now outside my body, above the table watching myself, knowing that I don't have a clue as to where to go with his question. I quit thinking about the question and focus only on the situation, panicked by my ignorance. I turn to my advisor, hoping that he would intercede and request that the questioning move on now that it is so evident that I can't answer the question, but his face is just like my interrogator's. The next few minutes (seconds? I cannot say) are filled with silences, my stammerings, my questioner's continued verbal battering with the others silently watching. It is clear to everyone at the table that I am lacking: I cannot perform the dance, sing the song, kiss their rings, or praise the wisdom of those before me. I will never be like them, so sure of themselves, no matter how much I study.

Three hours later at home: My husband is confused: why am I crying when I passed my comps? I strip the wax from my kitchen floor. A veneer, just like the one stripped from me.

A psychologist I'm not (see above). And even before I came to medical education I was uneasy with any move to pathologize behaviors, values, or ways of thinking that seem out of the ordinary, particularly women who don't act enough like "men" or who don't act enough like "women." I remember an amazing sense of relief the first time I heard a fellow student—a woman—express her insecurities about being so close to receiving a Ph.D. and feeling fraudulent about being there in the first place. After all, she said, I'm not that smart. A fluke, she called it, a mistake in the admissions process because she looked good on paper. She slipped through the cracks. Slid right by them. Deceived them about her abilities. Talked her way into the program. I nodded the entire time she was talking, saying me too, me too. I felt less freakish.

I felt like an imposter in the academic world, trying to wear the smart, self-assured, always-ready-for-a-good-intellectual-exchange persona I saw brilliantly enacted by my professors and peers. It was terrifying, living in that world. There wasn't a label for what I (and others similarly closeted) was feeling then, but psychologists were just beginning to call it the impostor phenomenon (Clance & Imes, 1978; Topping & Kimmel, 1985; Steinberg, 1986). These are feelings of being incompetent, or being a phony, laced with fears of eventually being "found out." We imposters tend to obsess about failure when we're faced with evaluation of any kind, we cannot internalize positive feedback, we consistently underestimate our abilities, and we attribute whatever success we might have to luck or hard work (Worell & Remer, 1992, p. 265). How does this happen?

As a graduate student it had been easy enough to hide in classrooms where interaction was not required, where thinking on one's feet was not expected. Most of the time I was able to shape a "confident image," convincing others that my internal state matched my cheery external demeanor. Plus, the ubiquitous activity of writing papers provided safe haven—I could lean on the thinking of others in private, construct an intelligent self on paper without the piercing gaze of professors and peers, and whatever criticism appeared was written on the paper, not my body, no matter how much I'd invested in that work.

II.

What would you think if I sang out of tune?
Would you stand up and walk out on me?
—Lennon & McCartney, 1967

Here come those same fears again, this time right before my first paper presentation at AERA in a symposium I'd organized on women and solitude. I am to read a paper along with three other women, plus the discussant (and the real draw to this session) Maxine Greene, who is my intellectual idol throughout graduate school and beyond. Of course I'm nervous, but unlike my oral exam I have my paper in front of me as a prop, and I intend to read it word for word. *(Speak extemporaneously with only notes? Never.)* But as the time to begin approaches, I watch people begin to fill most of the seats in the divided ballroom and I sense something more than the jitters, more than the now-familiar "I am not worthy" feelings carried over from my graduate school experience. Whatever is happening is frighteningly embodied: my heart is racing, I can barely catch my breath, and I fight the impulse to walk out of the room. I'm terrified because I have just decided that my paper is simplistic and trite, and that everyone will be listening in an embarrassed silence. I revert to old standbys that never work but now I am desperate: self-talk *(You know this stuff! They came because they're interested! This is a good paper! It's going to be published!)*, the rhythmic breathing of Lamaze, and searching for a friendly face on which to focus. Nothing helps, and the panic grows more alarming as I walk shakily to the podium. I don't think I can do this. But somehow I begin to read—no greetings, no chit chat with the audience. My voice trembles and cracks, but I read as fast as I can. I don't care if anyone understands what I'm saying because the faster I read the sooner I can sit down.

I vow never to submit a paper proposal again, tenure or not.

As a faculty member, my fears of being uncovered as a fraudulent take a different form: impostor syndrome meets stage fright. Most of the time I move through the world of academic medicine with energy and joy as I teach and write, grateful and astonished at my good fortune . . . until I am faced with a performance before my peers. My fear is almost debilitating. It is a fear of appearing ridiculous, which in academic crowds means to have poorly articulated, unsubstantiated, pedestrian ideas. We *are* our ideas when we are at the podium; never mind that I'm a good teacher and writer, or that I am an attentive daughter, a fervently devoted mother, or that I grow the most beautiful flowers in town. This tormenting fear at the podium makes no sense given my compulsive, often excessive, preparedness and is exacerbated by the terrible possibility that my "fear will break through the mask and become humiliatingly visible to all" (Marshall, 1994, p.134). Presenting academic papers, I discover, is much like Rosalind Russell's well-known description of acting, which is "standing up naked and turning around very slowly" (Frank, 1992, p. 190).

The doctors I work with would call this fear a "discrete social phobia" (Cirigliano & Lynn, 1992; Marshall, 1994). According to the *Diagnostic and Statistical Manual of Mental Disorders-IV* (APA, 1994), performance anxiety is a form of social phobia, or social anxiety disorder, that usually presents as persistent fear of situations involving scrutiny by others and concern about potential humiliation. The discrete form of this social phobia is when one's anxiety is confined to particular social situations such as paper presentations or other academic performances other than teaching. Adults with social phobia surrounding performance situations know their fear is excessive or unreasonable but are, nonetheless, "afraid that others will judge them to be anxious, weak . . . or stupid" (APA, 1994, p. 412). Oddly, and blessedly, many people who fear public performance are very comfortable in other social situations.

Prior to the performance, the symptoms of my fear are always the same. Kaplan's (1969) early work (and still consistently quoted) divides the symptoms into two kinds First, *blocking* is the sensation of having lost all of one's diligently practiced function (in my case, the publication-ready paper I've read countless times with ease) and the sense of control over one's speech and movement. Gabbard (1979) describes the feelings exactly:

Deafening palpitations, excessive perspiration, and dryness of the mouth are commonly noted. Uncontrollable trembling of the knees or hands is also frequently present. This characteristic stage fright experience is generally short-lived, extinguishing itself within moments of its onset, much to the relief of the performer. (p. 384)

Depersonalization divides the performing self in two, one a functioning self and the other an observing self, with the latter watching the functioning self "off at a distance, operating mechanically before an audience which is also perceived as quite distant" (Gabbard, p. 65). So much for the friendly face: the audience is a blur.

The "experts" have the origins of my fear all figured out, which only add to my shame. Psychoanalytic explanations (see Gabbard, 1997) abound, such as separation anxiety: Just as the child becomes terrified of abandonment by her mother, the performer often feels alone and isolated, paralyzed that the audience might get up and leave. This is a revival of a developmental conflict during the separation-individuation phase. Of course part of my fear is that the audience will be so put off or bored by my performance that they leave, but this does not explain my level of terror. Bergler (1949) sees it this way: At the core of my fears are oral fantasies of being devoured, or of being starved. Or there is the "indulgence in forbidden pleasures" theory—the performer is ashamed of the "exhibitionistic thrill" of performing in front of an audience. According to Gabbard (1997), shame is central to the experience of this particular kind of fear. I do not find any of these interpretations even remotely interesting or helpful, the Rosalind Russell definition involving nakedness notwithstanding. I uncover other psychological explanations for the development of this fear—denial of emotions, problems in communication, negative approach to the body, difficulties with authority figures and boundaries (Rappaport, 1989). I also learn that this fear will probably not go away, but the *physical* symptoms—not the emotional experience of fear—can be relieved through beta-blocking drugs (Cirigliano & Lynn, 1992): a pharmaceutical answer to a problem that has been medicalized by pathologizing the *individual*, not the culture that grows and nurtures such fears.

> The decision to treat a patient . . . is based on the extent and severity of symptoms. In some patients, occasional treatment with a low dose of a _-blocker, such as 20 to 40 mg. of propranolol taken one to two hours before the performance situation, is warranted—provided the patient's symptoms cause significant subjective disability. . . . Although some [researchers] have found that symptoms of severe stage fright in some patients persist despite the patient's repeated performance experience, the use of cognitive psychotherapy and behavior modification in conjunction with drug therapy may diminish the severity of symptoms over time. (Cirigliano & Lynn, 1992, p. 62)

Of course I take the drugs.

III.

Did I, my lines intend for publick view,
How many censures, wou'd their faults persue,
Some wou'd, because such words they do affect,
Cry they're insipid, empty, uncorrect.
—Anne Finch, Countess of
Winchilsea, "Introduction," p. 71

Growing up during the second wave of feminism but not yet benefiting from its hard-fought results, I wanted to be a teacher, wife, and mother. It never occurred to me, nor was it ever suggested to me, that I could choose from a much wider range of options. In my mid-twenties, I chose to go to graduate school alongside full-time motherhood, a marvelous opportunity at night as I cared for my children during the day. Amazed with what I encountered in those first classrooms, texts, and conversations, I fell in love with learning as a student all over again. But instead of eighteen-year-olds sitting next to me in class plotting the location of happy hour, I sat next to doctoral students who in their day jobs were school superintendents, college instructors, teaching assistants, or department chairs in prep schools, and who used references and footnotes every time they opened their mouths. I become an apologist for "not working" and uneasily began to feel that something was not right there: *I* was not right. Here, in the classrooms of graduate education, not in my inadequacies (or in my parents' childrearing patterns), was where my fears were conceived and nurtured. Like Madeline Grumet, I entered this world as a "grown-up woman" simultaneously caring for my children, and like her, "I was astonished to discover that only the public activities and interests of men were being studied as significant sources of contemporary education . . . somehow their serenade to society left me no part to sing" (1988, p. xv). In addition, she continues, "the experiences of family life, of bearing, delivering, and nurturing children, were absent from this discourse. Silent too was the language of the body, the world we know through our fingertips, the world we carry on weight-bearing joints, the world we hear in sudden hums and giggles" (p. xv). Now, over twenty years later, I realize that nowhere in sight in those classrooms was a discourse intended for me (Lewis & Simon, 1986). Not realizing this then, my response was to grow fearful and silent.

I pull out my well-worn copy of Adrienne Rich's essay, "Taking Women Students Seriously," still glowing and incisive decades after she wrote it. It is well worn because I read it often to remind myself of the bodies inhabited by my students, half of whom are women. Rich asks me to

listen to the voices of the women and the voices of the men; observe the space men allow themselves, physically and verbally, the male assumption that people will listen. . . . Look at the faces of the silent, and of those who speak. . . . As women teachers, we can either deny the importance of this context in which women students think, write, read, study, project their own futures; or try to work with it. We can either teach passively, accepting these conditions, or actively, helping our students identify and resist them. (1985, pp. 21–28)

Even though I was slow to realize it during those years of my professional education, I was not taken seriously because my days were filled with play-groups and story hours, reading to my children, feeding them, holding them even as they slept. Not only did my storyline fail to match those of my fellow students, I was also unable to adopt the all-knowing, all-powerful voice of the academy: I was/I had an unacceptable discourse in both content *and* form. I came to believe, as Jane Tompkins did, "that if we don't call attention to our-selves *as* women, but just shut up about it and do our work, no one will notice the difference and everything will be okay" (1989, p. 121). So I turned in on myself with a fierce self-scrutiny, a form of "self-erasure, an analogue to an obsession with thinness, a way of assuring ourselves and others that we'll take up less space—a kind of professional/pedagogical anorexia" (Greene, G., 1993, p. 17)

What I wanted to do, and what I could not do, was learn how to talk simultaneously about motherhood *and* Althusser's Ideological State Appara-tuses, or my son's first steps *and* Pinar's reconceptualization of curriculum the-ory, or my father's descriptions of growing up poor *and* Guba and Lincoln. But it was 1980, and I learned to pretend that whatever we were studying had nothing to do with my life because it—an idea, or theory, or writer—tran-scended the personal. I wish I could have, like Jane Tompkins, been able to say "to hell with it," but I didn't know then what I know now, that the public-pri-vate hierarchy is a "founding condition of female oppression" (p. 123).

Thus, in my mind's tug of war between silence and speech, silence won, a silence imposed by being ignored or dismissed by those in charge, or adopted as a strategy to avoid embarrassment. My mind, however, was never won over to such an unnatural state as silence: it continued to race and puzzle, to put together and take apart. But my speech was always turned inward, with the fear of hearing my own voice and of being heard too great a risk, its source not my anatomy or physiology but a function of my *situation*—a woman who could not meet the machismo gazes of academic rituals. I lived

the ever-present possibility that [I] will be gazed upon as a mere body, as shape and flesh that presents itself as the potential object of another subject's intentions and manipulations, rather than as a living manifestation of action and intention. The source of this objectified bodily existence is in the atti-tude of others regarding [me]. (Young, 1990, p. 155)

The rest is history (see above). Today, years later, a decidedly senior member of a medical school faculty, I have learned several discourses not intended for me by altering or hybridizing them just to the edge of what is acceptable to those who have power over my academic self. I have studied the map of academic life for routes of safe passage, and have learned where ambush is likely to occur. Ambush is, of course, unavoidable in the academy, its satellites (academic conferences and journals), and its cultural practices (paper presentations, so-called peer review, and the dance of promotion and tenure). These ambushes take many forms: judgment by authorities that one's work is trivial and unworthy of publication, or hazing ("pimping," as it is called in academic medicine) during oral presentations in the form of insistent, mean-spirited interrogation by someone in the audience.

With that sentence, I've circled this text, back to where I started: fearfully presenting what I know to others who judge the adequacy of my thinking. My body still wins during these moments—my heart, my lungs, my trembling hands, all tell me how frightened I am before I take my pill. I am resigned to this condition, for myself anyway. But I am not resigned for my students, and when I look around my classes and see a look or hear a silence, I will not rest. I will not let a student's silence, or mine, certify the system of teaching and learning in the medical academy. Perhaps she is shy; perhaps she is worrying about the test she just took, or her mother, or the loan statement she just received. Or perhaps she has discovered how disconnected her experiences are from the task at hand, how the material practices of medical education do not match what she thought being a doctor would be.

What I can do is try to make the environment into a demilitarized zone by "cleaning out the male curriculum . . . the process/product paradigm, the myth of objectivity" (Grumet, 1988, p. 186). What I can do is design experiences for students to speak persuasively, even podium-style, but with rules that forbid goading, bullying, or intimidating the one on her feet to think *fast*, respond *quickly*, to engage in point/counterpoint where a winner is required. What I can do, finally, is try to create classroom discourses that do not include fear of not knowing, of knowing this but not that, classrooms where texts of all kinds speak at the same time, each valued in its uniqueness, classrooms where phantoms of unworthiness can be released, or if not released, weakened with every breath.

FEAR OF SECOND BIRTH

Mary

My life is a series of synchronisities, I am happy to say. When Martha's piece on fear came to me electronically, I had just finished a piece I had written,

"Flight and Fear" (2002). Like Martha's, my piece was a response to the attacks on 9/11; my sense, like hers, that this new America we all now inhabit is an emotional desert. Where do we turn? What can we say? How may we live in this new, strange time?

And then Delese's piece came to me, speaking of a different kind of desert, that of the academy's dry dust. Delese recalls the moment of her dissertation defense when the question she could not answer, put to her by the impassive face of her inquisitor, caused her fear of being an impostor in an impossible land. Citing psychologists, she spins her story around the "impostor phenomenon": the fear of being found out—so prevalent a feeling among professional women operating in hostile patriarchies.

I have had both of these fears: the recent one of 9/11 and the professional one. Delese and I have been on some of the same panels over the years, and while I have never detected her fear in the wake of the impossible question from an audience member, perhaps she has not detected the same in me. We cover ourselves well. But now is the time for the uncovering, strangers no more, and so I share the fear I had of coming out after decades in the safe closet of social conformity.

First: the safety. I sought safety as the cave that would allow me to stay unborn. What was my fear of being born? Wasn't I already born? Didn't I have a mother (yes, she became lesbian) and a father (yes, he became homosexual), with a brother (yes, he was gay)? Oddly, my family background did not encourage me to make the changes my people made; in fact, the opposite. I was to be the straight one. So my childhood toys were dolls; my closet had laces, velvets, and patent leather shoes with straps; and my mother plotted for my marriage. She, an avant-garde woman editor, was my nineteenth-century mother who thought of a daughter as a duty. My father kept me infantile, the pot of gold at the end of his rainbow; and my brother fixed me up with his gay friends with whom I fell in love because they were just like him: funny, erudite, insouciant. But why wouldn't those fellows ask me out twice? It was all so confusing.

I was a constructed being. I adopted all the tags my family and others attached to me. I was obedient, pliable, nonopinionated. I had boy friends and girl friends and my best friend was my mirror. "Mirror, mirror on the wall, who's the fairest one of all?" Oh, how I understood that fear of competition, for it is the Queen's greatest fear, of course: Snow White will outdo her in the looks department. Fear, Bill Pinar (2000) reminds us, is inverted desire. Could the wicked stepmother of fairytale *desire* the princess? Was that why she went so far out of her way, into the deep forest of the dwarfs, to visit again and again the young woman seven mountains away? What an interesting twist that would be to the Grimm tale of fairies and queens! But growing up I knew nothing of desire, so acclimated was I to the dry winds of normalcy. Whatever twinges I may have felt for those who shattered my mirror were put aside, covered up, repressed. And so Snow White-me, "unsoiled/white as a bonefish" (Sexton, 2003, p. 400), lived like a sleeping virgin, keeping my unacknowledged fear at bay. Out in the bay were vague memories of childhood crushes, occasional dreams I could not understand, and, most certainly, genes. But, like the fairy tale princess who is essentially comatose, locked in a glass coffin, I was unwilling to look beneath the glass surfaces of my "life"—I had no reason to think my "life" was unauthentic to my self. I was gliding along, unborn.

Nobody I know remembers the trauma of birth. I turn to fiction to help here. Doris Lessing's "Through the Tunnel" offers a metaphoric account of the passage into birth in her story of a boy who comes out of his blissfully innocent relationship with his mother by accomplishing a physical feat of extraordinary danger. He swims through an underwater tunnel after four days of practicing holding his breath for a hundred and fifteen counts. Why he challenges death in this manner is the ontological question here. The task seems too great: "He was trembling with fear that he would not go, and he was trembling with horror at that long, long tunnel under the rock, under the sea" (2003, p. 865). Lessing's Jungian imagery of water, tunnel, and blood all suggest the extreme death-defying difficulties of the birth process through the narrow canal of one's mother. The boy's passage necessitates a "dying" to pre-oedipal innocence and unawareness so as to "birth" a fuller, more conscious adult self.

The second birth journey is no less difficult and fearsome; it, too, requires coming into one's own by shedding attachment. The security systems I had built around me had formed a hardened pattern; I functioned and played my part well, script in hand. I was attached to the demands of social intercourse. My dreams, however, gradually became insistent that I wasn't listening to my other self, I wasn't "living." These dreams had telling metaphors about transformed houses, little eggs, and forgotten scripts. My eros began building strength when I finally met Marla, my love; then, my dreams began getting downright audacious:

> I am getting married to an unidentified woman. It is to be a menage-à-trois. I dress for my entrance in secondhand clothes. I am vaguely aware that my attire is out of place for this wedding occasion. My husband sits at a picnic table. He tells of having bought an octagonal glass house for the three of us. I am excited about the new house, but my wedding partner stamps her foot in anger and says, "No! I will not live in a glass house!"

The thing was, I was still too afraid to do as my dream-wedding partner had done: to refuse to be on show in a house made of glass. I was too afraid to listen to the dream or see its meaning, so firmly had the wall of security wombed me. Had I paid the slightest attention, perhaps I would have noted the dream details of "secondhand clothes." Clothing images had recurred in my dreams during this period: I was obsessed with my outer appearance, my persona. Here the dream image was a little more insistent. I was borrowing hand-me-down ideas about gender and identity. And what about the octagonal shape of the new house, a sort of mandala? The dream was telling me I was desiring entrance into my truer "home." The dream was a beacon, beckoning me to see through the mirror of social ideals into the glass of transparent reals.

The archetypal psychotherapist James Hillman has this to say about glass:

> Glass in dreams, as windows, panes, is to permit seeing through. Glass is the metaphor par excellence for psychic reality: it is itself not visible, appearing only to be its contents, and the contents of the psyche, by being placed within or behind glass, have been moved from palpable reality to metaphorical reality, out of life and into image. . . . Glass is the concrete image for seeing through. (1975, p. 142)

While the dream was presenting me with an image for me to "see through" or to understand, I was, even as I recorded this dream, fearful. How could I leave my nice country club life? I was in love with another woman. But how could I leave the life that had been set down for me and that I had allowed? I felt, like Amy Lowell, "held rigid to the pattern" (2003, p. 658).

It took five years.

At first, I had no real intention of leaving the pattern. It suited me to retain the privileges of heteronormativity. I fooled myself into believing I was the clever conductor of a dual existence. I became good at lying. I told myself that I was a true Gemini with two selves. But as my passion for Marla grew and her impatience with my hypocrisy grew, I realized I was nothing more than an impostor in a pumpkin shell. I had to make a break for the sake of my life and the lives of those to whom I was lying.

Mine was the fear of coming out. What would people think? Those Republican aunts, uncles, and cousins? My colleagues, neighbors? My childhood friends, some with whom I had corresponded over the years? My greatest fear was that I would lose my son. Would he shun me, call me a disgrace? Having been constructed by others' ideas of who I should be, it was now time for me to decide for myself who I should be. The thought was terrifying, simply horrific. But I was comforted in these early stages by my dreams, my love, my son, and my cookie fortune (still taped to my computer): "Depart not from the path which fate has you assigned." I was on a journey bathed in tears. Like the swimmer boy, water was the element that helped prepare the way away from the dust of conformity. I was, as Martha writes, gradually able to "nurture" the fear I was having of alienation from others, realizing perhaps for the first time that the face I would be showing to the world in my new queer life had been there all along, only hidden under too many smiles. And now, having emerged on the other side of the tunnel, I am able to see through the dis-approving looks that come my way, realizing that, while I may seem strange to some, I am no longer a stranger to my self.

EXAMINING THE FACE OF FEAR

Martha

What I see in the face of another is never the whole story. Even my own reflection tells a false tale as I whisk through my morning routine, shaping a public persona before rushing toward the day. I work to create that confident image, convincing others. Convincing myself. But fear shadows the cheery demeanor, ready to seep into my stream of consciousness when the frantic pace slows or when I am confronted by news that shocks me to attention. Political events never envisioned have exploded in this new millennium. Planes toppling buildings—ghastly to be sure—have become fodder for fear mongering. I am a teacher. How can I help others make sense of roiling inter-national circumstances? Silence, of course, is curriculum, too.

Psychologists say that love is letting go of fear (Jampolsky, 1979). But fear is not a groundless emotion. It is a *response*. And fear is impossible to dismiss without first disentangling the self from the object(s) of fear. In fact, love and fear are both responses, though polar opposites. To glibly suggest the replace-ment of one response with its polar opposite, well, even the words don't come easily. They mock me as I write. It seems outside the realm of possibility to shift from fear to love without, at the very least, some stepping stones along the way. Fear to hate comes easily. But fear to love? . . . First the focus on fear-inducing people/events/conditions must be reexamined allowing additional, even contrasting images/ideas to creep into view. I must gently explore the possibility of shifting my gaze.

In the wake of imploding towers and tragic loss, childhood warnings about strangers return to consciousness with a new salience. Those I do not know or, more precisely, those I do not understand have confronted me in the pages of the daily newspaper, on the television screen, and from magazine cov-ers. These faces have been defined for me: crazy, evil, religious zealots. Seduc-tive descriptions. I am offered nationalistic emotions and flag-waving right-eousness to keep fear at bay—keep me from dwelling on these faces I fear. I am told that I can shift my attention to patriotism, comfort myself by focus-ing on my country's moral position on the righteous side of dualism. But what I see in the face of another is never the whole story. . . .

In occasional quiet moments, the seductive simplicity of this shift from fear to intense patriotism will not be ignored. Unwilling (unable?) to escape the glut of information that flows and flows, I read. Other images/ideas call out for a response. Why do they hate us so? asks one weekly magazine. The history I've ignored seeps through the cracks of public rhetoric. The magnitude of my ignorance presses me on. The questions raised are difficult. But they carry me to other images. Images that are connected to the faces I am told to fear. Images of children in war-torn, poverty-ridden countries. When did the faces of those screaming with rage cease to be children in pain and become instead the personification of evil? On which day? In which place?

There is no excusing the violence that snuffs out lives in a flash. But the images thrust upon me, chosen for me, can become a part of a larger collage—a contextualized scream. As the wide-angle view replaces the telescopic close-up, I can attempt to respond to human pain instead of human anger. And a response to human pain—my own pain, the pain of victims of violence in our own land, the pain of children and their frightened parents where bombs fly and terror ricochets from here to there—must stretch wider than fear. Bring in sadness, and frustration, and—in a fleeting moment I long to capture—pathos, even love.

Still, the uneasiness—fear—persists. My vulnerability is suddenly starkly clear. And the sensible response to vulnerability is fear. Fear clamors for my attention. But wait. I must stick to the images visible through the wide-angle lens. This sudden awareness of vulnerability—a shift in our individual and collective awareness, not in our state of being—establishes a new connection with the world community. As I look long and hard into faces from countries where vulnerability is integral to daily existence, there can now be—if I allow it—a flicker of recognition. Unable to maintain the separation that allows for self-interested objectification, an unsettling slippage occurs.

In a brief instant, faces merge, the enormous disparity between my life experiences and theirs evaporates. Not in a material way. Not in a distorted way that erases global inequities. But, somehow, in some almost imperceptible yet undeniable shift of consciousness, asymmetrical power relations that have maintained my unrealistic sense of security are slightly altered. The media replays the shocking event that brought my/our vulnerability—obscured during an extended, privileged period of insularity—into crisp focus. Can I shift my focus from these persistent images—allow the slippage to do its work? I-thou existentialism (Buber, 1970) leaves the pages of intellectual analyses and connects with beings from the other side of the world. Fear leads me to an uneasy identification with vulnerable Others. What I see in the face of another is never the whole story. . . . But exploration can begin and, as I explore, I find something of myself.

In an instant unexpected, Other has become familiar. My reflections have now become somber enough to slip back and forth between my previously constructed reality and Other experiences new to my consciousness. The newly troubling object of my attention, my own vulnerability, widens to encompass the reality of the vulnerability of all human life, even the vulnerability of the environment that sustains human life. My response shifts again. How can I want some semblance of security without wanting it for those Others that have suddenly taken up residence in my field of vision, their reality pressed into my awareness in ways that conflate I-thou distinctions (Buber, 1970)? Fear of vulnerability shifts with the shifting images. (For how long I cannot say; I am plainly mesmerized by my own existence.) To fear (or hate) Other is now to deny my own identification with the human—and inevitably vulnerable—condition.

And so a struggle ensues. How I focus my attention has everything to do with the nature of my response. Emotions fluctuate. Given the circumstances, is it any wonder I resist letting go of fear? This is, after all, new territory. Emotional deserts in foreboding mountainous regions. And fear suggests that I push aside my complicity in the way things are. Once I shake off the immediate response of immobility and shock, I must act in some way. "The strategic moment of action is not an innocent space; it involves elements of complicity" (McCoy, 1998, p. 6). In some halting, unclear way, I must decide. And because of my shifted gaze, my decision about responding has changed. Less certain. I need time. . . .

Fear compels a hasty response. It defends me from the need to deconstruct the world. My binary assumptions protect me from the hard work of deciding which fear is healthy and which fear is destructive. Hope may lie in being able to complexify the binary—move beyond us/them, good/evil. A more nuanced view of fear itself begins to emerge, so as to be nurtured. I revisit the question of fear and consider what seems at first to be an oxymoron—healthy fear. In the aftermath of September 11, in the ongoing crisis of arrogant nationalism between countries and political conflict within countries, simplistic answers that objectify Others and bring premature closure to enormously difficult questions *should* engender fear—healthy fear. Hold back the media. Retreat to a position of thoughtful repose. Search within.

But remain quiet and reflective? There is also that pressing fear of spaces, real and symbolic. Fear of gaping holes, once beehives of activity. Metal and humanity thrust together into the wounded ground. In New York, in Baghdad. I cannot speak. Modernity has given me answers. Rhetoric and distractions that fill in the empty spaces. Fast-paced, techno-dependent production and entertainment keep minds jam-packed. No spaces. Modernity wastes little time in filling the gaps. A "new war," enduring justice, victory over evil, nations with us or against us. Rhetoric shaped for a new millennium. Fear, I am told, is my enemy, the outcome of terrorist events. Embrace outrage. Bring on patriotism. In the face of terrorist evil, fear, I hear, must give way to vengeance.

Yet, expand the gaze, slow the pace, and there is a revelation that evil also resides in a history of political choices guided by self-interest, covered by patriotic rhetoric, untroubled by spaces that beg contemplation. I need the chasm—but the troops have been mobilized. I need to hold the simplistic answers of modernity at bay—but the battles for Baghdad, the battles for Felujah, the battles for "freedom" rage on. Talk of bringing the Others of the world into a Western version of civilization rings in my ears. Can I speak of this fear to others? This fear of quick answers and righteous justice?

I need time to think carefully and to choose words carefully. How can I balance the need for time, the need for reflection with the need to speak out? Listening, contemplating, stretching to new ways of seeing and thinking are essential. For despite talk of the need to replace fear with decisive responses, the answers are not evident. Spaces have been filled in with such haste. A sense of urgency wars with the desire to reflect and examine the intricacies of each decision. Quiet the talking heads, yes. But speak alternate views before it is too late. What can I make of this world immersed in disaster? How can my classroom become a space for searching carefully before developing the courage of conviction. Can I create a space where my students and I resist the call to look only at the ubiquitously provided Other? Widen the view? Contextualize the frozen images?

I am Other. Amid the hustle of obligations and deadlines, I need to gaze steadily into the mirror long enough to push back the press of passing time. Long enough to catch a glimpse of the slippage. What I see in the face of anOther is never the whole story.

SIX

Forgiveness

INTRODUCTION

Delese

Forgive: to give up resentment for an offender, to pardon. To give up resentment? Surely this is one of the most difficult shifts in thinking and feeling humans can make when they have been aggrieved, scorned, or hurt. And to forgive with real sincerity? Even rarer. Still, there is the often-quoted other half of forgiveness, if we are to believe Shakespeare's admonition in Lear: "Pray you now, forget and forgive." But then, he could not have been so naive about human nature as to suggest a kind of erasure from one's memory whatever word or action was injurious? Perhaps he merely meant to get on with it, over it, for as Martha writes, "As long as I am unforgiving, my energy for living is redirected toward a single characteristic or past action, event, or circumstance." She looks to the work and example of Hannah Arendt to make meaning of forgiveness and its central role in creating a more humane context for life. This includes forgiveness at the most personal level—forgiving ourselves, and at the most global—forgiving the world "as it has been passed on to us." And as we forgive ourselves and others, we ask for forgiveness from others, recognizing the always already brokenness of the world and those humans who inhabit it. "I boldly invite [students] to forgive me and promise to forgive in return," she writes. "Will we fail? Yes. That's the point."

Oh, we do not speak of such things in medicine. Doctors do not speak of it, and when I'm a patient I do not want to hear it, particularly my doctor's failures or the prediction that he will most certainly have more. But as I note in my piece, mistakes occur all the time in medicine; they occur because doctors are fully human and all humans make mistakes. Unfortunately, U.S. culture places unattainable standards of perfection on its doctors, as David Hilfiker writes, because

> we always look to shamans for magical healing, we always look to priests, the medical priesthood. There's a tendency to look at healing as a divine art, so there's something within people that expects divinity from our healers. But the profession has also encouraged them. (1989, p. 96)

And because of these expectations—not to mention the very real threat of litigation—when doctors do make mistakes, there are few forums for revealing and discussing mistakes, and almost no tradition of apologizing and seeking forgiveness from patients and their families. Moreover, nothing in their training prepares them for the sorrow and guilt they face in the aftermath of mistakes. I wonder how, where, and under what circumstances might forgiveness become a healing rite in medicine?

Mary's take on forgiveness blends the disparate moments forgiveness is sought and granted—in the confessional, between mother and son, and in the seemingly unworthy characters drawn by Flannery O'Connor—and how the forgiven "can begin again, afresh, in a grace state that forgiveness bestows." That is, as Mary points out through O'Connor's stories, "forgiveness is not judgment; it is grace," itself a part of God's mystery that O'Connor says "cannot be accounted for by any human formula" (1969, p. 153). Mary finds some of O'Connor's most unworthy characters—a smug, Bible-thumping racist, a condescending son, a hackneyed old woman who causes her family's murder—and shows how each is selected for grace, each "redeemable because they are able, at the end, to find their better beginnings." Perplexed, as always with these thoughts, I am reminded of Annie Dillard's thoughts on such mysteries which, "from time to time, seizes our lives, and reveals us startlingly to ourselves as creatures set down here bewildered?" (1990, p. 73).

FORGIVENESS: BEGINNING AGAIN

Martha

> Forgiveness is the Key to Action and Freedom.
> —Hannah Arendt

Hannah had it right, I think. And she should know. Plenty of opportunity to practice forgiveness during her lifetime. Persecution in her homeland—internment in a French concentration camp—married to one man and in a long-term, if unclear, love relationship with another, whose political views bound them together but often diametrically opposed her own (Kristeva, 2001). Yet her life was filled with action and, it seems, the freedom to think and to dream. She writes of action, freedom, and natality—*vita activa* and new beginnings. Arendt (1968) invites us to expand our thinking to a reexamination of public communication and endeavor and, if we accept her invitation to journey this direction, somewhere along the way we may be met by Buber's strong assessment of encounter and relationship (Buber, 1970).

As long as we cling to our judgments of others, we can feel justified in our resistance to Arendt's call to productive collaboration in the public sphere, "interaction." Oh, we can be self-righteously busy. But this kind of busy-ness is central to Arendt's different concept of *vita activa*. Despite the presence of others in our midst as we rush through our responsibilities, busy-ness has nothing in common with Arendt's interaction. They agitate against one another. Locked into a general pattern of unforgiveness, we can be comfortable with a systematically superficial life. We blame our own limitations, others, circumstances seemingly beyond our control, rather than grapple with the reality of our limited thinking. To stretch our vision, to move beyond the dailyness of experience, this seems impossible. To cover real emotions and get on with the tasks at hand seems expedient. But, avoiding authentic, complicated conversations (Pinar, 1995) has cold consequences. Both perpetrator and injured party chill to the bone.

Arendt sees forgiveness as an essential antidote for this truncated existence, this failure to take the risks necessary to participate in the creation of a public space where our individuality can contribute to and be molded by the unique contributions of others (Arendt, 1968). Can this be? Mary writes of expanded, relational understanding—perhaps even forgiveness?—in private encounters with her son and in O'Connor's writing. Can forgiveness create such a balm, extending our willingness to go on risking in a life inevitably fraught with pain, in relationships perennially plagued by misunderstanding, and in a world where violence and deceit run rampant? Can forgiveness be this useful in public, social settings? How much can we really expect from a forgiving encounter? What redemptive forces might be unleashed if teachers were serious about contextualizing their relationships with students with the salving (saving?) grace of forgiveness? Can we envision a curriculum of forgiveness? It seems a worthy investigation. . . .

Arendt quickly dispatches with any concern of forgiving those guilty of serious crimes. This is an important distinction, since the notion that forgiveness equates to a world without judgment or consequences is, given the human condition, unthinkable. There is, in the public realm, a need for judgment. But her focus is on the everyday life of communities. Her tone exposes her faith: "Startling unexpectedness is inherent in all beginnings" (1968, p. 178). When we relate to each other, insert ourselves into the space between, anything can happen. Thus the need for forgiveness. But, her hope, if we proceed with an attitude of acceptance and the willingness, seems unshakable: "man [*sic*] is able to perform what is infinitely improbable. . . . The revelatory quality of speech and action comes to the fore where people are *with* others and neither for them or against them, that is, in sheer human togetherness (italics in original)" (p. 180).

I like the sound of this being with others. It speaks to a human longing. A place of acceptance where we can find out who we are as we live out our lives together. Certainly the world needs this mutuality of experience, the plurality that makes forgiveness necessary, the possibility of acting together to sustain human affairs. Arendt uses the term "praxis" here. Key to the possibility of such action as understanding. The work of Pinar (1995) leaves no doubt that understanding is a form of praxis.

Forgiving others, living with a constant commitment to overlook when appropriate, to gently disagree without judgment of another, even a willingness to pound fists and let the ideas clash vehemently in an effort to move toward a better understanding and thus, toward effective action: This is more easily written than done. My way or the highway is the *modus operandi* of many relationships. What sort of miracle can bring us past this rugged individualism woven so tightly into the fabric of our national image? Not determination. Not practice. Something deeper must occur and this is where Buber's I-Thou becomes important (1970). Forgiveness of this sort is always contextualized by the infinite wonder and complexity of relationships; even a cursory read of Buber's microanalysis of relationships leaves us impressed (overwhelmed) by the beauty of being together. His notion of connection cuts across our usual ideas about boundaries. The real boundary, he says, is between those times when I accept another as a complete presence, as something more than an object, and those times when I am barely aware of a person (I-It), occasions when I view myself and others as beings without individuality (It-It), times of immaturity when group members remain undifferentiated (We-We), and times when groups of people are only viewed in opposition to one another (Us-Them). "Only as You become present does presence come into being" (p. 63).

But how does one get there, to this place of acceptance, to this "presence." Now comes the complicated part. Love. He uses the word unashamedly, calling it a cosmic force. Feelings vary, he tells us. We "have" them. But love occurs. "Feelings dwell in a man [*sic*] but a man [*sic*] dwells in his [*sic*] love. Love is between You and I [*sic*]" (1970, p. 66). His ideas seem to call into question talk in a public setting, even in a classroom, a relatively manageable public setting. It seems too lofty an ideal.

Still, talk of forgiveness is used as a driving force in major political efforts these days. The United States apologizing to Japanese Americans for the atrocities visited on them during World War II. South Africans exploring the act of forgiveness for seven long years through the operation of the Truth and Reconciliation Commission (Gallagher, 2000; Grunebaum-Ralph, 1997). Certainly such events are fraught with political maneuvering. Even small-scale efforts to forgive are complicated by issues of self-interest. But if acts of love and forgiveness can be approached in these historic events, it might be important to consider their potential in the classrooms we inhabit. Listen to Buber's hope. "When we stand in [love] and behold in it, all become You to Them" (1970, p. 66).

Yet even Buber's sense of expectation is tempered with reality. "The shifting of a person . . . from It to You and back again is often an intricately entangled series of events that is tortuously dual" (p. 68). We attempt to connect but our failures are considerable. Thus the need for forgiveness and, perhaps, the need to return to Arendt who realizes that love and forgiveness, while ideally inseparable, must be separated if we are to "constantly forgive" in our workings within *vita activa*—the active public life. Her realism makes sense. "If . . . only love can forgive . . . forgiving would have to remain altogether outside our considerations [of our public togetherness]" (1968, p. 243). In what strikes me as a stellar moment of clarity she substitutes respect for love. We may not *love* all with whom we share the public life but we can, perhaps, respect them, provided we look closely at her definition of respect.

> Yet what love is in its own narrowly circumscribed sphere, respect is in the larger domain of human affairs. Respect . . . is a kind of "friendship" without intimacy and without closeness . . . the modern loss of respect, or rather the conviction that respect is due only where we admire or esteem, constitutes a clear symptom of the increasing depersonalization of public and social life. (1968, p. 243)

This kind of determined respect can be enacted. Separate the doer from the deed. "Respect . . . because it concerns only the person, is quite sufficient to prompt forgiving of what a person did, for the sake of the person" (p. 243). Love, as Buber defines it, happens rather than is coerced. It may entail a decision (more a decision to stop ourselves from judging than to actively engage) but the decision includes a determination to receive the other at a level that may be unrealistic in public spaces. Buber inspires us through his explication of relational living. But Arendt gives us hope that respectful relationships can be intentionally created as we shore ourselves up with a forgiving spirit, determined to have these public/personal relations. "Forgiving and the relationship it establishes is always an eminently personal (though not necessarily private) affair in which *what* was done is forgiven for the sake of *who* did it" (p. 241).

And so I find forgiveness of the other within my grasp. Ideally, teachers might want to think about opportunities for students to become bonded, connected, a community of expectation and forgiveness where love provides possibility. But Arendt keeps our feet on the ground. Respect seems more doable. It can become the stable platform for the practice of forgiveness. With our feet thus steadied, we return to Arendt's claim that forgiveness redeems us from "irreversibility." Our interactions are unpredictable. They'll need to be forgiven on a regular basis. Begin with and maintain an attitude of forgiveness and we can "remain free agents . . . trusted with so great a power to begin something anew" (1968, p. 241).

> Forgiving . . . is the only re-action which does not merely re-act but acts anew and unexpectedly, unconditioned by the act which provoked it and therefore freeing from its consequences both the one who forgives and the one who is forgiven. (p. 240)

Life can go on: we can be active and free if we choose respect, choose to live with forgiveness as a given, and renew our commitment, moment by moment, to these choices. Tough words. Gentle words. An ambiguous response is understandable, even predictable, given the human and historic tendency toward cynicism. But isn't that the heart of forgiveness? The expectation that we will fail? That others will disappoint, even injure? Why else this need to begin anew?

In a world that seems on the brink of self-destruction we may be clinging to the one best hope—our ability to begin anew. We have little power over our circumstances, it seems. And who am I to suggest to those barely surviving in a hostile world that the offenses that oppress their lives be forgiven? I cannot. Yet I have experienced and read of a strange phenomenon of late. Native American friend without a trace of angst. Life dedicated to celebrating the centuries of contributions of indigenous people. Presenting this information in tandem with stories of annihilation that are horrific. No words minced, but not a whisper of anger, judgment, or revenge. Hispanic colleague working creatively and successfully to recruit and retain underrepresented populations at the university. Working in the face of raw bigotry. Daily. What marks his relationships with others? Forgiveness. New beginnings. Frustration, yes. But an ongoing willingness to begin anew, forgiving himself, others, and the world he has been given. Parents of murdered child visit and forgive the murderer. Not the stuff of novels where vengeance drives the characters into schemes that make for intricate, spell-binding plots. Instead, a simple response. New beginnings.

I shore myself up and begin a new semester with my undergraduate students who are eager to "make a difference" in a world gone wild. And I begin as I have for the last two years with the quote that began this written exploration. "Forgiveness is the key to action and freedom." Can they choose to forgive their own halting first attempts with large groups of children? The experienced teacher whose classroom they will inhabit who may teach in ways they find unconscionable? The student whose behavior keeps them up in the night? The curriculum that agitates against student learning? The district whose policies shackle creativity? The politician whose priorities are suspect at best? The professor who is giving it her best shot? I boldly invite them to forgive me and I promise to forgive in return. Will we fail? Yes. That's the point. Forgiving our unforgiveness is part of the deal.

But forgiveness is not the same as acceptance. It paves the way for a new beginning but it doesn't imply the action forgiven is somehow acceptable. Only that we are willing to move forward, putting the past behind us. Begin again. As we forgive can we form alliances that lead us toward changes in the state of the public world? In our quiet moments with ourselves. In our most intimate relationships. In small groups and classrooms. In community endeavors and political collaborations and confrontations. Not all will be responsive to change. We will not always be responsive to change. And so we choose our challenges. Forgive ourselves when we are unwilling to take the risk. Forgive others unwilling to engage in the process and move on. Unforgiveness only shackles us—rarely matters to anyone else. Stumble in our attempts. Make mistakes. Run away for a day. Return. Start again. "Natality" Arendt calls it. She should know. Her life story is one of continual new beginnings. Forgiveness is not a panacea. The problems remain, seeming to grow as risking muddies the water of relationships requiring us to face human frailties and the complexities of circumstances. But forgiveness allows us to continue to work, to be active. No small gift. It doesn't require optimism, only commitment to the struggle.

FORGIVENESS AND FOR ISNESS

Mary

"Forgive me, father, for I have sinned." So begins the phrase Catholics recite in confession, a ritual I used tremulously the many years of my conversion. Telling my venial sins caused dis-ease for me, a feminist, talking to a (usually) young (always) man of the cloth; still, his pardon and my subsequent penance exacted from me a flooding sense of relief. I had told an other, in the darkness of the confessional booth, that I had lied too often or drunk too much or said ill of my mother-in-law. Saying an act of contrition, I was forgiven. I was allowed to return to a state of grace. To be "returned" is to be as one was, once, originally, before the drums and clamps of everyday living. One can begin again, afresh, in a state that the church bestows on behalf of God's grace. So I believed when I accepted the church's principle of konfession [spelling mine].[1]

Julia Kristeva, critical theorist, linguist, and psychoanalyst, offers a different view of forgiveness. She agrees that the act of speaking is necessary but what is more necessary in her view is the simultaneous act of being heard by another in an aspect of private mutuality. In her capacity as a psychoanalyst

Kristeva says that the hearer can actually accompany the teller in a movement of mutual transformation and rebirth (2002). I understand her to mean that speaker and hearer, in a space made special by a particular kind of interaction, together, become involved in an act that "moves" the hearts of two. Her private sphere constitutes a sharing. The words "sharing" and "mutuality" point to what differs Kristeva's couch from the konfessional booth: relationship rather than principle (Gilligan, 1993).

I remember one such mutuality I shared with my son when I discovered a letter he had written about me. He had left the letter out on his desk in his cluttered room. I was cleaning up and of course discovered the letter lying there, out in plain sight. He wanted me to read his accusations. When I later told him this, he denied it vehemently, but I am sure that it was so. He must have felt he could not really talk to me, so why not talk to me through indirection and contempt? I read the letter several times in disbelief and shock and then took a long walk to discern how best to respond. When he came back from wherever he had been, I told him I needed to talk with him. I knew that this talk would be a turning point in our relationship—that I needed to construct the time and space for it carefully—since something in me had turned my son away. What I knew was we needed mutual forgiveness, not just he forgiving me but also me forgiving him. And so I devised a ceremony. I asked him to bring the letter down, not so he would read it and I judge it, or the other way around, but so that we could turn its contents into something else. We entered the back yard, an enclosure, and, as dusk was settling, I asked him to rip the letter into pieces and place the bits in an urn. Together we lit a fire. As the flames rose we watched the hurting words turn, phoenixlike, to ash. Over the embers we spoke new words to each other and offered new promises. The fire broke down the too-solid wall between us. We began articulating, connecting, speaking, hearing, burning away; we were making meaning. Through the ceremonial act of burning, the hurts my son felt toward me and my hurt toward him were able to be cleared onto a new horizon of understanding.

Like the words "sharing" and "mutuality," the word "horizon" suggests an important complication to the notion of forgiveness. Horizons imply relationship, one *and* oneness. The scenario sketched earlier of me in the konfessional booth was not a "horizon." The priest and I were not on equal terms. The Catholic Church, hierarchical through and through, is structurally vertical. The priest acts as an infallible source with unquestioned authority such that I, a penitent, must ask to be pardoned from a human act called a "sin" by the church and deemed a "sin" so as to keep me obedient to a set of cardinal laws (remember him?).[2] As Catholics practice penance, and as I willingly and obediently followed the practice, the phrase "I absolve you" uttered by the priest sets up the inequality. Once absolved, the problem vanishes. For the penitent, there is consolation; I used the word "relief." The relief is in believing that the error has been transcended, so long as I say my beads.

One problem with this practice is that authority to forgive resides outside the self. And with the church, ordained priests are the authors of belief. It is they who have the author-ity over those of us willing to conform to the belief system the church calls dogma. There are so many of us willing to conform in this way. My uncle is one. He joined the Mormons so as to know what to believe. My friend Gabrielle is another. She joined a cult so as to know what to believe. I was one. I converted to Catholicism so as to know what to believe. We are difficult people to reason with. We are full of belief. We have been trained with answers to problems. But as Marla observed of Gabrielle, she seems half-dead. While offering a perky presence, she nevertheless is flat behind the eyes, half dead in her imagination. Her imagination has been Christianized by belief.

Troubling this notion of forgiveness does not simply involve criticizing orthodoxies. There is a far more serious problem here with deadening imaginations. Imagination stops when problems are solved. When "sins" are forgiven, that is the end of that. When told that a group of people is "sinful," that clamps a label onto them. End of them. Forgive the Holocaust. End of that.[3] The ability to think more deeply is aborted when forgiveness provides a resolution to that which cannot be resolved by believing it away. Kristeva, however, suggests that thinking deeply is a meaning-making activity that occurs on "a horizon, something in the way of the other, the big Other" (p. 284). Metaphors, affects, and intonations are heard on a horizon, she says, which bring into play "the entire panoply of the psychic life" (p. 282) where questions lead on to openness.

Self and the big Other. Flannery O'Connor's writing is infused with the presence of "the big Other." O'Connor calls herself a Catholic writer, but not in any orthodox sense. In fact, her key religious word is not "belief" but "mystery," because mystery, as she says, "eludes formula" (1969, p. 153). I see her writing against orthodox Catholicism when she chooses as her typical protagonist the pious believer. She says of this sort of character, "he has reduced his conception of the supernatural to pious cliché and has become able to recognize nature in literature in only two forms, the sentimental and the obscene" (1969, p. 149). O'Connor goes on to argue that it is the business of the serious writer to write dangerous (her synonym for "obscene") fiction for believers, while it is the business of the church to protect believers from dangerous fiction (1969, p. 149). Anyone who has read O'Connor will know where she is going with this discussion, since violence is so much a part of her plots. But, like a blow to the blades during zazen ('kyosaku'), the act of violence or "breaking through" serves to awaken imaginations deadened by belief. Grace, that which returns one to an original state with God, is, as she conceives it, not kind and not simple. Grace is violent (1969, p. 112), found, she goes so far to say, "in the territory of the devil" (1969, p. 119). For O'Connor, God's mystery completely eludes the realm of sentiment or worthiness or righteousness, even. It eludes courts of law, even; cardinal law, even; common sense, even. O'Connor's notion of mystery, while steeped in Catholicism without sentiment, embraces Buddhism without beliefs (Batchelor, 1997).

O'Connor's concept is difficult, the sort of aesthetic Kristeva selects in order to grasp the idea of redemption. Forgiveness is not judgment; it is grace. O'Connor's idea of grace shares much with certain forms of Buddhism and Taoism, where the question of forgiveness is always already there, not something to be bestowed. If God acts in mysterious ways, O'Connor's God acts through the sun (she puns) in a surreal sky. In "Greenleaf" the sun is like a burning bullet (1978, p. 325). In "The Temple of the Holy Ghost" it is like "an elevated Host drenched in blood" (1978, p. 248). In "The Enduring Chill" it is "like some strange potentate from the east" (1978, p. 357). Her characters are smug in this oddly illuminated place; they take for granted that God has placed them above those of "lower" class or race. To their peril, they are oblivious to the beckoning of the sun. The characters see only what is literally in front of them in black and white, not the glaring colors nor the fierce, enacting light of a surreal landscape.

O'Connor, however, insists that grace occurs precisely to those characters seemingly most unworthy, most unforgiving. Her people, pious churchgoers and Bible thumpers, are unrepentant bigots, all—drawn from the rural South where she grew up and lived. Their focus is extremely narrow and selected. They read the Bible but do not understand Matthew's gospel: "And why beholdest thou the mote that is in thy brother's eye, but considerest not the beam that is in thine own eye?" (7:2–3). Her characters cast judgment on others in the hypocritical notion that they themselves lack fault. Nevertheless, O'Connor uses a character's eye as symbol for a viewpoint that perceives, suddenly, at the hour of death, a reality beyond the real. It is as if O'Connor gives to her protagonists, at the end, the gift of a prophet's eye, which O'Connor distinguishes from the eyes of the church (1969).

I find O'Connor's notion of a grace that lies beyond the horizon (a metaphor for beyond the norm) similar to—of all theorists!—Jacques Derrida. "Forgiveness should remain exceptional and extraordinary," Derrida writes (2002, p. 32), "beyond the . . . horizon of a redemption or a reconciliation" (p. 39). While O'Connor's words for forgiveness are synonymous with the words "grace" and "mystery," Derrida's are synonymous with "enigma," even "madness," which he describes as "a dream for thought" (p. 60). Forgiveness, for both, lies outside the realm of sovereign law or common understanding, extending the Abrahamic moral tradition far, far farther than many are able to go.

In "The Enduring Chill," Asbury, the spoiled and sickly twenty-five-year-old son of Mrs. Fox, is an intellectual with a very hard head. That is his problem. He is too fixed in his thoughts. Nevertheless, Asbury has come home to die on a day when his dying corresponds to the rising of the sun in the manner of an eastern potentate (O'Connor, 1978, p. 357). Early on we learn that he has a bloodshot left eye. O'Connor's metaphors suggest Asbury's wounded left side now becomes vulnerable, which is to say open, to a different kind of vision. Because he does not buy his mother's brand of religion, he shuts out her piety but finds a comforting attraction in her home environment. His mother's cow, for instance, really catches his attention: "a small, walleyed Guernsey was watching him steadily as if she sensed some bond between them" (p. 362), O'Connor writes. Asbury's bond is stronger with a cow than with either the local doctor or the local priest. That he cannot abide doctrine or traditional medicine suggests there is a wound in his hard-headed intellect that allows openness toward another, more Eastern way.

The vast background of the story provides what Kristeva might call the horizon for the big Other. The whitegold sun is seen "beyond the black woods that surrounded Timberboro," casting a "strange light" that intimates "a majestic transformation" (p. 357). O'Connor's treeline, in my view, symbolizes that which separates the common from the surreal, the rational from the nonrational, the eye of the prophet from the eye of the church, the other from the big Other, the Catholic believer from the Buddhist practitioner, the ordinary from the eschatological.[4] Asbury cannot see this horizon initially because of the mote in his bloodshot eye: he lives too enclosed in ordinary time. Still, it is he—the wounded one—who receives the terrifying and purifying presence of the Holy Ghost.

> A blinding red-gold sun moved serenely from under a purple cloud. Below it the treeline was black against the crimson sky. It formed a brittle wall, standing as if it were the frail defense he had set up in his mind to protect him from what was coming. . . . It was then that he felt the beginning of a chill, a chill so peculiar, so light, that it was like a warm ripple across a deeper sea of cold . . . the Holy Ghost, emblazoned in ice instead of fire, continued, implacable, to descend. (1978, p. 382)

This astonishing description accords with how Rudolf Otto characterizes numinous experience as "something inherently or wholly the other . . . before which we therefore recoil in a wonder that strikes us chill and numb" (1958, p. 28).

Grace—far from being gentle—is a force strong enough to dislodge the distorting mote. The mix of Christian and Eastern language in this story suggests O'Connor's acceptance of Buddhist ideas within her Catholic frame, particularly the passages that show the intersubjective quality of a cow and a man and her reference to an Eastern potentate. In another story, "Greenleaf," it is a bull that beckons the protagonist, a bull described as "some patient god come down to woo (Mrs. May)" (1978, p. 311). Here this bull-god forces itself on Mrs. May "like a wild and tormented lover" and gores her heart (the organ of sentiment and belief). Mrs. May offers no resistance, standing in "freezing unbelief" against a familiar O'Connor landscape of treeline and sky. At the end of the story, O'Connor offers an inversion of the pietà when she focuses on Mrs. May dying on the horns of the bull, "whispering some last discovery into the animal's ears" (p. 334). While O'Connor references familiar Christian ideas like the Host and the Holy Ghost and employs familiar iconography, she does so with a zenlike twist.

In "Everything That Rises Must Converge," O'Connor again focuses on sudden death with sudden awakening. The story takes place on a bus wherein Mrs. Godhigh (!) and her stuck-up son are traveling so that the mother can attend her weight-loss program. The bus provides O'Connor with a sort of waiting room or purgatory in which all forms of humanity converge before they reach their final destination. In this microcosm Mrs. Godhigh assumes she is better than her fellow travelers because of her social standing, remarking, "it's a wonder we can enjoy anything. I tell you, the bottom rail is on the top" (1978, p. 407). Wearing her imaginary dignity heavily (she is, after all, overweight), Mrs. Godhigh does not hear the resonance of her own Christlike observation—the last shall be first. O'Connor indicates with this resonance that Mrs. Godhigh, despite her patronizing attitude and old-fashioned bigotry, is not a hateful person. The story ends abruptly when Mrs. Godhigh has a heart attack and dies on the street. O'Connor makes it clear that while the mother does not reach her literal destination, she is called "home" to her larger destiny: "home" taking on a wider meaning in a new way (Smith, 1999).

Why is this woman selected for grace? Are her prejudices "forgiven"? Because her heart can be attacked she is vulnerable, just as Asbury is vulnerable in his eye. To signal her transformation from belief to sudden enlightenment, O'Connor describes Mrs. Godhigh's distorted face. "One eye, large and staring, moved slightly to the left as if it had become unmoored" (1978, p. 420). The other eye acquires strange insight, seeing "nothing" in her son's face. At the last, Mrs. Godhigh sees the waywardness of her son's vacuous views and becomes "unmoored" from the anchor of her own biases. Released, she sees beyond the horizon to a hidden presence of a divinity that is cosmic and awe-full, in the manner of Teilhard de Chardin, with whom O'Connor had a lively correspondence, and who remarked that Christ can be felt in "the realities reputed to be the most dangerous" (in Eliade,1990, p. 85). Being open to the beckoning world and dying to old habits are also necessary steps in the walking of the dharma path (Batchelor, 1997).

Violence and enlightenment form a particularly awe-full twosome in "A Good Man is Hard to Find." Again we find characters in transport, a metaphor for a necessary psychic movement. In a car are a family of four and a grandmother, who is O'Connor's pick for enlightenment. Their journey to Florida is interrupted when the grandmother insists on a side trip to visit an old plantation she grew up on and which she wants to show her grandchildren. She thinks they would enjoy what she thinks of as the good old days when houses had six white columns, driveways had oak alleys, women were

ladies, men were suitors, and black children were pickanninnies. The grandmother lives by kitsch phrases and trite ideas and holds impossibly simplistic
views of the ways things used to be—before things were messed up by inte-
gration. (She shares a Lott with certain modern day Dixiecrats.) Her ignorance notwithstanding, the grandmother notices the multicolored quality of
God's green world:

> Stone Mountain; the blue granite that in some places came up to both sides
> of the highway; the brilliant red clay banks slightly streaked with purple; and
> the various crops that made rows of green lace-work on the ground. The
> trees were full of silver-white sunlight and the meanest of them sparkled.
> (1978, p. 119)

By these observations, she shows herself to be potentially capable of a broader
vision.

The grandmother's character, like that of Asbury, Mrs. Fox, and Mrs.
Godhigh, has an inner coherence that makes her a candidate for enlightenment. Like Mrs. Godhigh, she believes in her heart all the trashy notions of a
bigot, but she is able to discard these notions in a flash when deterred from
her straight and narrow path. The grandmother insists on a detour. The side
road is so bumpy that the car upends in a ditch. Here the family meets their
fate when three escaped convicts discover the mishap and without provocation
kill the family, one by one. But this does not occur before the grandmother has
an epiphany. She recognizes in the Misfit's face a similarity to her own: "The
grandmother had the peculiar feeling that the bespectacled man was someone
she knew. His face was as familiar to her as if she had known him all her life
but she could not recall who he was" (1978, p. 126). When the Misfit says,
"Jesus thrown everything off balance" (p. 131), this thought echoes the grandmother's, though coming from opposite sides. In the territory of the devil the
grandmother finds her own opposite self and loses her beliefs.

Here we have a riddle. Opposites unite in most unlikely sources: a faint-
hearted old woman and a mean-spirited young man: an innocent and the
devil. What they have in common is their shared instinct of going off the
beaten path, suggestive of their intuition that what matters finally, in the end,
at the time of one's death or of one's birth, eschatologically, is not of ordinary
concern. Just before he shoots the grandmother, the Misfit proclaims a most
mystical idea uttered in a most coldblooded way: "She would of been a good
woman . . . if it had been somebody there to shoot her every minute of her
life" (p. 133).

What would it be like to have a revolver at one's head every minute of
one's life?

It would be impossible not to think final thoughts. It would shock
human stupidity out of the brain and sentimental gush out of the heart. It

would catapult one into a state of unpacking, disgorging, reversing the drift of habitual responses and automatic impulses. It would blow away a lifetime of ordinariness in an instant of utterness. It would be an existential confrontation of the first order at the last minute. It would be a pivot in time when the fullness empties and the emptiness fills, when immediacy breaks into old patterns and offers a glimpse of reality that is simultaneously more familiar and more elusive. O'Connor plays with these paradoxes in her fiction because she sees that the mystery of being is itself a paradox.

O'Connor shrouds in mystery the final moments of her characters who have demonstrated, despite their flaws, an inner coherence that is suddenly awakened. Her characters are caricatures in a cartoon world until that final moment of their dying. And then they go "home" beyond the treeline that separates belief from imagination. They seem to accept with a calmness the baffling urgency of their dying, which in itself is a living in isness. Questions lead on to questions. They do not recite any learned words, receive absolution, or solve the riddle of the universe. They leave all those old learned habits behind. They have within them what James Hillman calls a daimon, "the inescapable and necessary pattern" which the daimon "remembers" (1996, p. 46). While they may not be deserving in terms that a law court might rule, these characters are tranquil because they connect, at the end, with their better beginnings. They are called home to themselves. If, as David Smith reminds us, contradiction is at the heart of life (1999, p. 25), then dying would seem to be, in Flannery O'Connor's particular brand of Buddhist-Catholicism, enlivening. And Forgiveness gives way to isness.

"MISTAKES WERE MADE": ADMITTING (AND FORGIVING) MEDICAL ERROR

Delese

A diagnosis presumably missed. A patient through a presumed lapse, does poorly. The patient dies despite all measure. The physician . . . feels deeply responsible. And profoundly guilty. And unforgiven.
                                        —LaCombe, (1999, p. 444)

Very few people have a clue about the ubiquity of medical mistakes. Somehow most of us operate with the belief that doctors don't make mistakes—at least not on us or someone we love. Mistakes are those newsworthy items we read about in the newspaper or in the *Enquirer*: "Doctor removes wrong leg" or "Healthy heart removed from woman undergoing hysterectomy." Our doctors wouldn't miss a breast lesion in our yearly mammogram, order Zyban instead Zydone, or fail to inform us about possible long-term effects of HRT.

Unfortunately, mistakes occur all the time in medicine. According to an Institute of Medicine report, "To Err Is Human," medical errors cause between 44,000 and 98,000 deaths annually just in U.S. hospitals, and that medical error ranked eighth among the leading causes of death in the United States—higher than breast cancer, car accidents, and AIDS (Kohn, Corrigan, & Donaldson, 2000). Another study of three training programs in internal medicine found that 45 percent of residents reported making at least one error, 31 percent of which resulted in someone dying (Wu et al., 1993).

Mistakes occur most often when doctors are inexperienced or when new procedures are introduced (Weingart et al., 2000), not because of doctors' arrogance or sense of omnipotence. In fact, LaCombe speaks of the "secret sense of utter inadequacy" doctors often feel upon entering the profession, noting that "it requires supreme arrogance for a young physician to feel adequately prepared for anything" (1999, p. 444).

> There is this crafty pedagogical trick we play upon our young trainees, whom we cause to believe they fight alone at the front, while all the time we roam behind the lines, supervising them in surreptitious ways. When a patient dies, the physician feels suddenly alone and the "tyranny of the shoulds" boils in the young physician's brain. (p. 444)

But feeling alone begins long before doctors get their hands on patients. It begins the first day of medical school when students learn that the person sitting next to them may not be someone with whom to share feelings because of the toxic competition that saturates the whole process. Medical students quickly learn the high cost of not knowing, of not being on top all the time. Pimping, a time-honored "pedagogical" tool, occurs on teaching rounds when the most senior members of a team ask questions of trainees, often obscure facts associated with patients' illnesses, and often in rapid-fire succession. Attending physicians pimp fellows, fellows pimp residents, and everyone pimps medical students: kick the dog, medical style. Not knowing, or the *appearance* of not knowing, becomes something everyone hopes to avoid.

Atul Gawande's essay "The Learning Curve" (2002) is one all would-be patients in teaching hospitals would be wise to read before admission. A surgeon himself, Gawande unflinchingly admits that "like the tennis player and the oboist and the guy who fixes hard drives, we need practice to get good at what we do. There is one difference in medicine, though: we practice on people" (p. 55). His essay traces how as a first-year resident he learns to insert a central line into a patient's chest, a procedure that involves numbing a spot on a patient's chest then threading an eight-inch line into the main blood vessel into the heart. Complications occur in fewer than one case in one hundred—if the doctor is experienced. But he was not experienced, and as he prepared to do his first procedure, disasters "weighed on his mind" about what could go wrong:

> The woman who had died within minutes from massive bleeding when a resident lacerated her vena cava; the man whose chest had to be opened because a resident lost hold of a wire inside the line, which then floated down to the patient's heart; the man who had a cardiac arrest when the procedure put him into ventricular fibrillation. I said nothing of such things, naturally, when I asked the patient's permission to do his line. He said, "okay" (p. 52)

Gawande fails to complete the procedure successfully on his first attempt when he "kept spearing his [patient's] clavicle instead of slipping beneath it." On his second attempt with a different patient he "stabbed the needle in too shallow and then too deep." On his third patient "again, it was stick, stick, stick, and nothing." All three times a more senior resident took over, and no one died or was seriously hurt (pp. 54–55).

But what of the more senior physician's mistakes, those not attributed to inexperience? The most compelling, forthright account of medical mistakes written by a contemporary doctor in the United States is by David Hilfiker, who disclosed how he terminated a much wanted pregnancy in error in the *New England Journal of Medicine* (1984) and ultimately in his memoir *Healing the Wounds* (1985). A family doctor in rural Minnesota in the late seventies and early eighties, he often practiced medicine, including obstetrics, without the benefits of technology found in larger academic centers. After one of his patients missed three periods but had four negative pregnancy tests, he decided that a dilation and curettage should be performed to remove what must surely be the tissue of a dead embryo, and his patient agrees. He did not order an ultrasound to confirm what his experience told him; such a nonroutine procedure (for that time) would have required a car trip of a few hours and money his patients didn't have. But during the D&C, things did not go as he expected:

> There is considerably more blood than usual, and it is only with great difficulty that I am able to extract anything. What should take ten or fifteen minutes stretches into a half-hour. The body parts I remove are much larger than I expected, considering when the embryo died. They are not bits of decomposing tissue. These are parts of a body that was recently alive. (Hilfiker, 1991, p. 378)

After the procedure he told his patient and her husband all he knew for sure without letting them know what he suspected. Two days later when his patient called him tearfully reporting that she passed some recognizable body parts, he made an appointment with them to tell them what he ultimately learned from the pathologist, that he had aborted a living, eleven-week fetus. They were crushed.

Hilfiker's guilt grew over the weeks and months after the procedure, guilt and anger not only for his mistake but also for the expectation that doctors will be perfect. "We are not prepared for our mistakes," he writes, "and we don't know how to cope with them when they occur" (1991, p. 379). What does happen is that doctors hide their mistakes from their patients and other doctors because open discussion of such errors is banished except in very specific forums. And what happens, Hilfiker maintains, is that when doctors are unable to ask for forgiveness for their mistakes, they are cut off from healing: "We are thwarted, stunted; we do not grow" (p. 380).

But as the personal stories of Gawande and Hilfiker show, and as the startling results of the Institute of Medicine's study indicate, mistakes happen. The culture of medicine, set apart and above from the "laity," has rarely focused on apology, and even less on forgiveness from patients. The reasons are fairly straightforward. The first and most obvious reason is that doctors get sued for their mistakes, and U.S citizens are a litigious lot when it comes to what they expect from doctors who make mistakes. Jury awards to patients now average $3.49 million (Treaster, 2001), while claims paid to patients in malpractice cases average $384,282 (Walsh, 2001). Malpractice insurance for some specialties—obstetrics or surgery—are often more than $100,000 a year for coverage in some states (Treaster, 2001); a neurosurgeon in south Florida may pay as much as $200,000 for coverage (Stolberg, 2002). Why would anyone admit to an error when the financial stakes are so high?

But there are other reasons doctors do not apologize or seek forgiveness for an error they committed. Such an admission places the doctor in jeopardy of considerable negative consequences, some of which are professional: "damage to one's professional reputation and perceived authority, loss of referrals and income, an increase in malpractice insurance premiums, and diminished chances of professional advancement" (Reitemeier, 1997, p. 355). Other reasons are deeply personal: Hilfiker did not seek forgiveness from his patient and her husband because he believed they had suffered enough grief without having to deal with his guilt and sorrow.

Thus, doctors rarely openly admit error and apologize to affected patients, yet the emotional impact on those who commit a medical error is intense, including remorse and a sense of inadequacy (Wu et al., 1993). And because of the possible legal repercussions,

> a curtain of denial and nondisclosure, and a code of conspiracy of silence are created by [doctors]. Another myth is then maintained: the perception that mistakes are rare and atypical. Because there is little or no room for imperfection, and because mistakes are believed to be rare, there are few available forums for revealing and discussing mistakes, and no acceptance and support if disclosure by professionals does occur. (Smith & Forster, 2000, p. 40)

But there's an irony here. Numerous studies have shown that doctors who avoid discussing mistakes with patients and their families may be inviting what they are trying to avoid: "A poor relationship with the physician, poor delivery of information, and negative communications by the physician may actually increase litigious intentions" (Witman, Park, & Hardin, 1996, p. 2565). That is, in the existing doctor-patient relationship—one presumably based on trust, respect, and altruism—apologies may be even more important than in other circumstances because the trusted caregiver turns into the enemy. Levine (2002) believes that patients sue doctors who make mistakes not just for financial reasons but because they feel "abandoned and aggrieved, in ways that better communication and acknowledgment might alleviate." Moreover, she continues, doctors have always known "the importance that families place on knowing what happened to loved ones and the frustration they feel when stonewalled. If there were more openness, including apologies, some lawsuits might be forestalled . . . without so much emotional toll on families" (p. 241).

And, perhaps, there would be less emotional toll on doctors themselves. Hilfiker suggests that the unattainable perfection demanded from doctors is, in part, archetypal: "We always look to shamans for magical healing, we always look to priests, the medical priesthood. There's a tendency to look at healing as a divine art, so there's something within people that expects divinity from our healers. But the profession has also encouraged them" (1989, p. 96). He proposes that one way to change this is for doctors to bring *themselves* into the process of healing, not just their expertise. Only then will doctors know how to feel their patients' pain, "and the only way to be able to feel a patient's pain is by being willing to face your own," he says. "So those of us who work with people at that level need to get out of our technical selves and be able to share our own pain and move into their pain" (1989, p. 97). Such sharing, it seems, may include admissions and apologies, and sometimes seeking forgiveness—for one's mistakes, for one's limitations, for sometimes seeming unresponsive.

But who is forgiving whom? Perhaps doctors' asking patients for forgiveness is too great a leap in a litigious culture where error-free diagnosis and treatment is expected. Certainly medicine itself isn't having a conversation about forgiveness: with only a few exceptions, the voluminous literature on medical error does not even address apology much less forgiveness. *Disclosing* error is as close as it gets, usually in a passive construction: "Mistakes were made." Even at that, if doctors were to apologize for error, what are they apologizing for? Mistakes resulting from lack of expertise or lack of knowledge? Mistakes resulting from carelessness? Mistakes resulting from fatigue or burnout? In his classic essay on medical mistakes, Lucian Leape argues that "errors must be accepted as evidence of system flaws not character flaws" (1994, p. 1857). If that is by far most often the case, what does an apology from a doctor to a patient or family really signify? What if the illusion of infallibility inculcated in doctors throughout their training along with the inhumane work environment of residency programs were actually the primary causes of medical error? Wouldn't it make more sense to focus on the hierarchical values, training rituals, and epistemological assumptions underlying medical training that force expectations of an error-free practice? Leape argues that

> role models in medical education reinforce the concept of infallibility. The young physician's teachers are largely specialists, experts in their fields, and authorities.Authorities are not supposed to err. It has been suggested that this need to be infallible creates a strong pressure to intellectual dishonesty, to cover up mistakesrather than to admit them. The organization of medical practice, particularly in the hospital, perpetuates these norms. Errors are rarely admitted or discussed among physicians in private practice. Physicians typically feel, not without reason, that admission of error will lead to censure or increased surveillance or worse, that their colleagues will regard them as incompetent or careless. Far better to conceal a mistake or, if that is impossible, to try to shift the blame to another, even the patient. (p. 1852)

Is it any wonder, then, that doctors almost never seek forgiveness, even for deadly mistakes or those that cause permanent injury, disability, or emotional pain? There is no forum for doctors to discuss their feelings of sorrow or guilt for having made an error, and nothing in their training prepares them for the aftermath of mistakes that they will all most surely make. Instead, Hilfiker writes, "we either deny the misfortune altogether or blame the patient, the nurse, the laboratory, other physicians, the system, fate—anything to avoid our own guilt" (1991, p. 386). And as Martha suggests, as long as someone is unforgiving of themselves or others, their energy for living is "redirected toward a single characteristic or past action, event, or circumstance."

Of course, some might argue that there is a forum within medicine for the discussion of mistakes, namely, "M&M"—the Morbidity and Mortality Conference, which usually takes place once a week at nearly every teaching hospital in the United States Attendance is mandatory for everyone from department chairs to medical students, for here is where mistakes are discussed (passive construction intentional) with the hope of uncovering how the mistake happened and how it can be prevented. It is a practice protected from legal intrusion, which is why it can exist. According to Gawande, the reports of error in these conferences "involve a certain elision of detail and a lot of passive verbs." No one screws up a procedure; the procedure "was attempted without success" (1999, p. 49). Obviously, this is not a place for doctors to deal with the guilt and sorrow of harming a patient, much less patients' and families' grief or anger.

Returning now to the two examples of medical error cited earlier, we might ask if Drs. Gawande and Hilfiker should have apologized or asked for forgiveness. If I were the patient on the receiving end of a resident's awkward attempt at inserting a central line in my very sick body, I would—I think—feel comforted, even touched, by such an apology from a young and scared doctor in training. I don't think it requires forgiveness. But if my much-wanted baby had been aborted in error, I think an apology is the minimum gesture I would expect from a decent and compassionate doctor. But apology does not require or assume forgiveness. In fact, is forgiveness necessary? I don't know; I am inclined to believe that Hilfiker was right: a doctor seeking for-giveness from a patient or family he or she has harmed may be asking too much of someone already consumed with grief and sorrow. In fact, it strikes me as a bit solipsistic.

But forgiveness does have a place in these scenarios and others like them in the ongoing drama of medical care, and that place must begin within the profession itself. I'm not talking about a new and improved M&M confer-ence, or the development of a secret society where confessions are heard, but rather a changed professional, institutional, and educative ethos where sup-port and emotional healing are present at every turn for fallible doctors (and students) who have made mistakes that harm patients. "The emotional impact is often profound," Leape writes, "[yet] physicians are typically isolated by their emotional responses" (1994, p. 97). Without ways to help doctors deal with their mistakes, mistakes which will most surely occur because doctors are humans, this dilemma that has no name because it cannot be spoken will con-tinue to exist. "I am a healer," Hilfiker writes, "yet I sometimes do more harm than good. . . . At some point we must all bring medical mistakes out of the closet" (1991, pp. 386–87). When that begins to happen, perhaps doctors can begin again, wiser, afresh, each day with each new patient, in their commit-ment to heal, and to do no harm.

SEVEN

Light

INTRODUCTION

Delese

IT SEEMS THAT LIGHT, whether noun or verb, is usually associated with something good or positive, particularly in contradistinction to dark. Martha speaks of "the inner light" and "the light in children's eyes," of "lighting the way for students" and "being struck by light-giving understanding." She also speaks of the light extinguished by teaching practices and curriculum prescriptions, of silence as darkness, of schooling that silences. But Martha is also concerned with the sustainability of her own journey toward light. "How," she asks, "can I ask my students to move beyond the explicit, required curricular notion of enlightenment if I myself fail to make the journey? . . . Central to this process is my own willingness to go deep. There's light in there. I know it." Fanning the flames, even the flames of confusion and struggle, is what Martha describes as central to her project of teaching, a project where she and her students learn to reflect each others' lights, together illuminating and even changing the world.

Mary's reflections on light arise from an entirely different orientation. "Dark is not the absence of light," she writes, "but that which makes the things I might otherwise overlook come alive to my senses." She resists the Enlightenment dualisms of light and dark, good and evil, dualisms bifurcated even more intensely since the tragedies of September 11, urging us (as Maxine Greene does) to "get rid of these damn discrete particles" (2001, p. 2). Dualistic thinking is usually up to no good (even here I cannot resist the polarities!), for here is where categories come into play, each begging for content to be sorted neatly into their respective containers of thought. I am reminded of Terry Tempest Williams's words that ward off such categorical, static thinking: "Identity is no museum piece sitting stock-still in a display case, but rather the endlessly astonishing synthesis of the contradictions of everyday life" (2000, p. 78). And contradictions do indeed abound when we think only in designations of good and evil, Mary reminds us, for human nature is complex, a composition of "opposite tendencies both good and evil, light and dark."

In my piece I examine light mostly as verb, as a teacher trying to understand how we teach our students to notice things, how this is foreground (lit, and thus important), while that is background (dimmed, and thus less important). Even in a postmodern world where "light is everywhere and on demand" (Morris, 2002, p. 10), I wonder how my medical students, when listening to patients' stories of their illness, decide what is relevant and what is not, or which accounts are more trustworthy or reliable and which are not. Using Ann Fadiman's eloquent anthropological exploration of the colliding worlds of U.S. medicine and Hmong culture, I examine how what captures our attention may be the least relevant dimension to another observer of the same phenomenon. She turns the spotlight fairly and compassionately on the two seemingly disparate cultures: here on the unflinching force of parental love in a poor refugee family struggling to protect their gravely ill daughter Lia and ancient Hmong healing traditions from the absolutism of Western medicine, there on her skilled, caring, tireless physicians who try to save Lia's life. How do our gazes become so focused, so singular, that we fail to see? Annie Dillard says that "we are most deeply asleep at the switch when we fancy we control any switches at all" (1977, p. 62). My medical students must surely learn to see humans in all their rich, diverse, and contradictory ways of making sense of health and illness and dying; how can such attentiveness be nurtured?

NURTURING LIGHT

Martha

They come with wonderful intentions, my students. They feel enlightened, mature. And they want to pass this enlightenment on to children. It's a predictable comment. "I want to be a teacher because I love to see the light in a child's eyes when they understand." Laudable rationale. But understand what? 8 times 4? The capital of Mississippi? Perhaps more deeply: The causes of the Civil War? Or even more interpretive: The injustices of colonization? I don't mean to cast aspersions on these educational goals. But think again about the light in a child's eyes. Surely it is shining there when there is a sudden sense of accomplishment or understanding. I've enjoyed those shining moments myself. As a teacher. As a mother. As a friend. But what of the light of wonder? What of the less flashy light of steady concentration as a child searches for her inner self, her view of the world, her voice?

There's a lot of talk about silencing these days. Fine (1992) describes it in the extreme. "Silencing signifies a terror of words, a fear of talk" (p. 115). Those who hold power or fear difference choose to silence. I imagine silence as darkness. The personal darkness of invisibility. I'm not there. My presence is absent. It is a darkness that creeps into my life unexpectedly these days. I'm more assertive now, more able to play the collegial, collaborative, move-toward-the-goal game. But occasionally I find myself suddenly cloaked once more. Yearning for light. Fighting to be visible. I remember my days of being so aware that I was not-male, not-faculty, not-tenure-track. The light seemed to be shining at the top of a ladder that I needed to climb. But now, I waver. Is light really up there, out there? Is it something to be captured? And I wonder again about the children. My students are right, of course, to be looking for the light within children. But will they find the time and courage needed to ponder their own perceptions, search for their light within, and encourage their students to do the same? If, as many of us have claimed, school experiences and teachers unwittingly silence students' voices (Delpit, 1988; Fassinger, 1995; Jones & Gerig, 1995; Simpson & Erickson, 1983), what will come of their determination to enlighten their students?

A rough judgement, to be sure. Schooling as silencing. But in 1916, Dewey was already talking about "congestion in the curriculum." And think of all we've added since then! Apple (1993) refers to the deskilling of teachers. Who needs extensive skill when the day is scripted, saturated, systematically overloaded? Intensification of the work (Gitlin, 1990) of teaching is a contemporary version of Dewey's curricular congestion with the focus shifted from curriculum to the act of teaching and, by implication, the teacher. Silencing. I'd say so. The glimmer of personal understanding snuffed out, or never really kindled. In all the hurry, all the hustle and bustle of covering ground and accountability, the voice of the inner child—student's or teacher's—is seldom heard. I imagine the glow, the light that would accompany those conversations. Conversations that are more complicated, more reflective. And I wonder, What do my students know about fanning the flames of personal understanding until each of their students begins to glow? How many of them have struggled in significant ways to find their own voices, their own light? Have I?

A difficult question emerges. Has the search for voice, my determination to take the longest, most difficult journey inward, been quenched in an academic community, a politicized environment? How can I ask my students to move beyond the explicit, required curricular notion of enlightenment if I myself fail to make the journey? Lighting the way for students should not only be an invitation to them to find their own voice, their own view, their own pre-view (Greene, 1995). It should also entail an obligation to quiet the voices that drive us on as we listen for our own thoughts, wait for our own glow of understanding to emerge. I want to adjust my undergraduate syllabus, include playdough and music in our experiences. Push past the educational rhetoric of doctoral seminars and ask the elemental questions. Playdough and music here, too? How best to encourage creation and productive conflict? Can we talk about the elephant in the room—our very beings—that everyone sees (if superficially) but no one addresses? But central to this process is my own willingness to go deep. There's light in there. I know it.

I was seven, I think, walking on a narrow pathway beside my neighbor's garage, on the way to play in his backyard. There was a window in the garage—four panes, all smudged with dirt. I caught a glimpse of my reflection and the moment was suddenly etched into my memory. Not just my blurry image but the dirty window, the trees wafting in the breeze, the smell of spring, the anticipation of play. I thought, "How wonderfully odd this all is!" Spring, trees, buildings, friend, and me. It was a flash of insight. An awareness of myself and my surroundings. Perhaps my first metacognitive moment. A sudden light emerged from within. I think it changed me forever, for I remember it still. And in an occasional quiet moment I return to that light, reminded of the magnificence and strangeness of existence.

I'm reading the introductory section of a curriculum manual. It's heavy and cumbersome. I'm an undergraduate, studying to be a teacher. "Seven-year-olds tend to be day-dreamers," it says. I'm transported back through time. Yes, I think. How wonderful. I remember my reflection-in-the-garage-window experience. When I teach seven-year-olds, I must remember this. It will help me to understand them. But the sheer weight of the book catches my attention. It is filled with the prescribed curriculum that might keep me from nurturing the goodness of the child's natural impulses. I worry a little, but move on. Ironic. As I think back now, the tone of the introductory information in that manual was not about nurturing the inner light of children. No, its aim was to use predictable stages of development and build on those in ways that would allow more efficient coverage of the curriculum. As a fledling teacher I was being coached on how "best" to interfere with that day-dreamer—get her refocused on prescribed learning.

My father is stressed. It's something about snow shoveling and teenagers who don't have enough sensitivity to get up and clear the way for the day when the snow is deep, his schedule even deeper. I should feel chastised but suddenly there is a moment when I see him as a real person. He's not just my dad. He's an overloaded, frustrated human being. He was a child. He will be an old man. He's like me. And right now he's stretched and angry. Perhaps all the moments thereafter that were part of our switching from child/parent to deeply connected friends began just then. Through the years we understood each other, and we didn't, as is the case with all friends. Now he is gone from this magnificent, strange world. I can't bear the thought of having lost him. It helps to remember that moment when I was struck by the light-giving understanding of him as a human being on a journey, just like me.

Do my students know I am a struggling human being? Do they identify me as merely filling a role rather than sharing my life? The hours I've spent with them, children, young adults, experienced teachers: have those been time well spent? Do they realize that they have changed me immeasurably—as I undoubtedly changed my father and he me? How much light have we drawn from each other? Which moments were worth having? I fear there were many hours lost to prescription and expectation. But my father is gone and some day I will be gone and the students that will fill my tomorrows deserve real experiences (Pinar, 1992). We need to ask authentic questions, struggle toward understanding, fan the flames of confusion until we have discovered something of worth.

John F. Kennedy is dead. I am sixteen. All I can think about is the weird controversy over his being the first presidential candidate to stroll in public without a hat. How could we have cared about hatlessness? How can he be dead? My grandfather is dead, and now this. Life is temporary. Terrible acts of violence can catch us off guard, shatter our sense of security. I try to stifle the fearful thought. He's in heaven, I believe, like Grandpa. So why this frightful emotion? Something to do with my own mortality, my own vulnerability. Hardly a moment one would characterize as filled with light. And yet, my generation was changed that day. Many took his legacy of volunteerism seriously and tried to juggle that through an upcoming decade of rebellion and outrage. Do my students know the reasons I'm teaching a foundations of education class? Do I? Do they understand how the political climate of the sixties informs my current concerns about social injustice? How often do I examine the roots of my current choices and passions? How much light has come from the darkest moments of our experiences?

Do schools allow the darkness of reality to nurture the light of compassion? Thirty students in our care—can we still take the time to allow life to seep through the doors, down the hallway, and into the classroom? Life is messy, sometimes dark. Will we shove that reality aside and learn "appropriate (who decides?) social skills," carefully crafting a nonproblematic, pleasant response to daily events? Is our fear of the darkness related to our decades (centuries?) old pattern of failing to trust teachers to share the world with children, create meaningful, relevant curriculum?

To find the light, the inner light, we must first trust ourselves and each other to be with our students in ways that will move us through life to learning. Dewey (1900) advocated learning through occupations. All right. But shouldn't we also learn through the relational, through the interpersonal, through the troubling circumstances of life? And, perhaps most importantly, shouldn't we allow the darkness of society, the difficulties of life, to challenge us and our students to struggle toward understanding that will enlighten not only individual learners but also our communities and our country?

I am a young teacher in a faculty meeting dominated by male voices that fail to see that their silencing is oppressive. They are entitled. They are full of themselves. I can sit still no longer. I rise, quite surprised at myself. Others are surprised, too, and into the silence that hangs in the air I mention the time and another commitment as I make my way to the door. Hardly a confrontation. But it was, for me, a moment of light. The beginning of a growing commitment to gender equity. I leave the room feeling exhilarated but not really understanding. Light that has been kept dim through years of socialization does not emerge easily (Johnson, 1981). Yet I remember the moment as if it were yesterday. The gentle flame that flickered that day now fuels my commitment to talking openly about gender and sexual orientation to my students.

I teach young women, mostly. Living in a conservative community, many of them remind me of myself as a student before the second wave of feminism. They talk of the convenient match between mothering and teaching, teaching as preparation for mothering, women as natural caregivers. I usually have one or two males in the group. Amazingly, the young women often fail to see the differences between their comments, their demeanor, their sense of appropriate engagement and those of male student(s) who embody a different understanding of gender. The women have good hearts. Yet they embrace oppressive ideals. How deeply can I ask them to dig on a personal level when many of them believe deeply in their views of patriarchy as divinely inspired?

I persist. We dig deeply into gender issues. I am tired from the task. Yet these are often authentic conversations, complicated conversations that can leave us feeling simultaneously troubled and energized. The exhaustion may be an indication that something good is happening. I don't know. But it's quite possible that we are too seldom exhausted when teaching and learning. I'm reminded of working on the campfire when the wood is damp, the sky is dark with clouds, and we are cold and hungry. A cheer pierces the gloom when the sparkling embers flicker into flame. The fire will still need tending, we know, but the wood is ignited and the light will increase as we carefully choose bits of wood to feed to the tinder.

There are more moments of light to attend to—the process is just that, a process. A lifelong journey. My students and I have work to do. But, what's this? I am dogged by a nagging fear shaped by years of techno-educational rhetoric. Schwab (1978) suggested that Dewey's progressive ideas were more than teachers could handle. The inner conflict my fear raises continues. I ruminate and then I become livid when I connect this distrust I still harbor about the history of the supervision and control of women. My own complicity in this process, the dimming of the light in so many of us, is appalling. I must, I see now, encourage my students to teach progressively. In just a few semesters they will be expected to wield instructional strategies that maintain the status quo, that pave the way from the private to the public sphere (Grumet, 1988). We name them keepers of the next generation. Lip-service— if we tie their hands with constraints and make demands that edge them— their very selves—out of the classroom. Tragic. Imagine the journey we and our students could take if we trusted teachers to go beyond what curriculum requires. Imagine this shift accompanied by a reallocation of our collective resources toward teacher development and support—a provocative shift from current massive investments in prepackaged, prescribed curriculum.

Fine (1992) challenges us. "A self-critical analysis of the fundamental ways in which we teach children to betray their own voices is crucial" (p. 138). It begins with our own reflecting. Teacher educators talk about preparing teachers to be reflective practitioners (Labosky, 1991). The idea is to get educators to consider their practice carefully, to reflect on their thinking, planning, and the act of teaching. Perhaps we need to broaden our understanding of reflection—think about a teacher's opportunity to reflect the light of each of her students. First, it must be encouraged, discovered, nurtured in them and in ourselves. The challenge will be to stop "delivering" curriculum. In our best visualizations of authentic classrooms, we can take the risk of going deep and delving into our perceptions. We can truly be reflective practitioners, reflecting the light students graciously share with us. As we break our silences together, we may cast a light that will illuminate and even change the world.

HOLDING FLASHLIGHTS
Delese

I.

"I see the light" is a statement not about objects but about understandings: actions.

—Morris (2002, p. 13)

When I was a child we would make tents out of blankets that we had put over the clothesline in the backyard. While we waited for dark, we would assemble our sleeping bags, transistor radios, books and board games, dragging them out to the airless, hot tent. My mother would make popcorn, which we would put in small brown shopping bags, holding our hunger until later. One of the last things I would locate to take to the tent was a flashlight, a true staple of the backyard sleepover. Even in familiar environs, the light it emitted would guide us back to the unlocked back door to the safety and comfort of being inside. It also provided light to the unknown under our feet as we snuck around the neighborhood peering in windows, giggling nervously. Back in our sleeping bags, the flashlight's beam would shine on the impenetrable wool blankets above our heads, illuminating the darkness in the tent and casting shadows from our small bodies. And each of us, when it was our turn to hold the flashlight, would invariably hold it under our chins for the desired scary effect, or against our hands, the light shining through the translucent skin of our fingers. Whoever held the flashlight determined not merely what we could do, but what we could see. We were in need of light, even with our knowledge of the environment around us.

Yet, once we move past our childish fascination with lights, light becomes something we do not notice until we can't control it. We expect light at the flick of a switch. We are acclimated to lights, according to David Morris, who argues that "postmodernism is light everywhere and on demand":

> All-night diners, twenty-four hour markets, and round-the-clock casinos typify a world where artificial illumination suspends time. Somewhere in every city a television is always on. Skylights add a luxury touch to car and home. Strobes, spots, and color lasers pump up the sexual wattage of rock concerts and bowling alleys. The huge cultural shift that has brought us from oil lamps to night baseball, however, is more than an instance of progress in technology. We have altered our relation to light. . . . Most people in the developed world have generally, quietly, forgotten about light. (2002, p. 10)

In our always lit land-of-plenty, in our Internet-, image-, sitcom-, decibel-driven world of books on tape and Sharper Image white noise that constitutes our waking and slumbering consciousness, we have indeed forgotten about light, about the solitary beam; we have forgotten how to listen for the oboe while the rest of the orchestra plays.

To teach is to hold the flashlight. To teach is to stand in the light of others' flashlights. To teach is to pass the flashlight. To teach is to have more than one flashlight. To teach is to remember the distinction between *lux* and *lumen*, "the source of the radiation and the sheer luminosity created by it" (Arnheim, 1996, p. 78). Being a teacher in an always-lit world is a challenge when trying to help students and ourselves discern particular lights. In medical education, this is exceptionally trying, for medical students are taught early on that they are in control in the doctor-patient interaction: they determine what is important to investigate, how much time is allotted, if and for how long questions are permitted. None of us in the United States really needed a French intellectual to tell us about the medical gaze: we've all been under it; we recognize its feel; we recognize that the doctor always gets to hold the flashlight.

Because I am a teacher of language and literature, I am especially interested in point-of-view, or as I have been using the term here, the flashlight holder. For medical students to become adept at recognizing the power held by those who get to tell the story is for them to become better doctors. Of course, even when patients do get to tell their stories, they are hugely restricted by their own fears of what's wrong with them, their concern for "taking up the doctor's precious time," their doctors' constant interruption and dismissal of their questions and concerns they bring with them, and sadly, their doctors' disinterest, misunderstanding, rejection, or utter ignorance of views not arising from "science" and medicine.

II.

> Although the Hmong do not agree on just how many souls people have . . . there is a general consensus that whatever the number, it is the life-soul, whose presence is necessary for health and happiness, that tends to get lost.
> —Fadiman (1997, p. 10)

The Hmong people have a saying, *hais cuaj txub txub*, which means "to speak of all kinds of things." These few words characterize a highly complex, elaborate world view shared by the Hmong people: Everything in the world is connected, no event occurs in isolation from others, and "you can miss a lot by sticking to the point" (Fadiman, p. 13). These beliefs about how the world operates characterize not only Hmong thinking but also any attempt to render Anne Fadiman's remarkable book, *The Spirit Catches You and You Fall Down: A Hmong Child, Her American Doctors, and the Collision of Two Cultures* (1997), into an orderly commentary. In fact, throughout the book Fadiman narratively enacts the culture she so skillfully and respectfully chronicles: Because the Hmongs themselves cannot be neatly characterized in ways Westerners easily understand, any attempt to describe them in a language not their own cannot be a linear, "rational" exposition. "The long way around," according to the Hmongs, "is often the shortest way from point A to point B" (p. 95). Fadiman beautifully takes the long way around so that upon finishing the book, readers are profoundly affected by the rich history of the Hmong people, yet perplexed by what American medicine can and should do for non-majority groups, many of them immigrants, who do not share—or *care* to share—the majority culture's values and beliefs. Having students read Fadiman's generous, inquisitive, humble, and always respectful back and forth lighting of Western medicine and Hmong culture was my attempt to worry them about all our differences, how differences are ordered and valued depending on who's in charge, and how differences are played out in health-care settings where the stakes can be so high.

The book is a story of clashes—the larger one between Hmong culture and U.S medicine, the more specific one between doctors and a family over the care of a child. Lia Lee was born in 1981 in a U.S. hospital to Foua and Nao Kao Lee, recent Hmong immigrants from Laos. At the age of three months, Lia had her first epileptic seizure, or as Hmongs view this mysterious occurrence, "the spirit catches you and you fall down" (p. 20). Five years later, after countless seizures, seventeen admissions to the county hospital, routine miscommunications and misunderstanding regarding medicines—her anti-convulsant prescriptions changed twenty-three times in four years, with new directions given each time to a mother who did not read or understand English—Lia has "the big one," a two-hour seizure secondary to septic shock (p. 140). Considered brain dead by her doctors, Lia was lovingly viewed by her parents not as dead but as a little girl whose soul had fled her body and become lost.

Throughout the book, Fadiman takes readers on a historical excursion into Hmong culture, which has been marked from the beginning by one "bloody scrimmage" after another, with occasional periods of peace. The Hmong have always responded to "persecution and pressures to assimilate by either fighting or migrating—a pattern that has been repeated so many times, in so many different eras and places, that it begins to seem almost a genetic trait" (p. 13). Indeed, their desire to be left alone, whether in China or Laos or California, is one of their most problematic features—problematic as determined by the majority culture wherever they are. As Fadiman notes, the Hmong have never had a desire to rule over anyone else but merely want "to be left alone, which . . . may be the most difficult request any minority can make of a majority culture" (p. 14).

Alternating with chapters tracing Hmong history are chapters detailing Lia's unfolding medical problems, particularly her doctors' dogged attempts to keep her seizures under control with medications whose regimens her mother only partially understood and accepted, and the Lees' frustrations with American doctors who did not understand what they, her parents, believed was causing their child's seizures and what should be done. In fact, the doctors caring for Lia never asked her parents what they were doing to heal her because it never occurred to them to ask, even though most Hmong people readily accept "a little medicine and a little *neeb*"—a middle ground that uses both medicine and healing spirits (p. 106). Still, Fadiman chronicles these clashes in deeply insightful ways, blaming neither the Lees nor her doctors, always mindful of the complex, competing narratives arising from Lia's illness. To speak of Lia's illness and the medical response to it is, truly, to "speak of all kinds of things" (p. 12).

If nothing else, and even before opening the book, the mysterious title catches your attention, along with the picture of a beautifully adorned child on the cover. Fadiman's profound sensitivity and understanding of both Hmong culture and American medicine present questions, not arguments, that teachers and students should ponder: How do doctors achieve cultural understandings of patients that give illness context and meaning? How should doctors honor their patients' cultural beliefs and practices that may be in opposition to standard medical practice? Where does the soul fit into the practice of American medicine? And in the quintessentially Cartesian world of medical thought and practice, what might be gained from the Hmong practice of *cuaj txub kaum txub*—to speak of all kinds of things—as we contemplate the mysterious connections between the body and spirit? Fadiman writes:

Hmong culture . . . is not Cartesian. Nothing could be more Cartesian than Western medicine. Trying to understand Lia and her family by reading her medical chart (something I spent hundreds of hours doing) was like deconstructing a love sonnet by reducing it to a series of syllogisms. Yet to the residents and pediatricians who had cared for her since she was three months old, there was no guide to Lia's world *except* her chart. As each of them struggled to make sense of a set of problems that were not expressible in the language they knew, the chart simply grew longer and longer, until it contained more than 400,000 words. Every one of those words reflected its author's intelligence, training, and good intentions, but not a single one dealt with the Lees' perception of their daughter's illness. . . . Almost every discussion of cross-cultural medicine that I had ever read quoted a set of eight questions, designed to elicit a patient's "explanatory model," which were developed by Arthur Kleinman. . . . I thought the Lees might have answered his questions [this way] after Lia's earliest seizures, before any medications had been administered, resisted, or blamed, if they had had a good interpreter and had felt sufficiently at ease to tell the truth. To wit:

1. *What do you call the problem?*
   Qaug dab peg. That means the spirit catches you and you fall down.

2. *What do you think has caused the problem?*
   Soul loss.

3. *Why do you think it started when it did?*
   Lia's sister Yer slammed the door and Lia's soul was frightened out of her body.

4. *What do you think the sickness does? How does it work?*
   It makes Lia shake and fall down. It works because a spirit called a *dab* is catching her.

5. *How severe is the sickness? Will it have a short or long course?*
   Why are you asking us those questions? If you are a good doctor, you should know the answers yourself.

6. *What kind of treatment do you think the patient should receive? What are the most important results you hope she receives from this treatment?*
You should give Lia medicine to take for a week but no longer. After she is well, she should stop taking the medicine. You should not treat her by taking her blood or the fluid from her backbone. Lia should also be treated at home with our Hmong medicines and by sacrificing pigs and chickens. We hope Lia will be healthy, but we are not sure we want her to stop shaking forever because it makes her noble in our culture, and when she grows up she might become a shaman.

7. *What are the chief problems the sickness has caused?*
It has made us sad to see Lia hurt, and it has made us angry at Yer.

8. *What do you fear most about the sickness?*
That Lia's soul will never return. (pp. 259–60)

III.

If we are blinded by darkness, we are also blinded by light.
—Dillard (1974, p. 23)

What Fadiman has done is to shed light on the complexities of competing world views wherever they arise, and she did so putting down her pencil, unplugging her laptop, finding the most respectful entry into Hmong culture in Merced, California, and inviting the Lees and the rest of the Hmong community to illuminate the world they inhabited, the same world inhabited by U.S. doctors whose understandings of *lux* and *lumen* take into account, when all is said and done, only the light of scientific-based Western medicine, which seems at times to overpower all other sources of light. The doctors' understandings of Lia, evidenced by the thousands of pages of her medical record, were truncated, biased, and confused by their "more is better" attitude, in much the same way we think of light.

"What is the effect of covering the night sky with a smoglike haze of light?" asks David Morris (2002, p. 22). To light everything always is to eliminate darkness, shadows, and the nuanced light of dawn and dusk. We cannot see the flashlight's beam in environments of ubiquitous light. "After light," Arnheim suggests,

the eye rejoices in shadow, the mind gives it meaning. . . . Religion and literary convention make much of the light that dispels darkness, but that is not really what it does, for the power of light is finite. It only pushes darkness further away. (1996, p. 336)

As teachers, we can work against blindness caused by too much light.

THE DARK OF LIGHT

Mary

None of us stands outside humanity's black collective shadow.
—C. G. Jung

It is telling that the word "enlightenment" means such different things in the West from in the East, and in that difference such a story lies. Western Enlightenment of the seventeenth and eighteenth centuries brought the "light" of reason, logic, and scientific experimentation as a celebration of the mind's capacity to sort things out. To be enlightened in the West meant to become more knowledgeable about the outer world, its laws and histories. Eastern enlightenment seeks to rid the mind of rational busyness. To achieve Eastern enlightenment, one must alter or redefine the usual, logical frames of reference. One enters a mental impasse, a muddied darkness we could say, out of which one might become "enlightened"—aware of something greater than what the mind can comprehend. Interesting that the Romantic revolution of the nineteenth century, which made dark forays into imagination and the occult, saw, with an Eastern sense, that mystery's shadows contain numinous light.

Light with its shadows makes me think of my mother.

It is my earliest memory. I am four. I remember only this one incident of her life with me before she left the house. My mother is putting me to bed, something evidently she did not do often. She stands at the door, then she closes the door but does not turn out the light. I feel abandoned, utterly. Why did my mother not turn out the light? I am left in too much lightness. I intuit in a flash that I am not in my mother's universe. By her not turning out the light, I am my mother's darkness. Years later I think, rather, that my mother then and for decades after saw me only in lightness. I set now the task to seek the darkness that lay between us and to find there some knowledge of ourselves.

A year before my mother died she told me she was dying. "I don't believe in your Madonna or Christ," she told me. "When I die I believe I will go through the green light in that crystal." She pointed to a crystal hanging in a window opposite her bed. Her belief in the absolute purity of insubstantiality dazzled me. And her calm acceptance of her dying was sheerly poetic. Indeed, I think my mother, without studying it, had a Buddhist notion of enlightenment, seeing no distinction between herself as a subject and the green crystal as an object. At her dying time she was awakening, I think, to her wisdom mind.

Now, as I write this piece, it is the Season of Light, December. We light the Hanukkah candles and sit with the flames until they go out. Their frail light gives dimension to the darkness of the room. I see the darkness. In winter afternoons, the light is pale, thin. I see the outline of trees. The sky is closer, drawing my eyes to nearer things like the dead leaves on my summer plants. Dark is not the absence of light, but that which makes the things I might otherwise overlook come alive to my senses.

There is, too, a Christian light throughout our town: windows have candles in them, trees have lights, churches have candlelight services, carols are sung outdoors by holding a light. In Santa Fe, little bonfires, called luminarios, are lit on Christmas Eve; in the bayou country of Louisiana, large bonfires are built and lit with kerosene: all these to warm the Christ child's coming. The interplay of cold and hot, dark and light make of the winter months a veritable complex of opposites.

But with a mind groomed on Enlightenment polarities, light in post-9/11 represents all that is Good while dark is Evil, like the "Satan" we pursue in Afghan caves, Saddam stockpiles, or the Axis newly named countries. Since when has the world been bifurcated into Good and Evil? Why this predilection to equate evil with darkness? Are we blinded by living in an always-lit world illuminated by a mere flashlight point of view? What does it do to the other mind, the wisdom mind, to put onto those who do us harm all notions of Evil, shrouding ourselves in the cloak of Goodness? I say this in the time, in Advent (when waiting is what we do), to talk about "the dark and light of the imagination," as Maxine Greene puts it. She goes on to say, "the Romantic imagination starting in the nineteenth century, sort of had to do with Freedom From the taken for granted or constraints, and not Freedom For. I think that's another thing we have to infuse somehow in the curriculum that gets rid of these damn discrete particles" (2001, p. 2). And what is surely damnable is the impulse to place blame, articulate either/ors, castigate the Other—without examining our own darknesses.

Western Enlightenment thinking has returned in the second millennium. Is this Yeats's rough beast slouching toward Bethlehem (1959, p. 185)? "The darkness drops again; but now I know / That twenty centuries of stony sleep / Were vexed to nightmare by a rocking cradle." These lines haunt. We are too full of "passionate intensity" (p. 185). The angels that crowd The Christmas Shop are puny white, lacy things. Santa is jolly and round. American goodness reeks of angelic purity and plump righteousness. In this season of light there is too much light, like my neighbor's white, girly angel blinking atop the tree.

Where is enlightenment vision in all this? Such a vision might be less clearly defined (Good vs. Evil). It might be, indeed, fearful, fascinating, troubling. Angels, Rilke tells us, are terrifying. David Miller blames Christianity for lightening angels by whitening them iconically. "They are dark. Ask Jacob. . . . They are to be wrestled" (in Sardello, 1995, p. 125). If the angel of the Lord were to come down now, I am thinking he would dazzle us by his fury. In this new war against the most hated Other, we are blinded by our intensity to rout out the evildoers. "One would do well to possess some 'imagination of evil,' for only the fool can permanently neglect the conditions of his own nature. In fact, this negligence is the best means of making him an instrument of evil" (Jung, 1958, pp. 96–97).

What might an "imagination of evil" consist of? I think we have to do no more than go into a deep sleep and open ourselves up to the world of our dreams. If we are at all honest about these night forays, we would have to admit to seeing, bubbling up from our own sources, some pretty unpleasant images. These might be lewd, poisonous, bizarre. We quickly might want to forget we dreamed these images, for to see us behave during the light of day, we are all pleasantness. But, once again, head on pillow, we return to the recesses of conscious thought where the unconscious resides. Incest, sorocide, fratricide, suicide, homicide—all the "cides" of myth—are there as well, within. An imagination of evil at the very least acknowledges inner darkness, and rather than projecting what shames us onto the Other, sees the compensatory function of dream. Dreams remind us that human nature is complex, not simple; a composite of opposite tendencies both good and evil, light and dark. Dreams re-mind us, put us in the other mind. And if we can teach ourselves to see these dark images, maybe we could temper our oh-so-clear ideas about what constitutes evil. If that fans the flames of confusion so much the better. We should admit to our con-fusions.

I think the ability to see dark images is what Michael Eigen refers to as seeing "creative horror" (2001, p. 93). He speaks of Oedipus, but he could as well be speaking of our own era of horror. He writes, "Tragedy rubs our noses in what we would wish out of existence. We see ourselves in the mirror of events and gasp" (p. 93). There but for the grace of God go we.

Seeing darkly requires more than literal seeing. After all, we can physically see only 5 percent of the "real" world: that segment of the spectrum located between red and violet. This means that 95 percent of all other existing light is invisible to our literal vision (Vogel, 1974). We need, then, to rely on sources other than that which is available to us through our senses. For Eigen, this source is God, since "there is no place outside God" (p. 95). What this means is we cannot go around saying Good is Us and Evil is Them, because Good is God and Evil is God, too. The two go together. God is everywhere, and Eigen lists the places lest we are afraid to stretch the thought: "the Holocaust, racial cleansing of every sort, mass starvation and oppression in Africa, terrorist bombings" (p. 95). This is a difficult concept to grasp. All we can do, perhaps, is gasp at such awful possibilities. But we need to remember that this dark incantation of horror is paradoxically creative, in the sense that the "staying with ghastly things," as Eigen puts it (p. 96), turns and creates a light born of pain. We need the light not of Enlightenment reason, where opposites separate, always, but of enlightenment's vision, where ecstasy makes a fire of stasis, and con-fusion reigns.

EIGHT

Motherhood

INTRODUCTION

Delese

MOTHERING FROM THE MIDDLE, as Martha calls it, has to do with being here and there, or not here and not there; feeling pulls from both ends; operating on both/and, either/or, a little bit of this, a little bit of that. She speaks of how her "mothering has shifted and changed through [her] ages—dramatically" as she moved from the predictability (and then, desirability) of traditional, modern mother to a way of being a mother that sometimes seems detached from her "motherness." Her piece is really about the malleability of life, moving along not in a predictable, preplotted, MapQuested sort of way, but with a tentativeness, a make-it-up-as-we-go-along way, relying on what we know and what we don't know, making up new rules, breaking old ones, then breaking the new ones, perhaps. Like Martha, I recognize this as both mother of young adult children and as daughter of a mother approaching eighty. I have the view from somewhere—*here*, based on memories, some astonishingly beautiful, some painful; the persons my children, my mother, and I have all become and are becoming; my now hybridized beliefs about the "good" mother and the "good" daughter, the impossibility of these labels yet the ongoing desire to still live up to them in some unknown way. In Martha's assessment—one I lean toward very much at this moment—perhaps "all we can give our children is our embodied experience, our struggling attempt to shape a journey in the midst of conflicting and mixed messages."

In "What's the Matter with Mom?" Mary writes about the various pathologies associated with mothers and the pat cultural response to humans' maladjustments such as paranoia, hysteria, even schizohrenia: It's their mother's fault. That doesn't even begin to account for the evil and deformity evoked by fairy tales: mothers eat their young, and "witches and jealous queens do terrible things." Citing mothers found in Emily Dickinson, Virginia Woolf, Charlote Perkins Gilman, Doris Lessing, Jamaica Kincaid, and Margaret Atwood, Mary shows us how "mothers can't win; they are trapped on the rung of the rank," victims all of "patriarchical power" that "paternalized to death their inner selves." Their choices, she suggests, are limited: to be "traditional" or to develop "subversive" ways around the problem. Mary learned from her own mother that subversiveness is not always consistent with traditional mothering and came to understand how little she cared about her mother's mothering and how much she cared about her mother's legacy.

Interesting, this talk of legacy. Legacies imply things handed down—traits, values, ways of living in the world. Mary sees her mother not only in her face and body but also in the tilt of her tea cup. In my piece, I wander into the broken legacies my daughter must face not knowing her birth parents. Over a quarter century ago and still today, I wonder about this other mother who for reasons we will never know decided she could not, would not raise her newborn daughter. Not like the open-book transactions of today's adoptions within the United States where adoptive parents know everything from educational level of grandparents to propensities for nearsightedness to athletic prowess of birth parents, we were given no information except the stamped "Koren" beside both "mother" and "father." Without stories, she must surely have invented them, as I have, of her birth mother and the circumstances that brought her to us, the life she might have led, and yes, that other mother's hair and eyes and tilt of her tea cup. And while transnational adoption "advertises itself as both humanitarian relief and the fulfillment of parental desire" (O'Brien, 2001), there are too many untold stories of how, and why, reproductive labor among women is enacted disproportionately by race, class, and location in the world in "transnational circuits of exchange" (Castananda, 2001, p. 296).

As Mary writes, "Mothers matter," in all their varieties, circumstances, and locations.

MOTHERING FROM THE MIDDLE

Martha

"It's a great movie. You'll love it!" My twenty-three-year-old daughter has picked up a video tape for us to watch. My eighty-five-year-old mother is visiting from out of town. My seventeen-year-old son decides to watch it with us. My spouse sits in, but after the film is over he is savvy enough to sense an impending deep and intense review session and evaporates before the final credits have begun to roll.

The movie begins simply enough. The plot is straightforward. Beauty pageant run by rigid and controlling mother and her strange son becomes the setting for a bizarre series of murders. And, of course, the evil mother gets it in the end. The fast-paced insanity takes aim at the superficial and lays bare the hollow existence of the characters. No traditions remain sacred. No fan of beauty pageants, this should be cathartic for me. But no holds are barred in the deprecation of friendship, family, and, ironically—Minnesota Lutherans. At least we're not from Minnesota. The language and the biting humor have their way with us and we each have a generationally appropriate response (with the exception of my spouse—did I mention that he slipped out the back way?).

My children are entertained. They are laughing uproariously. The system, the culture, the whole world is bankrupt and they are loving every minute of it. With my mother present I am acutely aware of every detail that could be offensive in much the same way as when we view a questionably bawdy movie with children. I personally find the movie too over-the-edge to be funny. *Okay*, I'm thinking. *The world's a superficial mess. But do we have to see the multiple dimensions of moral collapse in full and loving detail and call it entertainment?* I glance at my mother. She's a trooper. She's watching and frowning some, although I think she's too interested to waste time being offended. What a woman. But she's not liking this.

Afterward, the conversation begins. First, the youngest generation. They've noticed our reserved response. "Didn't you think it was hilarious? We think it's a riot. So do our friends." They admit there's quite a bit of "language" and the content is intentionally offensive. But that's part of the humor, they insist. "That's why it's so dang funny! You can't fix the world. Laughing at it is the only answer."

Then Grandma weighs in. "I think it's terrible. Why would you want to watch something like that? The people are all just self-interested and messed up. It's like those talk shows on TV where everyone tells about their horrible problems. I don't want to see people behave like that. It makes everyone feel like the world's beyond hope."

Finally I chime in. I'm caught in the middle somewhere. "Sure the world's riddled with disaster and superficial responses. Systems and institutions are corrupt and people are driven by the bottom line. I know that. But I don't want to watch that writ large and call it entertainment. These are serious issues. The movie just trivializes them. I don't find an exposé of cultural reality funny. Put it in a drama or a documentary."

My offspring listen and try to understand and we do the same. The conversation that ensues allows us a window into each other's perspectives and continues for a long time. Somewhere in the midst of the words I begin to hear a subtext that is with me still. My mother grew up fully entrenched in a modernist perspective. Entertainment for her was all about making the country look good. Especially during the war years. Her nineteen-year-old brother was killed in World War II. She still cherishes movies like *White Christmas* and *It's a Wonderful Life*. In these dramas, the world has its problems but, in the end, the good shines through. Modern to the core.

I'm a child of the sixties. We mainstream kids naively thought our generation was the first to discover blatant hypocrisy, systemic bigotry, and rampant greed. We felt quite brilliant. (We were, of course, echoing the progressive impulses of liberal reformers and muckrakers from preceding generations— Jane Addams, W. E. B. DuBois, Sinclair Lewis—but in a new era, struggling anew with this tension between hope and despair). Others were enlivened by the civil rights movement and "discovered" social activism. We knew the system was abusive and that the power brokers cared little for the powerless or the earth. But we believed we could escape or protest loudly enough to make a difference. We listened to the Rolling Stones and Bob Dylan and we watched *Easy Rider*, wondering how certain our hope really was. We clung to the belief that we had options.

My children grew up in the information age. I'm not sure when they came to understand that governments, institutions, even the local police might not have their best interests at heart. But now I would guess they lost their innocence at a much younger age than I previously had imagined. Media messages were spewed into their lives with alarming force and, although I tried to control their early exposures to the world, there's no measuring how quickly the perceptive minds of children grasp the tenor of conversations. Highlights of the day's news and everyday conversational banter and humor brought them a steady social analysis of the postmodern world. Their grade school lives were punctuated by critical theory àla Doonesbury and Dilbert.

So there we were, each of us a product of our generation. And I began to wonder. How does a mom from the sixties mother in a postmodern age? If our view of the world is so socially constructed, so must our mothering be (Chodorow, 1978). Our mothering has shifted and changed through the ages (Ehrenreich & English, 1978). My mothering has shifted and changed through my ages—dramatically. And now I find myself stranded in the middle—no longer captivated by modernist visions of patriotism (or even Marxism), yet not fully ensconced in the postmodern era.

The world has been shifting into this postmodern milieu for some time. Seinfeld-land. But the political rhetoric of modernism has intensified in the news media. We face a fragmented, illusive, new challenge to a world view still certain of its rightful dominance. And tragically, as the war of words and worse escalates, the social construction of culture is trumping our initial and appropriate speechlessness. All around us people are sounding their voices. Strangely collective voices. Finding words—troublingly unified words. Good vs. Evil. Us vs. Them. You are with us or against us. Binaries abound—a veritable goldmine for deconstructive activity (Derrida & McDonald, 1982). And I find myself thinking of the dilemma of the postmodern mother.

I feel caught in a gulf immortalized by the continual heated arguments between social revolutionaries and postmodern theorists. I've rejected Harriet Nelson and June Cleaver. I've tried to choose my own path for mothering. But it seems my choices lead me to a fragmented and frenetic—postmodern?—model of Mother. If I am, then, postmodern Mother, or at least, some iteration of her, does this mean that all cohesion has left the room? Left my life? Once I was haunted by traditional, modern Mother. Now I feel a new specter creeping—a personal dilemma of sorts. And a quintessential postmodern dilemma at that. . . . Choosing my own path, owning my desires, I find myself caught in a neverending race of busyness that leaves me precious little time to live out my motherness. As I rush out the door I am tempted to run back in the back way. Revisit a simpler, slower time. Refuse the ruse.

Perhaps an analysis of postmodern Mother—who still bears the traces of a false, modern construction of liberation—the I-can-do-it-all model—can inform my thinking about this world in which I live and the future I strain to envision. She is on the move. She skates across the surface of life, lacking a predictable pattern of experience. She gazed wide-eyed with the rest of the world at recent political events, the shockwave now dubbed "9/11." But does her casting first as one Mother and then Another give her any insight into the spread of cruelty across the globe? What will she tell her children? What will I tell mine? Does my story, so seldom spoken, provide a view from the margins that sheds even a small ray of light on the state of the world? Will I be able to convey any wisdom born from my daily rounds that will help bridge the gap between everyday maternal circumstances and rampant and troubling world ideologies? Or is my sometimes surreal, fast-paced existence erasing me in a postmodern version of the invisible mothers of fairy tales?

Richardson (1990) addresses the strange limbo of being caught between two perspectives. She confronts the puzzle of how researchers can exercise their authorial voices without doing violence with their words. She suggests a "progressive-postmodernist" rewriting of the research endeavor. Perhaps she can help me mother from the middle. "The progressive impulse is to give voice to those who have been silenced, to speak for others" (p. 27). There it is. The siren song of my youth. "The postmodern impulse has been to deconstruct the difference between sign and signified" (p. 27). Ah yes, my Other voice, my new understanding, nurtured in the academy. Who am I to speak for others, especially given my whiteness and my secure economic status? If mothering is about sharing our impulses with our children, passing on passion, my dilemma persists.

But Richardson goes on. "A progressive-postmodernist rewriting, however, proposes that because all knowledge is partial and situated, it does not mean that there is no knowledge or that situated knowledge is bad" (p. 27).

She draws on Haraway's work (1988). "There is no view from 'nowhere.' . . . There is no view from 'everywhere' except for God. There is only a view from 'somewhere,' an embodied, historically and culturally situated speaker" (p. 584).

I've wrestled with this tension. In my research. In my writing. In my life. Have the skirmishes prepared me in any small way to mother meaningfully? What can my "embodied, historically and culturally situated" view be? And how does it shape my relationship with my children? The word "embodied" lingers in my mind. Perhaps—and I speak tentatively if not "under erasure"— all that we can give our children is our embodied experience, our struggling attempt to shape a journey in the midst of conflicting and mixed messages. Perhaps this is especially true when we straddle dual (multiple?) perspectives. It is the embrace of tension in our lives, the determination to think from whichever standpoint makes sense in a situated context, that may bring the most meaning.

My mother gave herself to me—and still does. Now, in my middle years, I see her gift with new eyes. I can only hope that my children will continue to receive what I can offer with their changing eyes as they journey through experiences not unlike mine and my mother's yet shaped by a world beyond our earlier imaginings.

Mothering from the middle may maintain the simultaneity of fast-paced fragmentation and progressive commitment to social justice priorities; it may stop me in my tracks, call me to focused action. No recipes here. Knowing my knowledge is partial makes me cautious. Believing in the importance of response-ability and the beauty that persists within the broken human condition makes me hopeful. And so I remain—cautiously hopeful. Perhaps the right response from Mother in the Middle.

MOTHERHOOD, DESIRE, AND TRANSNATIONAL ADOPTION

Delese

> I could not have anticipated that this family formed across the continents would seem so clearly the family that was meant to be, that these children thrown together and with me and with each other, with no blood ties linking us together or to a common history, would seem so clearly the children meant for me.
>
> —Elizabeth Bartholet (2001, p. 192)

It is a bit like the old adage about giving birth: it's the most quickly forgotten pain. Except with adoption, you feel no pain, only amazement and joy and overwhelming gratitude. I wish I could retrieve these more visceral aspects of the moment my daughter was handed to me at the airport twenty-seven years ago, but now I rely on slides when the urge appears. The first image: a clock on the wall, documenting the time her plane landed. The second image: the airplane. The third: an off-duty flight attendant—her escort from Korea— handing a bundle to my husband, who had bullied himself to the front of the line. The fourth, fifth, and the rest of the images: my husband and I staring at and nuzzling and kissing this beautiful six-month-old baby girl, dropped from the sky into our arms.

Twenty-six years old and just given a verdict of irreversible infertility, my husband and I immediately knew that adoption was the route to complete our family, which then consisted of the two of us and our two-year-old son. At that point, we wanted a healthy baby of any color, but except for a brief blip in the 1960s when transracial adoption was acceptable, black babies were being placed only in black homes, white babies only in white homes. (Even today, many child-welfare professionals continue to insist on placing children with same-race parents [Bartholet, 1999, p. xii].) The year was 1975, and the shortage of healthy white infants had arrived with a fury, a shortage created by the legalization of abortion, by the reduction of social stigmas surrounding single motherhood, and by the availability of more effective birth control methods (Bartholet, 1999; Ragone, 2000). Between 1972 and 1973, there was a 33 percent increase in the number of children adopted in the United States from foreign countries, precisely the moment "that American women won the right to decide whether or not to carry a particular pregnancy to term" (Solinger, 2001, p. 22), thereby ending pregnancies that might have produced adoptable babies. Impatient, we, along with thousands of other U.S. citizens, began to search internationally for a baby because if the United States could- n't find one for us, certainly some other country could. Leading us to a loca- tion outside the United States was also the fact that Korean adoptions were very common, affordable, and easily conducted.

Before World War II, international adoption was almost unheard of in the United States. In fact, between 1935 and 1948 fewer than fourteen chil- dren per year immigrated to the United States (Babb, 1999, p. 47). In 1948 Congress enacted the Displaced Persons Act, which allowed three thousand sponsored children left parentless by the war to enter the United States. Holt Adoption Agency, which linked us to our daughter, was formed by Harry and Bertha Holt in 1957, and eventually became this nation's oldest and largest international adoption agency. In recent years, an average of ten thousand children born in other countries have been adopted by Americans every year (Bartholet, 1999; Babb, 1999). In the 1990s, with the opening of Eastern Europe and China, more Russian and Chinese orphans were adopted than children from all other countries combined, and in 1999, sixteen thousand immigrant visas were issued to "orphans" coming to the United States from all over the world (U.S. Department of State, 2002). "Orphans," I might add, is a legal term denoting a child who has been abandoned or legally relinquished (Gailey, 1998), and speaking from personal experience, it is a term that helps adoptive parents forget that their child's birth parent(s) may still be alive.

I could write pages about the questions one is asked when one or two tall, blue-eyed adults have in tow a blond-haired, blue-eyed boy child and a black-haired, brown-eyed Asian baby girl. In our experience, almost all such questions were inappropriate and annoying. Most questioners treated our daughter as if she were an inanimate object, unaware of their looks, their questions, their dismissal of her less exotic brother who clearly could see that he didn't warrant much attention. Such scenarios play out the master narrative that kinship is strongest where there are genetic connections between parent and child. That is, the family unit is rooted in nature, which includes the myth that "genetic connection makes attachment expected or even automatic" (Gailey, 2000, p. 23). Thus, when a child so obviously not the genetic offspring of two parents appears, cultural expectations for that child's adoptive family kick into gear: adoptive parents are rather heroic people who are "saving" children— orphans, that is—from tragic circumstances in the "Third World" or "developing" nations. Several scenarios can be selected here to make tidy sense of the orphan's birth mother: she died in the warfare of that country (often involving the United States directly or indirectly), or, similar to domestic "unwed mothers," she was irresponsible in giving birth to a child she couldn't afford to feed, clothe, or shelter *or* a child she didn't want, but was responsible enough to give the child to people who were able to do so. Some particularly ignorant people—total strangers—ask if we know anything about her "real" parents.

The profile of the adopting parents is, of course, the polar opposite of the birth mother. Currently in the United States, transnational adoptive parents are relatively wealthy, nonacademic, heterosexual, white professionals. In one study, the annual incomes of these adopters ranged from $65,000 per year to close to $1,000,000 per year. Without the latter figure, the average annual salary of the group was $120,000 (Gailey, 2000). Similar to other expensive, nonreimbursed reproductive technologies (for surely adoption is assisted reproduction), transnational adoption is generally not available to the poor; the average cost of adopting a child from a country outside the United States is around $42,000 (Gailey, 2000). Without a close look at the class- and race-based issues embedded in the practice, transnational adoption "advertises itself as both humanitarian relief and the fulfillment of parental desire" (O'Brien, 2001).

Anna is two years old. We are visiting my mother in the hospital, where she's recuperating from surgery. Anna is restless and wanders around the room and finally out the door and into the corridor. I get up to follow her and find her stopped dead in her tracks watching a resident who is outside mom's room reading her chart. Anna tracks her every move, and as the resident, who is female and Asian, walks into mom's room, Anna quickly follows with her pudgy arm extended toward the resident saying quietly, "Anna . . . Anna." I realize that Anna has never seen an Asian face up close, and recognizes the resident's face as similar to the one that stares back at her in the mirror. In her fair-skinned, fair-haired, fair-eyed family, this is perplexing to her and perhaps exciting. I feel sad and some hard-to-describe shame. I realize then that as my baby grows up she will never experience the taken-for-granted family banter I remember and still enjoy when we speak of our astonishingly similar Wear legs or our Wear thin skin or Wear this or that, all tied to our DNA.

The National Association of Black Social Workers (NABSW) has the following to say about transracial adoption as it pertains to adoption within the United States:

> Black children should be placed only with Black families whether in foster care or for adoption. Black children belong, physically, psychologically and culturally in Black families in order that they receive the total sense of themselves and develop a sound projection of their future. Human beings are products of their environment and develop their sense of values, attitudes, and self concept within their family structures. Black children in white homes are cut off from the healthy development of themselves as Black people. (Castaneda, 2001, pp. 281–82)

Opponents of transracial adoption—and by association, I would assume, much transnational adoption—imagine both race and culture as inhering in the child, "invoking children as a natural—that is, racial—resource that must be protected" (Castaneda, p. 282).

What were we thinking about race when we decided to adopt a baby from Korea? I have trouble accessing those thoughts now, but not the ones about wanting, simply, a baby. Like most young women, it never occurred to me that the very elemental biological process of reproduction might not work; in fact, I spent a great many years trying *not* to get pregnant and many agonizing spells waiting for a sign that I was not. When told that I could not give birth myself, I went after alternatives with a vengeance, and as I think about it now, a particular U.S.-type vengeance informed at once by my own temperament and class privilege. If I can't find a baby to complete my family here, I'll go anywhere in the world to do so. My focus was exclusively on a baby and her availability, not the conditions in which she would became available. That is, the woman who gave birth to her did not receive much of my attention or sympathy, other than the usual concerns about her health.

As I write these words twenty-seven years later I am, of course, ashamed, but I also recognize now what I did not realize then: after being denied her biological reproductive choices, the zeal of a woman desiring a baby cannot be matched. No, there is an edit needed here: the zeal of an economically privileged, well-educated, politically savvy woman desiring a baby cannot be matched. The actual needs of my yet-to-be-found baby girl or any other form of humanitarian impulse associated with "rescuing" were not part of my consideration any more than they were when I was trying to get pregnant on my own. For me, reproduction or assisted reproduction was about my desire, and my husband's desire, to create a family.

Of course, once our daughter arrived we were a transracial family, but I also recognize, uneasily, that we must have known we were choosing a daughter who was "ambiguously or acceptably tan" (Gailey, 2000, p. 23). In fact, according to one investigator of transnational adoptive families, "race [is] a submerged motive for most couples. . . . One woman said international adoption was a way of 'making sure you get a blue-ribbon baby'" (Gailey, 2000, p. 44). In addition, these couples

> seemed to assume that the poor in another country were healthier or more morally upright than the poor of their own country. If they talked about their children's birth mothers—and some simply talked about their children as orphans—the picture was presented of an unmarried woman with few options. . . . While this is doubtless true . . . some of these children's birth mothers were married women. (Gailey, p. 51)

The proposition that maybe the children would be better off if the money being paid for the child were merely given to the birth parent(s) if they were in the picture is never seriously considered

Anna is in junior high. She does exceptionally well academically, but like many girls her age, she desires to be pretty and popular and blend in. She is in an awkward state between childhood and womanhood, and the plump, pig-tailed, childish charm that used to make people smile and stare has receded, replaced by braces and a more a serious demeanor. The only Asian in a junior high of three hundred students, she has decided that she wants to be a cheerleader. I keep my mouth closed; she knows exactly where I stand, having withstood my gendered ruminations for years. She perms her long, shiny, beautiful black hair; I offer no opinion because I don't know what to say because the effect is unattractive. During that same period she becomes unusually quiet when faced with taking her family's health history for a science project. If adolescence is all about identity, what must she be going through?

Unlike the NABSW's conceptualization that ties the child to her community because of their shared race, the transnational adoptee's racial makeup does not have the same linkage to any given community. With her particular racial makeup, this child is completely mobile, allowing her to move from one racial community to another. Moreover, when a white family adopts a black child, it imports a child that is racially other, because the child carries with it a given racial makeup. But this makeup quite specifically and insistently has no cultural content. Racial difference here cannot and in fact must not be associated with cultural difference. And while the child may have a racial identity, that identity is entirely individualized . . . the child is constituted in terms of a racial difference that is utterly surface, a racial makeup, a color, to which cultural difference or community belonging is necessarily attached. (Castenada, p. 283)

Today Anna is an intelligent, sensitive, passionate, and beautiful twenty-seven-year-old physician. How do I explain the kismet that brought her to us to love and raise? As she has grown into this extraordinary person, I find myself increasingly drawn to her birth mother. Who was, or possibly *is*, she? Of course, we—her mother, father, and brother—have had some influence on the person Anna has become. I see some of my traits and sensibilities in Anna; many make me smile and some make me wince. But what of that other person, the other mother whose name was stamped "Unknown" on her adoption papers? What circumstances led to the stamp "Abandoned" on those same papers?

Solinger argues that whatever the conditions that lead babies and children into circumstances that make them "adoptable," the potential adopter comes to view the child as a separate entity from her birth mother, "even when a mother is involved with her baby and nearby, even if there is no hard evidence that the baby is, indeed, an orphan" (2001, p. 26). Such reports have emerged from more than one location: In 1975, a spokesperson for the U.S. Immigration and Naturalization Service reported that they had "no persuasive evidence" that the children brought to the United States during Operation Baby Rescue from Cambodia and Vietnam were in fact "orphans or . . . abandoned by their parents"; in 1991 another INS spokesperson said that if Romanian adoptions were investigated "probably 30 percent of all approved foreign adoptions would be questionable" (Solinger, 2001, p. 26).

Castaneda (2001) argues that reproductive labor among women is enacted disproportionately by race, class, and location in the world in "transnational circuits of exchange," and that women from the so-called sending nation are viewed as the "cause of overpopulation, unable to care for the children they produce . . . [and are] sources for a steady supply of children" (p. 296). Once here, the transnational adopted child becomes a mutable body, a site of family making, and in most media constructions, a site of racial and global harmony as well. What is not seen in those constructions are the reports of baby selling or of baby brokers who prey on young and poor women. Solinger (1998) maintains that

the public discussion of the burgeoning domestic black market and the market in foreign babies . . . almost never referred to the fact that the babies "for sale" already had mothers. Instead, it focused on the desperation and hope of the mostly white, middle-class couples seeking a baby: their risks, their disappointments, their joy when they finally succeeded in acquiring a child. The relinquishing mother, foreign or domestic, was every bit as invisible as the white, middle-class birth mother had been in the 1950s and 1960s when it was she who provided the babies for adoption. Probably most Americans do not realize how profoundly the motherhood "choices" of middle-class women—to get abortions, or to become single mothers (both of which choices diminished the pool of babies who might have been available to others), or to become adoptive mothers—indirectly created or directly depended on the definition of other women as having weak, or coercively transferable, motherhood rights. Nor was it always clear how much motherhood "choices" had to do with money, for both the women who had it and the women who did not. (p. 389)

Some critics would even tie transnational adoption in the United States as a "capitalist strategy" for building and maintaining the white, middle-class family through socialization of the international child into American hegemony (O'Brien, 2001). Such a discourse, O'Brien continues, conceals the inaccessibility of contraception, abortion, medical care, and other economic realities that force women in developing nations to either abandon or legally relinquish their children.

But this is not the only way to read transnational adoption. Transnational adoption does not create, according to Elizabeth Bartholet (2001), "the socioeconomic conditions that result in some people and some groups and some countries producing children for whom they are unable to care. It is a symptom" (p. 191). Ongoing efforts, including our efforts as privileged academics who write, are required to reverse conditions such as poverty, lack of adequate food, inadequate or nonexistent medical attention, and poor housing, not to mention access to birth control and other reproductive choices. And as Bartholet points out, adoption of children from countries where these conditions persist is not inconsistent with these efforts.

Moreover, Bartholet reads transnational adoption with a deeper symbolic meaning and potential. Is she waxing so eloquent to ward off those who raise difficult questions requiring closer examination of our actions? I don't know. Here is what she says:

International adoption can also be understood as a particularly positive form of adoption, with prospective parents reaching out to children in need rather than fighting over the limited number of healthy white infants available for adoption in this country. The fact that these families are built across lines of racial and cultural difference can be understood as a good thing, both for the parents and children involved and for the larger community. These are families whose members must learn to appreciate one another's differences while experiencing their common humanity. The evidence indicates that they succeed in doing so. (1999, pp. 142–43)

Motherhood can now be "achieved" not only through the traditional biological method or through adoption, but also through the various reproductive technologies involving in vitro fertilization, egg donation, or surrogacy. One woman's eggs are harvested, fertilized, and implanted in a second woman's uterus, both of them under contract by a third woman who will become the resulting child's "mother" . . . but who are those other women? What is their relationship to that child? These are strange questions.

My relationship to Anna is simpler. A plaque hangs in our kitchen, one found in many adoptive homes. It is sentimental and syrupy, yes, but it is so true, these feelings I have for my daughter who taught me that motherhood has nothing to do with giving birth:

> Not flesh of my flesh,
> Nor bone of my bone,
> But still miraculously my own.
> Never forget for a single minute,
> You didn't grow under my heart,
> But in it.

WHAT'S THE MATTER WITH MOM?

Mary

In Western psychology until only recently, mothers have been held largely and solely responsible for the raising, gender training, and social adjustment of their children. Melanie Klein's (1975) good breast/bad breast theory, W. R. D. Fairbairn's (1954) theory of the nonvalidating mother, Nancy Chodorow's (1978) social construction of mothering, Jacques Lacan's (1981) tragic look from the mother, André Green's (2001) "dead mother syndrome," Donald Winnicot's (1987) "good-enough mother": all place mothers center stage in the dramatic unfolding of their offspring's character and development. This prominence is often steeped in blame. A mother's responsibility is charged when children go astray. It is the mother who must be held accountable for any number of syndromes her children develop. We can point to the real protagonist in the drama of our maladjustments when we develop paranoia, hysteria, neurosis, psychosis, schizophrenia, gastroschisis, depression, tics, obesity, bunions, bad hair: Mother did it to me.

Except for Mother Hubbard and Mother Goose, fairy tales—those stories we heard at Mother's knee—do not feature mothers in any prominence.

One way to look at the lack of mothers in fairy tales is to discount her altogether. By herself, Mother is zero, zip—one who is preserved from experience, one who is not quite a person. Robert Penn Warren once remarked that a poem is not quite a poem if it is too pure (1971). The same could be said of idealized or absent mothers.

An exception to Mother's invisibility in fairy tales is the mother in "Jack and the Beanstalk." She is the archetypal hag, mother to Jack, a lazy fellow in a fatherless world. Jack earns his mother's wrath when he trades their only cow for beans. Furious at her son for his hapless swap, the mother spills the beans and sends Jack to bed without supper. Awakening the next day, Jack becomes a man. The spilt beans have produced morning wood in the form of a phallic beanstalk, which Jack of course climbs. At the top of the stalk is a giant's castle, where Jack becomes reborn when he hides inside the kitchen kettle, fights the ogre, avenges his father's death, steals the money bags, descends to his mother, and becomes rich. But what are we to make of Jack chopping down the phallic beanstalk—an act, by the way, that delights his mother (Opie, p. 225)? It would seem that for all his bravura, Jack returns from his adventure in the sky doomed to happiness in the motherworld as an emasculated hero. Mother is behind this fiasco. According to the child psychologist Bruno Bettelheim,

> The mother in "Jack and the Beanstalk" fails her son because, instead of supporting her son's developing masculinity, she denies its validity. . . . Jack's mother . . . stands revealed as the foolish one because she failed to recognize the development from child to adolescent. . . . This story teaches . . . that the (mother's) error is basically the lack of an appropriate and sensitive response to the various problems involved in a child's maturing personally, socially, and sexually. (pp. 192–93)

A possible explanation for the mother's error is to see her as an inadequate substitute for the father. Fairy tales, collected most famously by grim brothers, usually feature either failed mothers or phallic mothers. As if to draw attention away from the fearsome aspect of Mother, she is often disguised in fairy tale as the stepmother, stepqueen, crone, witch, godmother, grandmother, or widow-hag. Mothers may be left out of the tales we tell our children at bedtime, but they emerge nonetheless in the form of deformity. And they do big, unsubtle things. These substitute mothers wolf down their children, throw them into ovens, poison them with combs, or abandon them by the cinders. Highly charged mother-moments in fairy tale imply that behind the mother substitute lurks the figure of Mother herself. Even in absence her presence is malign.

Two of the most common assumptions about Mother would seem to be either she is not a person in her own right or her savagery makes us sick. Emily Dickinson's mother is characteristic of the first assumption. Typical for her time, mid nineteenth century, Emily's father's bossy patriarchal authority rubbed out her mother's ability even to speak. As Cynthia Griffin Wolff observes, Dickinson's mother's mode of discourse was indirection: she communicated her wishes "through a complex and often inefficient game of verbal hide-and-seek" (1988, p. 39). In a letter to the publisher Higginson, Emily went so far as to assert, "I never had a mother" (in Turco, 1993, p. 91). Wonderfully for us, Emily Dickinson used this negative dynamic between her parents to energize her poetry. When critics write of Dickinson's minimalism—the power of words as well as their limitation, her cryptic use of language, the slant of her rhymes—they are actually noting how Dickinson gives voice to the silences of her mother tongue. Literally. By withholding, by using suggestion, by not filling in the gaps of meaning, Emily writes in such a radically different way that she depaternalizes the notion of authority, elevating instead the realm of the unsaid. "Tell all the Truth but tell it slant / Success in Circuit lies," she puns (1985, p. 862). Before her time, Emily Dickinson was a poststructuralist.

Virginia Woolf is another of my literary heroes whose mother was a background figure. But in Woolf's case, as Louise De Salvo (1989) so brilliantly has shown, her mother's pose as "The Angel of the House"—idolized in a Victorian poem of that title as "the best half of creation's best / Its heart to feel, its eye to see" (Patmore, 1993)—was only a pose. That "Angel" kept an eye out for patriarchal privilege to the utter damage of the children. DeSalvo relates how Woolf's personal history consisted of a mother who conspired with the men of the family so they could gain access to the daughters' bedrooms. Through a subterfuge of maternal, steely silence, fathers, brothers, half-brothers, and uncles all exercised their members on virtually every female in the house, except on the mother. The woman on whom Mrs. Ramsay, in *To the Lighthouse*, is based, DeSalvo writes, was none other than Virginia's "cold iron" mother (DeSalvo, p. 118).

Interestingly, for all the brilliance of Louise DeSalvo's reading of Virginia Woolf's mother, DeSalvo is less clear about her own mother. Or perhaps she undertook intellectual work to deny the need for emotional work. In her memoir *Vertigo*, DeSalvo tells us of a blissful early childhood with her mother when neither father nor sister were in the scene: Father was off to war, sister had not yet been born. For Louise, life then was idyllic. But when the family rounded out, she tells us she was sent to Long Island for the summer months to stay with relatives. During that time only vague memories surface. After that time, Louise tells us she became subject to certain physical ailments that seemed to make her disappear—she fainted a lot and became very thin, having lost the appetite for her mother's food. Also at this time asthma literally took her breath away. As Louise's attitude toward her mother changed from adoration to confusion, she began to remember scraps of those Long Island holidays when she was a child; and finally she recalls the missing detail of sexual abuse of her by her aunt:

> I have had my first flashback. I remember the summer in Long Island, the
> light coming through the Venetian blinds, the bathtub. I am back there, I am
> back there, I am nine or ten or six or five or four, and I am so afraid that I
> am hardly breathing, I am so afraid that I dare not move, and as time stands
> still, I circle down, circle down, toward that dark still point at the center of
> the spinning vortex of memory. (2002, p. 102)

They say that the subjects we choose to write about choose us. As a graduate student writing on Virginia Woolf, Louise DeSalvo offers a ground-
breaking study of the pathology of the Victorian family of which Woolf was
an example. Louise DeSalvo was also an example of family incest and family
silence. But for all the power of her memory, Louise DeSalvo does not make
connection between *it* and her mother's silence or dumb nonknowing; *it* and
her bouts of physical illness; or *it* and her stuffed rage against her mother. The
entanglement, though, is there:

> I think that my life is beginning to resemble my mother's. I don't go out of
> the house except to do my exercise walking or unless I have to. I stop seeing
> my friends. I cancel speaking engagements. I'm afraid to go anywhere, afraid
> that whatever I do will precipitate a bad attack. . . . Sometimes, when I let
> myself think about her, I realize that I'm still angry with her. For not being
> the kind of mother I wanted. I know, though, that I held myself back from
> her because I was afraid that if I loved her deeply, I would become like her,
> but I've become like her anyway. (2002, p. 252)

Louise DeSalvo's memoir ends with a scene at her mother's death bed.
Commenting on Louise's cold hands, the mother says in her usual use of trite
expression, "Cold hands, warm heart"; to which Louise snaps back, "Cold
hands, cold heart, in my case, I'm afraid" (p. 260). Why the anger? Why the
verbal cruelty? Why the mother's aphorisms? Silence has many ways of speaking, as do the rages that make a body sick.

Curiously, Emily Dickinson, Virginia Woolf, and Louise DeSalvo could
all turn the absent or silent mother into a force that would shape the energy
of their creativity. Woolf's prose, like Dickinson's poetry, is elliptical. Mrs.
Ramsay (in *To the Lighthouse*) has traditionally been read as an abstract portrait of the ideal of womanhood: She is admired by all, she is well inten-
tioned, and she is beautiful. She emerges, however, as an enigma to readers
unfamiliar with how incest operates in a house where the mother is silent.
Thanks to Louise DeSalvo's code-breaking book on Virginia Woolf, we now
read Virginia Woolf differently. We discern that, for all of Mrs. Ramsay's
outward appearance of normalcy, this mother cannot attend to the smooth
running of the household, even with the help of servants. The house is in literal disrepair: the wallpaper is fading, meals are not on time, the greenhouse

has broken glass, and bedroom doors lack locks. These outward signs hint toward inner collusions. A student incest survivor (having read DeSalvo's book) once told my class incest can happen when mothers turn away from facing disrepair. It can happen when mothers choose not to see. Woolf so structures her prose to give the sense of being inside a situation where surfaces are disguises, the real drama occurring underneath, behind, between, or inside events. The plot is straightforward enough—if it rains, the family and their house guests cannot take an excursion to the lighthouse. But the pages contain many other, incomplete, opposing, seemingly disorganized schemes: fairy tale snippets; pieces of poetry; half-formed thoughts of this character, that character; arrangements of fruit on the table; arrangements of sand on the beach; the tap-tap of cricket balls; a scarf; a stocking; a pig's skull in the children's room. All these pieces take up lengthy prose descriptions which form their own little plots. Woolf *wants* to distract the reader; distraction is how sexual abuse works inside a household. The truth is that the house guests, with the unspoken permission of the mother, engage in the larger, hidden plot of sexually abusing the children. This is just like what happened in Virginia Woolf's own house, with Virginia Woolf's own mother. Fiction mirrors fact.

The second assumption about Mother, that her sickness makes us sick, is the subject of fiction, drama, essay, and memoir. Sick mothers in fiction have various illnesses: the woman in Charlotte Perkins Gilman's *The Yellow Wallpaper* suffers from postpartum depression; Susan in Doris Lessing's "To Room 49" suffers from suicidal depression. Laura Brown in Michael Cunningham's *The Hours* suffers from suicidal depression. Then, too, the mother in Jamaica Kincaid's *Autobiography of My Mother* is portrayed as a colonized self who in turn colonizes the daughter. The almost-mother in Margaret Atwood's *Surfacing* is tormented by the repressed memory of her abortion; and the almost-mother in Maxine Hong Kingston's *No Name Woman* was raped, and because rape is a disgrace upon the family, she throws her baby down the well. Some of these sicknesses arise from the temperament or inclination of Mother, that toilet breast we love to hate. Others are caused by repressive systems which no amount of logic or persuasion can alter.

Amazingly, the nineteenth-century feminist-dramatist, Henrik Ibsen, had a metaphor for the evils of patriarchal, hierarchal mindthink that results in women's illnesses. The metaphor is found in the character of Dr. Rank, in *A Doll's House*. Dr. Rank, we learn, has inherited his father's venereal disease; he is sick. But Ibsen is punning. The inherited sickness is that of "rank," which is like the patriarchy itself, where women are of lower rank than men but are to accept blame for the children's ills. Torvald Helmer makes that clear: "Almost everyone who goes bad early in life has a mother who's a chronic liar," he declares (Ibsen, 2003, p. 685). Hierarchy itself is "rank" with a disease that makes mothers sick. Nora slams the door on her husband and children (the loudest door slam in literary history) not because she is sick but because her husband can see her only as a silly child, or worse: a doll.

In all of these several works, mothers can't win; they are trapped on the bottom rung of the rank. They are victims, in one way or another, of a patriarchal power system that paternalizes to death their inner selves. Adrienne Rich analyzed the problem of the failure, guilt, and lack of choice in mothering when she said, "to be a female human being trying to fulfill traditional female functions in a traditional way is in direct conflict with the subversive function of the imagination" (1985, p. 2052). The key words here are "traditional way," and "subversive function of the imagination." The words conflict with each other. Either a woman must be "traditional" or she has to develop "subversive," imaginary ways to get around or under the conditions of personal imprisonment inside patriarchal patterns.

My mother was subversive. Brought up in Philadelphia as a Quaker, she fulfilled many of the traditional duties as a young woman. She "came out" as a debutante, she graduated from an all-girls college, and she married in her thirties. The problem was, as Rich defines it, she had a "subversive" imagination. Mothering was just not on her list of life goals. Holding salons in Cambridge during graduate school at Radcliffe, where the likes of James Agee came to read plays and discuss George Kittredge's philosophy or I. A. Richards's new literary critical ideas, Mother was an artist-writer in the making. Her diary, year 1932, charts her active social and intellectual life: "Read first act of Hamlet aloud—how I adore that play," she entered, February 13, 1932; "Tea with Phil and Amy very cunning and newly wed. Jim (Agee) came in very tight while we were having supper, stayed to read Acts 2, 3, 4 of Hamlet. Ted Spencer also came in. Discussion of Queen's guilt" (February 18, 1932). Several days later, on leap year, February 29, 1932, the diary ends. It is the day she begins a job in an office with Edward Aswell. She writes, "The big adventure begins and this diary ends because from now on my life will be strictly regulated." How prophetic! She intuited, even before she married my father, that her life would be "strictly regulated." This, from a woman who had held salons, discussed the latest critical theories, read plays in her drawing room, fostered an active intellectual life! Is it any wonder that *this* woman, who became a mother to Edward Aswell's children, in a 1940s village, would become sick?

My mother's nervous breakdown occurred shortly after I, her second child, was born. I have always attributed her sickness to the intolerable, for her, condition of suburban living in the forties. She was isolated. But more to the point, she was not meant to stay home with the babies. When she became hospitalized, first at Bloomingdale then at the Philadelphia Institute, she essentially gave over the child caretaking to my father; and while she protested that the men—her father and husband—colluded in the divorce agreement about the children, something about her protest never rang true with me. It simply wasn't done that the courts would allow custody of the children in those days to the father, unless my mother had agreed that she was "too sick" to mother.

She wasn't too sick, however, to continue her literary interests. For fifteen years, Mother had a successful editing career with *Harper's Bazaar*, mothering the work of Truman Capote, Eudora Welty, Jean Stafford, and others. A note on her by the photographer Rollie McKenna describes her perfectly:

> As fiction editor of "Harper's Bazaar" in the forties and fifties, [Mary Lou Aswell] discovered many gifted writers. . . . Mary Lou was brilliant, witty, often depressed and genuinely camera shy. The only picture I took of her was at a party where, characteristically in basic black, she stood out—small, dark and magnetic. (1991, p. 48)

Mother's literary works were extensive. She wrote and published mystery novels and researched material for a book on her Quaker background. She also edited two avant garde collections, one called *It's a Woman's World: Stories from Harper's Bazaar* and the other, *The World Within: Fiction Illuminating the Neuroses of Our Time*. In her foreword to the latter Mother writes:

> Which of us, in this age of freedom from certainty, has not been brushed by that terrifying wing (of madness)? Think of the commonplaces of our speech: "I thought I would lose my mind"; "it drives me mad"—empty as they may be of emotional content for most of us, they survive because their meaning has at some time pierced the shell of the cliché for every mother's child of us. (Aswell, 1947, p. vii)

Speaking as that mother's child, I can say how little I fret over her mothering skills, how much I care about her legacy. I see her in my own face and body. I drink tea the way she does—bending into the cup—I share her snobbisms, if not her brilliance. I admire her work, knowing how that could never have happened had she lived the traditional life. Had she lived in the house as a mother when I was growing up, I am quite sure that her depressions and neurotic behaviors would very well have made me sick. But that didn't happen. The only madness I can claim is my initials, MAD. When she died, I was so consumed with sadness that I wrote in four days a piece called Mother Matters. It was an outpouring of memory as well as an account of her dying. I meant it as a hymn to her. So, it is not that something is the matter with Mother, it's the other way around. Mother is the matter about which we write. Without Mother we would have no material. Mothers matter.

NINE

Teaching

INTRODUCTION

Mary

DELESE'S PIECE REMINDS ME of so many classes with so many of those students who are Over It. Over you with your enthusiasm for the book, over the book with its repetitions and unnecessary sexuality, over liberal humanism. What is coded with their attitude, Delese perceives, is resistance to talk of AIDS, behind which lies a deeply held bias against homosexuality. She wonders, Are there some values and beliefs so firmly instilled in humans that they are beyond teaching? What a great question. In a culture where values can be zapped with the remote, the slow pace of reading and entering another's world can be, I suppose, tedious—especially if the slow pace takes one unerringly where one does not wish to go. I wonder that same question about values and bias when I face the misogyny of my computer art students. They disguise their disdain for women by that Over It attitude. I taught Clarissa Pinkola Estés's book, *Women Who Run with the Wolves*, in my myth class one quarter. Big mistake. "Isn't this a bit too feminist?" one boy asked. Obviously, he had nominated himself to pose the question they all, especially the girls, had been gossiping about. The hostility toward the subject of wild women astonished me, dismayed me. Delese expresses some of this astonishment and dismay with her medical students who resist reading a book meant to stretch their empathy, if not their imagination. The fault lies not with the assignment. There is an issue here about the Over It attitude that we teachers face when introducing ideas that come up against firmly held biases. But the whole thing is, What other point is there in teaching but to challenge those firmly held biases?

Martha's take on teaching reminds me of my own student years of, as she puts it, disengagement. Ah yes, I remember those hours at those desks, scribbling. We were to learn logic, I recall: a math requirement. I found it more amusing to write down his sentences not for my notes but so I could imitate him back at the dorm. The subject did not, to put it mildly, engage me. Subsequently, Martha found herself on the other side of the desk, a terrifying place to be. She discovered something I think any good teacher knows: to teach, one must be subversive. She found her teaching to be personally incompatible with the structure and nature of schooling. Instead of teaching "school," she began to think about herself and her students as real people in a real world. She asks if there is a place in the classroom for weeping. Good thought. Very good thought. I have only had a few classes where there was weeping, but I will tell you those were the memorable ones. Those were the ones of engagement, all eyes working. The entire classroom atmosphere changed and we became, for one another, real people.

My own take on teaching in this chapter is via a circuitous route. I use a dream to prompt thinking about what has weakened my teaching. Two images provide what Roland Barthes (1981) might call the "punctum" of the dream. The word means "sting" or "sensitive point in an image." The two images are Clearing the Grasses and Released Snakes. Both images relate with what Delese and Martha call for in the teaching-learning act: a clearing away of dearly held beliefs so as to release more startling, perhaps even frightening, ideas. If our students are disengaged or just plain blasé, the teaching act could use more sting so that learning might begin.

TEACHING: A RETURN TO WONDER

Martha

I remember speaking the words without having planned them. "Teaching has become an integral part of my identity." It was 1998 and I was introducing myself as part of a presentation to the faculty I now call my colleagues. Whatever did I mean? Was it the absurdity or the unexpectedness that caused this moment to etch itself into my psyche? In any event, the words have stayed with me, echoing from the margins of my consciousness as I have settled into this current chapter of my life in educational settings. I spoke the words with what I imagine seemed like unwavering confidence; as if I knew myself well and, more remarkably, as if I had a clear understanding of the nuanced complexities of teaching. Now, in retrospect, as I find myself engaged in yet one more shift in my view of what counts as "good teaching," I marvel at my cavalier assertion, evidence of the masks I have worn that have fooled even me.

In keeping with an educational tradition begun by Pinar and Grumet (1976), the place to initiate a search for understanding may be with a look backward. An autobiographical turn to the past may bring me to a more complete understanding of the present and lead to a vision of the future that is worthy of commitment. Slattery and Rapp (2003) believe "proleptic hope" can be born through this increased understanding, a kind of momentous insight that can spur us to ethical action. For reasons to be elaborated later, I am in search of this hope.

> In the process of investigating educational ethics, we reiterate our funda-
> mental notion that ethics cannot be separated from our autobiographical
> journey. . . . The complexity of our lives makes the study of critical ethical
> issues of education an imprecise science at best. However, the process of
> struggling to understand the complexity of our lives is for us the beginning
> of wisdom. (p. 67)

I didn't enter the career of teaching mindlessly. In fact, I resisted it mightily. It's a story I've heard from some of my preservice teachers; amazing that the dynamic continues. I wonder at its tenacity and at the gender implications of its persistence. My mother was a teacher. My older sister. My aunt. They/I tell the tale. I had a sense that destiny was driving me and a nagging worry that my choices, which I perceived as limited in 1965, might have dreadful implications. I feared I might disappear completely if I chose teaching. Nursing and secretarial work were my perceived alternative options. Money making would only be an issue until I married and had children, or, until a catastrophic event that my as-yet-unknown husband might die and I would be forced to have a life outside the world of domestic tranquility. Just writing these words reminds me that I was far from awake to the world beyond my traditional family structure.

Annie Dillard tells us she "woke in bits, like all children, piecemeal over the years" (1987, p. 11). She was terrified of the day when her waking moments would be continuous and "she would never be free of herself again" (p. 73). This is an understandable emotion from a child's perspective, looking forward. But too much shelter, too much naiveté is limiting—suffocating?—when viewed in retrospect with the sense that deMello (1992) may be onto something when he claims spirituality and depth of understanding are dependent upon a continual waking up from cultural messages that have been carefully taught.

> When we start off in life, we look at reality with wonder, but it isn't the intel-
> ligent wonder of the mystics; it's the formless wonder of the child. Then won-
> der dies and is replaced by boredom, as we develop language and words and
> concepts. Then, hopefully, if we're lucky, we'll return to wonder again. (p. 126)

And so, nursing it would be. In preparation, I candy striped. (Hospital volunteers who wore red and white striped pinafores—clearly made with girls in mind—were dubbed "candy stripers.") But teaching would have its way with me. Several encounters with groups of children left me convinced (against my will) that I preferred the aroma of sweaty children to the smell of a hospital. Still, I cried the day my acceptance to a small teacher's college arrived. I remember the feelings that accompanied the tears as loss—I had lingered between the glorious possibility of two choices and the future was now narrowed to one. One that I had resisted intensely. I forcibly pushed the panic aside, and left for school.

I plunged with abandon into every aspect of college experience, with the exception of my schoolwork. My disengagement was, I think, symbolic of the future that I didn't want to face. Occasionally a course caught my attention and I would wake up a bit. Doctrine was required and I had a remarkable, leftist professor who expected us to dig and to think. Historical, metaphorical interpretations. I was more than intrigued. But these wakeful experiences were few. Miraculously, I moved quarter by quarter through the system, enjoying the away-from-home freedom and making fast friends who were as disengaged from their coursework as I. School had never captured my attention, really. By my junior year, fifteen years (think of it!) into the process, I had managed to do the work necessary to make the grades without ever taking school seriously. During the final quarter of that year, I found myself face to face with student teaching in a fifth-grade classroom. This was it. The limbo of educational indifference was coming to an end. These were real children and my life snapped into crisp focus.

I scoured the teacher's guides in preparation for my first teaching. In what seems now to be a single day event, I discovered that I had never in my life enjoyed anything as much as envisioning the combination of students and learning opportunities. I was overwhelmed with relief. Fortunately, my enthusiasm was contagious for my depth of understanding of the process of teaching was barely enough to get my feet wet. I suspect the students responded well to me because of the skills I had developed while avoiding serious engagement with schools: perspective taking, love of life (I had never connected this to formal learning), a spiritual commitment not much more mature than theirs, and just passable guitar playing and singing.

I think now that what made me a well-liked and respected teacher for the nine years I worked in elementary classrooms had something to do with my personal incompatibility with the structure and nature of schooling. From the beginning, I was committed to teach in ways that would not replicate my own monotone experiences. I was well acquainted with disengagement but passionate about creating activities that would be alive and important to students. A chance to wonder—for them and for me. Comparatively speaking, I was a pretty good teacher. But my enthusiasm ran much deeper than my insight. I learned from experience, took classes, shifted from parochial to public schools all the while searching for increasingly effective ways to reach children with the good news I hadn't discovered until I was twenty years old: school can be a part of one's reality; learning changes one on the inside. Thus began my identification with teaching. But, looking back, I can see that my vision of good teaching then was just the beginning of the journey.

Now, thirty plus years hence and deeply engaged in the education of pre-service and inservice teachers, I know how difficult good teaching is. My students look to me for answers and I supply them instead with questions, urging them to join me in the quest. I've moved from the "aha" of realizing the connections between school and perceived reality to the struggle of facing school's and my own complicity in perpetuating myriad realities that should never be. Critical theoretical perspectives have provided me with a language for the feelings about schooling and teaching that I had wrestled with for years. Feminist perspectives have raised my consciousness, shaken the foundations of my world, and left me changed forever. I began my teaching at the university level determined to invite my preservice and graduate students to struggle with issues that I wished I had encountered before my teaching career began. Students often resist the information in my foundations of education class. I search for ways to engage them in an open search for understanding without alienating them and succeed—some of the time. I have attempted to build on their well-intentioned desires to "make a difference" in the lives of children. But I am always unsettled by the knowledge that they will face institutional inertia and the weight of a lifetime of feel-good history and cultural traditions. Slattery and Rapp (2003) say it well.

> Current educational philosophies and structures often militate against teachers and students becoming actively engaged in releasing the imagination, critically analyzing ideas, experiencing the romance or passion in the curriculum and understanding culture and society. The hermeneutic circle that seeks conversation and understanding is perceived as dangerous, for teachers and students might become engaged and empowered. . . . The possibilities are endless; the resistance is immense. (p. 89)

And now I am envisioning another year of teaching aware of the immensity of the task. Long gone are the days when I viewed my task as a teacher as seeing to it that students become engaged in the learning, although this is no small goal. Teaching, Huebner (1991, p. 1) writes, is a creative process of "healing, re-integration, re-membering, and re-collection." Slattery and Rapp suggest it is about developing "teaching convictions." That resonates for me. It's not enough to get the word out about oppression, to invite students' written and verbal response to the facts. The impulses that have moved me to integrate art and music into my courses, the moments I have given over to painful, pushing conversations, the times I have stood determinedly with students, refusing to back away from the topics that seem risky in the religiously and politically conservative community that permeates our lives together—these are the times we have come closest to Dewey's notion of educational experience.

> What avail is it to win prescribed amounts of information about geography and history, to win ability to read and write, if in the process the individual loses his [*sic*] own soul: loses his [*sic*] appreciation of things worthwhile, of the values to which these things are relative; if he loses desire to apply what he has learned and, above all, loses the ability to extract meaning from his future experiences as they occur? (Dewey, 1938, p. 49)

Even reading Jonathon Kozol's stark exposés (1991; 1995) is insufficient. Somehow, in the face of increasingly conservative educational decisions and movements, my students and I will need the power of experiences that move beyond expected curriculum. Words will not be enough. Educationally engaging activities will not be enough. We need hope. Proleptic hope. The kind of hope that draws on the past, enlivens the present, and moves us toward a future of greater equity and justice—simultaneously.

There is, after all, a spark in my past that still ignites my commitment to a life shaped by educational endeavor. Once I wanted what was best for my students—mostly white, middle-class, privileged children. Now, of course, the whole world pours into our homes daily and with little effort we can come to understand that the only education worthy of the name must take into account the unconscionable inequities and pain that are rampant both in the world and within the world as our planet groans under the weight of our failure as stewards. Techno-rational, narrow-minded educational schemes that serve the political good of power brokers at the expense of the hearts and minds of our students are immoral. Not misguided. Not insufficient. Immoral. Somehow we must envision together, my students and I, a future where we will be able to act morally. Wanting what is best, not just for a few, but for all of us, and envisioning a path that contributes to that dream—that's what teaching must be.

I will need new tools. Slattery and Rapp (2003) insist on the centrality of aesthetics. I am persuaded. We will expand our use of social artifacts—videos, artwork, art experiences. Can we dream together? Imagine? Struggle? Even weep? And *wonder*? Perhaps real learning begins and ends with wonder. Can we look within and look back so that we can begin to grapple with the present and the future together? There are parts of me still cautious and shaped by convention. I've pushed the boundaries in the classroom—or at least I have tried. But this call to moral teaching will require more risk. Ironically, the profession I resisted with such determination has always had a hold on me. The grip is tightening.

TEACHING IN THE GAP

Mary

A dream: I am leading my students on a field trip to Washington, D. C. My colleague has selected a more appropriate place for her field trip. I worry about the book I have selected for the class, *Pride and Prejudice*. My colleague has selected *Catcher in the Rye*, a much better choice. The students are lining up on a grassy knoll, waiting for the lesson. The point of this field trip seems to be to raise the snakes from their holes. I have a stick with which to push back the grass and release the snakes. They are smallish and brown. I have no fear whatsoever; why should I? The process is slow but I am reassured each time one of the snakes is released.

The power of the snake. Releasing power. My power. Good, female power from the ground, good chthonic power. This dream is different from other before-school-begins dreams, which usually feature me in charge of a room of completely out of control students. The usual dream: I am trying and trying to get the students' attention, but either my voice or their clamor prevents my being heard. But in the dream detailed above, despite my sense of competition with my colleague whom I view as infinitely more competent than myself, there is that central element, the spine of the text, of the snakes gently being released. That is the word: "released." What an encouraging way for me to begin my next quarter. I must remember this dream.

True story: I am at a wedding supper of the same colleague with whom, for some ridiculous reason, I feel in competition. Seated next to me is a colleague who is, it turns out, a medium. The trumpets are blaring, the dancing has begun, we are between courses. I mention to my colleague that Christmas Eve is a difficult time for me, since my mother died on Christmas Eve eight years ago. My colleague bends his head to the floor. "She is a small woman," he says. "She is with another woman with cowboy boots on." So begins the next several minutes in which Geoff channels my dead mother. I bend my head to listen not to the trumpets but to the channeling. This is a most improbable scene. Like a dream. He goes on to describe my mother. I know this is a true rendering. Between pauses, he tells me what he hears: my mother is happy for me. "What is m and m?" he asks. I tell him that must stand for Mary and Marla. "She is happy for you," he repeats. "A ring," he says. "You have a ring of your mother's." (I do). I ask him if she is happy. "She tells me she is finally unleashed," he says.

There it is again. Release. Unleashed. My mother would be happy to be unleashed? This surprises me, since she certainly unleashed herself from the expectations of blue blood Philadelphia by moving out to Santa Fe and living with Agi, the woman in cowboy boots. But perhaps not. Perhaps even in her liberation from the patriarchy there were strictures of living in the all-woman culture of artistic Santa Fe. I always felt she resented having to play hostess to Agi's clients.

Unleashed. Release.

Back to the dream. My inappropriate book, *Pride and Prejudice*, would seem to be the dream's intuition that what is good for the canon may not be good for "the university in ruins" (Readings, 1999). Too much pride, too much prejudice. More appropriate, certainly as suits the landscape of the dream, is *Catcher in the Rye*. Recall Holden's imagination, picturing himself with kids playing in a field of rye: "What I have to do, I have to catch everybody if they start to go over the cliff. . . . I'd just be a catcher in the rye. I know it's crazy, but that's the only thing I'd really like to be. I know it's crazy" (Salinger, 1966, p. 173). Like Holden's life's ambition, my dream lesson of releasing the snakes sounds crazy. But that may be the only thing I'd really like to do as a teacher, metaphorically push back the grass and release the snakes.

In a less crazy articulation of this idea is the fiercely argued book by Bill Readings, *The University in Ruins*, in which some "crazy" ideas are discussed—among them the notion of excellence as a problem. "Excellence," he writes, "marks nothing more than the moment of technology's self-reflection . . . the optimal input/output ratio in matters of information" (1999, p. 39). Information, accountability, outcomes assessment, closing the gap: these are the code words for the standards and testing movement that has made the university the handmaiden of industry. Information is that which can be scored by scantrons and marked on pretest/posttests. Information satisfies the bureaucratic longing for exhaustive accounting, such as that which characterizes prisons, barracks, or the National Basketball Association. But information—what Edward Said (1983) refers to as "informationalization"—has become its own culture, one that feeds on the sort of educational self-help, how-to books that line the shelves of Barnes and Noble.

My students are dubbed the Information Age students because they grew up with easy access to computer click-button data. Rather than read, they game. Their humor is comic book attuned. I need not rant about the decline of truth, logic, and decency because those are the code words of subjectivities brought up with male, heterosexual, white biases. Pride and prejudice. But as a teacher to art students, many of whom are majoring in digital media or product design, I recognize the different set of attentions my students bring to my lessons in the classroom. This brings me back to the dream.

Skill building is not the answer to the gap in generations between my students and me. Nor is the admonition to "close the gap" that satisfies administrators seeking answers to, among other things, the difference between pre and post testing scores. Test more often! Drill skills! Build facts! Ahh, facts, lifeless facts. These urgings satisfy a pedagogy that keeps administration concerns central (this morning's headlines, bold print: "Schools make huge gains on Iowa Test of Basic Skills") (*Savannah Morning News*, 1999). These urgings ensure that privileged points of view hold sway. No, it is time to push back the grass, as my dream put it, so as to "decenter the pedagogical situation," as Readings puts it (p. 153).

The snakes that the dream urges me to release are highly symbolic because of their containing an ancient wisdom. According to Jungian psychologist Joseph Henderson, the snake, with its ritual of skin shedding, offers a different kind of knowledge from that ordinarily occurring during daylight consciousness. "This is the knowledge of death and rebirth forever withheld except at those times when some transcendent principle, emerging from the depths, makes it available to consciousness" (Henderson & Oakes, 1990, p. 37). The sort of decentering that the dream suggests is, of course, not the sort suggested by Readings. But I think a parallel exists between two kinds of sweeping-away, or decentering. One is spiritual, as in the snake symbol; the other, pedagogical. Both have to do with making negative space available for the emergence of something entirely outside systems of regulated ("daylight") thought. Readings even echoes Henderson's phrases and Henderson's Jungian ideas with the following radical definition of thought. "Thought," he writes, "is an empty transcendence . . . that throws those who participate in pedagogy back into a reflection upon the ungroundedness of their situation" (Readings, p. 161). Imagine a classroom where students and teacher are "ungrounded," where what is thought is an "empty transcendence"—a third term, a differend, something neither teacher nor student owns.

These ideas undo common assumptions about teaching. They are big ideas. So too my dream. With its stark imagery of grass and snake in an "inappropriate" educational setting, the dream is what Jung calls a rendezvous with destiny, or a Big dream. Jung writes:

> I have often examined many such dreams, and often found in them a peculiarity which distinguished them from other dreams: they contain symbolical images which we also come across in the mental history of mankind. . . . They occur mostly during the critical phases of life, in early youth, puberty, at the onset of middle age . . . and within sight of death. (1969, p. 291)

This dream occurred at a critical juncture in my teaching career when I was past midlife but unable to tap into my crone power with young art students bored and resistant to my courses in literature and writing. On the one hand, administrators were telling me to "hold the line" and be traditional. On the other hand, my experience with these students was unlike anything I had encountered before. It wasn't just that so many lacked basic skills. It was more that they were used to zip zap technology, having been brought up on a diet of computer games, zines, noir film, Tarantino plots, and the like. Because of a male-induced action literacy, students of both sexes demonstrated misogynist attitudes. A pervasive antifeminism manifested itself as disdain for anything promoting female-centered writing, criticism of patriarchal art, or my feminist method of teaching as "dwelling."

Nevertheless, the dream was directing me to access the inner snakes. By making room for the snakes, clearing away the grasses, the dream was prompting a radical return to my original feminist impulse to dwell. Dwelling, associated less with external action than with inner discipline, is another way to think about time and how it is spent with others, in the classroom. "To discipline an impulse" Michael Adams writes, "is consciously to avow it . . . or to regulate the expression of it" (2001, p. 418). What I needed to do was release and unleash. But release into what and for what ends, I was not sure.

As I dwell on the dream, with its implication of the powers that lie below and within, I enter the gap phase of wisdom. This is the space of not-knowing essential for eventual knowing of the "real-nothing" or "imaginal something" (Adams, 396). It is a clearing. Clarissa Pinkola Estés reminds us that the creative force seeks just such a clearing, gap, or hollow into which to flow. "The wild creative force flows into whatever beds we have, those we are born with as well as those we dig with our own hands. We don't have to fill them, we only have to build them," she writes (1992, p. 299). Using the dream as a teaching image, I wonder if I am able to open the gap in the classroom. I wonder if my art students are human beings "full of inner words" (Bakhtin, 1986, p. 118).

Bill Readings's remedy for these wonderings is to dwell inside the ruins, in a move of what he calls "dissensus." I understand him to mean that the teaching act is no longer consensus or even dialogue, since both terms imply "misplaced pedagogical commitments to autonomy" (p. 156). What has ruined the university has been its abandonment of the ethical obligation to think the question. "We are left, then," he says, "with an obligation to explore our obligations without believing that we will come to the end of them. Such a community, the community of dissensus that presupposes nothing in common . . . would seek to make its heteronomy, its differences, more complex" (p. 190). Clearing the table of all prior assumptions leads the way open for a thinking beside one another, no one superior to another, no meaning reaching a final end. Into this loose-endedness might come the snake of wisdom.

The aforementioned remedy, like my earlier discussion of a dream's psychopomp, could sound too idealistic or romantic or spiritual for some. Or could it just be that pedagogy in the gap is actually a revolutionary idea? Recall Lacan's notion of "speech beyond meaning" (in McGee, 1992, p. 71), Levinas's insistence on "the Other" of "the absolutely Other" (in Lyotard and Thebaud, 1985), or Lyotard's disavowal of a common horizon of truth (1979). These are difficult ideas, meant to challenge "the most disastrous effects of misunderstanding" caused by clarity (Readings, 184). Rather than pretend to transparent meaning, clear understanding, or the tying up of loose ends (all boxes that students can tick on faculty evaluation forms), dissensus offers an "abyssal space" for new relational thought (Readings, 156).

The gap as the place to begin in the ruins is admittedly risky business. Undergraduates (particularly) come into the classroom expecting information, answers, and bytes to add to their knowledge base. But that is the problem and that is the cause of the boredom. To set up a different dynamic is to change the direction of thinking and the bases of knowledge. The new call is for interruption, suspension, and lostness. The task involves a move to "producing the unconscious as the work of the text" (Lather, 2000, p. 303). Then a different kind of knowledge appears, one that jolts us all out of the familiar. In the gap, we can go to work. We can think. We can dwell.

(MIS)TAKES ON TEACHING

Delese

Always chance is powerful.
Always let your hook be cast.
In the pool where you least expect it,
there will be fish.

—Ovid, *Ars Amatoria*

I was expecting fifteen students to show up. That's what the roster indicated anyway. The one hundred and five second-year medical students had been divided into small groups for discussion of the book, and these fifteen were mine. I walked into the conference room a few minutes before the 2:00 class, a bit anxious at seeing only three students seated at the table. I busied myself with activity, even though all I had with me was the text and a folder with my notes. I opened the folder, pretending to read but really trying to decide how to open the discussion, a decision I usually make on the spot after reading the students and their mood. Two more students walked in. Uneasily I glanced at the clock. It was 2:00 on the nose. I'd wait another minute or two, I thought, acutely aware of the silence in the room, conscious that the students weren't even talking to each other. A very bad sign.

I began, choosing professorial formality despite the informality of the setting. "Well, we might as well get started. . . . Perhaps more are coming," I said without a smile or hint of irony. "You've been asked to read a literary text as part of an infectious disease course. We decided on this text because of the timeliness of the topic, its readability, and . . . well, it's a *good book!*" Aware that I was already in defensive mode—where *were* the remaining ten students?—I continued to drone on, providing literary background about the book and its author, and finally asking a series of rapid-fire questions to get discussion going. The silence was thunderous.

The idea for reading literature in the midst of a basic science class was, we all thought, conceptually elegant. My colleague, a microbiologist, was putting the finishing touches on a new month-long infectious disease module for second-year medical students when he realized that while the syllabus was appropriately full of viruses and bugs in all their origins and treatments, it was completely lacking in *stories* of illness. As Arthur Frank points out, the modern experience of illness is defined overwhelmingly by technical expertise—what doctors and other experts say about a person's illness and how it will be treated, mostly in unfamiliar, specialized language. As patients, people *become* the stories found on the medical chart, stories that are conflated with the actual experience of being ill. This is the way medical students learn about disease. Reading literature is one way to reinsert the ill person's story, unmedicalized, back into the education of doctors. "Help me pick a book," my colleague asked. "We'll have everyone read it and build in some time for discussion."

I could not have been more delighted, not to say surprised, by his request. The medical humanities, hardly newcomers to the medical curriculum, are still often viewed by many faculty and students as secondary to the "real" work of learning basic science and clinical medicine. Most humanities courses are separate, often parallel, to other course work: over here is where you acquire skills and habits of doctoring in the language of objectivity and rationality; over there is where you luxuriate in literature, ethics, philosophy, or spirituality in the language of subjectivity and emotion. Yet for willing readers, literature is a rich, complicated, provocative source of exploration into the multiple and conflicting practices of health care. Literature bids us to take an imaginative leap into another person's world, pushing us into ourselves to those places where our values and beliefs are made, stored, and often unexamined. Literature, as Dorothy Allison describes it, is "the lie that tells the truth, that shows us human beings in pain and makes us love them" (1994, p. 175). This was what we wanted students to encounter as they read literature in this particular setting—very human bodies who, in all their varieties, are always *someone's* mother, husband, or child.

We decided to choose from the abundant literature of epidemics, which have always evoked remarkable artistic/literary responses. The range of choices was wide, from Giovanni Boccaccio's *The Decameron*, to Albert Camus's *The Plague*, to Gabriel Garcia Marquez's *Love in the Time of Cholera*, to Paul Rudnick's *Jeffrey*, to name a very few. We finally decided on physician Abraham Verghese's memoir, *My Own Country* (1995). In doing so we played the doctor card (medical students would find him more credible than other writers) and the relevance card (medical students had grown up with AIDS). What we did not anticipate was the vehement negative response from students when they heard this was part of their assignment.

Of the five students who showed up, two had read the entire book, two had made it halfway through, and one had not even attempted to read it ("I thought I'd come to class anyway and see what I could get out of it"). The two who had read half were the most outspoken in their criticism of the book.

"It is so repetitious," Ann said. "A patient comes in. Dr. Verghese begins taking his history, and it goes on and on and on. All their stories sound alike."

"And the details of his patients' lives—where does he get off asking them such intimate details?" Paul added. "Why does he have to know when his gay patients 'knew' they were gay? Why does he ask them all those personal details about their sexual practices? Actually, I think he was enjoying all this *too* much. Maybe he does have issues with his sexuality, just like his wife thought."

I was instantly annoyed. "Well, it *is* a memoir . . . a doctor reflecting on his life as an infectious disease doctor in the era of AIDS, sharing his patients with us, and yes, most were gay. He wasn't treating them for a cold or the flu—hopefully he was going to be taking care of them for a long time and felt that he could give them more compassionate care if he knew them really well."

Paul, quickly: "Think he asked those kinds of questions about his patients with, uh . . . emphysema? I'm sorry, his sexual history taking was too much. I had to put the book down."

Ann, nodding in agreement: "I agree. I found the book almost pornographic in its details. This was more about the sexual practices of gay men than I care to know. I think you can give excellent care to people without knowing what they do at truck stops. Do we need to know if they practice safe sex? Of course. Do we need to know all the details? No. I finally stopped reading it too."

Theoretically, this was supposed to be going differently. Martha Nussbaum, among countless others, writes convincingly that engagement with literature readies one for moral interaction. Cultivated through literature, the narrative imagination can foster the growth of a "sympathetic responsiveness" to others and how the circumstances of their lives shape them. According to Nussbaum, literature "both inspires intense concern with the fate of characters and defines those characters as containing a rich inner life. . . . [T]he reader learns to have respect for the hidden contents of that inner world, seeing its importance in defining a creature as fully human" (1997, p. 90). The ability to imagine what it is like to be someone else—here, what it is like to live not only with a terrifying disease but also with the loathing and fear it evokes—is poorly fostered in medical training. Unlike the history taking exhibited by Dr. Verghese, most students learn to pare *down* patients' stories with inductive precision that moves toward classification and diagnosis. And without a narrative imagination, students are less inclined to venture toward their patients' rich inner lives, thus keeping those patients members of classes and categories: gay men, "the poor," welfare moms, difficult patients. Reading literature, we believe, can be a corrective against such categorical thought.

So why didn't this book "work" on more students' narrative imagination? Why hadn't it promoted sympathy and respect for persons with AIDS, particularly gay men who had contracted the disease, given the large number of admirable characters found in the book? Why were so many students unwilling to travel with Verghese in his own journey of self-awareness? Why were so many students unwilling to take the risk of identifying with the characters in the book? Are there some values and beliefs so firmly installed in humans that they are beyond the reach of sympathetic readings of literature?

Here, in this class, the hidden contents of Verghese's patients' inner worlds were indeed laid bare to readers, but instead of evoking sympathetic responsiveness, the contents turned many of them away from the page. I was angry with the more outspoken students for their barely masked homophobia, incredulous at their alarming lack of insight about the range of people for whom they would be providing care. The more stories I heard from other faculty about similar comments made in their classes, the more I wanted to pin the blame on something. *How*, I wondered, *do these overtly biased students get into medical school? The admissions process obviously breaks down frequently if we can't weed these guys out before they get here. If this beautifully crafted book evokes charges of "pornography," the problem obviously rests with students, not with the assignment.* Or so I thought, until my critical gaze finally circled back to me and my expectations for this experience.

Literature and medicine *is* an elegant pairing, each informing the other in fluent, inspired, often provocative ways. Reading imaginative literature about illness can provide insights and understandings to readers that are unavailable in medical texts. Yet, for these assertions to be realized they must be part of a larger pedagogical practice we did not provide for students in this setting. When I finally got around to examining the assignment—listing a literary text as a required reading and two weeks later blocking out time to discuss it—I was struck with how superfluous it must have seemed, wedged into the corner of a syllabus firmly committed to the scientific and clinical basis of infectious diseases. Under those circumstances, at best its reading might induce what Megan Boler calls passive empathy—when "our concern is directed to a fairly distant other whom we cannot directly help" (1999, p. 159), here to Ed and Bobby, Fred and Otis, and Vickie and Clyde, Verghese's wonderfully developed characters.

What was sorely missing from this educational experience was teaching. That is, what is in question here is not the literary work but the reading practices that were, or were not, encouraged when students were asked to read *My Own Country*. Without adequate time for faculty to guide students *as they read*, the text is less likely to realize its evocative possibilities, to induce empathy, or to incite readers to self-reflection, embedded as it was in the midst of course work that recognizes and rewards very different reading practices. Because the discussion of the book was to take place after it was read, I was unable to encourage aesthetic, critical, and sympathetic reading practices in students as they were getting to know Verghese, the conditions of his patients' lives, how his colleagues responded to persons with AIDS, and the strain that his work put on his family relationships. I am inclined to believe, given the setting and the conditions under which students were asked to read this text, that they did not have the skills to read it with close aesthetic attention, "considering the ways that its form conveyed a content, a view of what is worth taking seriously, and what the world is like" (Nussbaum, p. 102). I am also inclined to believe, given their other obligations in microbiology, immunology, pathology, and pharmacology, that they did not read it critically as a political text that could transport them into the lives of disenfranchised people who need to be respected and understood, especially by care givers. And while some students may have read Verghese's portrayals of persons with AIDS compassionately, I am not inclined to believe that they engaged in much self-scrutiny as they read, rethinking their assumptions or considering their obligation to work against the injustices illustrated in the text. These lacks represent teaching mistakes—I realized that I had orchestrated a superficial, looks-good-on-paper assignment that may have worked against what I hope to achieve.

I spot the familiar cover of the paperback. Leaning back in his chair in a library carrel nestled deep in the stacks, a student is reading *My Own Country*. I'm surprised—the discussion of the book was two weeks ago. I don't know this student, but still, I'm curious.

"So, what do you think? Enjoying the book?"

He looks up, straightens up, and puts the book down. "Yeah, I do like it. But it's taken me a long time to get through it. I'm not used to reading this kind of stuff."

"Did you go to the discussion of it?"

"No . . . I decided not to go because I hadn't finished it and I didn't want to ruin it."

"You and a lot of other students. Was that the reason that most students didn't go? They hadn't finished the book?"

"Nah. Most of the students who didn't go figured it was too much trouble for only three test questions." He smiles with some embarrassment. "Then there were those who said it was too gay."

"Hmmmm . . ." I paused. "So, did you learn anything new about persons with AIDS or taking care of persons with AIDS from reading this book that you didn't learn elsewhere in the course?"

He thought for a few moments. "No, not really. But it's a good story, and Verghese is such an awesome doctor. Now I just want to see how it ends."

I smile and walk away, reminded again that the shortest distance between two points is not always the straight line connecting them.

Notes

CHAPTER 3. DISGRACE

Mary

1. I finish my revisions to this chapter one hour after Senate Majority Leader Trent Lott resigned his position, December 20, 2002, because of his infamous blunder recalling fondly the days of segregation before our nation had all of its "problems." Nothing still so divides our country as the issue of racism, and racism's true colors are revealed in such quick, top-of-the-head, off-the-cuff, winging-its. Lott's remarks show how bigoted sentiments often lurk behind nostalgic utterances.

CHAPTER 6. FORGIVENESS

Mary

I am grateful for the discussion and suggestions made on a draft of this chapter presented at the 2002 Bergamo Conference. I owe special thanks to Gaile S. Cannella and Radhika Viruru for troubling my remarks.

1. I use the unusual spelling in the manner of Kafka's *Amerika* (New York: Schoken, 1962), to indicate his theme that justice is a form of discipline. This thesis is similar to that of Michel Foucault in his *Discipline and punish: The birth of the prison* (Trans. Alan Sheridan. New York: Vintage, 1995), where he claims that forgiveness is a method employed to extort and criminalize.

2. As I revise this chapter, the resignation of Cardinal Bernard Law, Archbishop of the Diocese of Boston, has been announced, December 13, 2002.

3. For an extensive study of the problem of "forgiving" an event like the Holocaust, see Marla Morris, *Curriculum and the holocaust: Competing sites of memory and representation*. Mahwah NJ: Lawrence Erlbaum, 2001.

4. I spent several class periods wondering aloud what O'Connor (1978) may have meant by designating O.T. and E.T. for two of her characters in "Greenleaf." The designation seemed important. The students and I played with a number of ideas—old testament/end testament; old time/end time; ordinary time/end time; ordinary time/everlasting time. We went around and around. Finally, we decided on ordinary time/eschatological time, since both are Christian ideas. Eschatology concerns itself with "end" matters, like death, judgment, the future state; while ordinary time concerns itself with earthly matters. In arriving at that idea, I think we "unearthed" a key component of O'Connor's religious view.

References

Adams, M. V. (2001). *The mythological unconscious*. New York: Karnac.

Allison, D. (1994). *Skin: Talking about sex, class and literature*. Ithaca, NY: Firebrand.

American Psychiatric Association (1994). *Diagnostic and statistical manual of mental disorders*. 4th ed. Washington, DC: American Psychiatric Association.

Anderson, A. (2001). *The powers of distance: Cosmopolitanism and the cultivation of detachment*. Princeton, NJ: Princeton University Press.

Anzaldùa, G. (1999). *Borderlands/La Frontera: The new Mestiza*. San Francisco: Aunt Lute.

Apple, M. (1993). *Official knowledge: Democratic education in a conservative age*. New York: Routledge.

———. (2001). *Educating the "right" way*. New York: Taylor & Francis.

Arendt, H. (1968). *The human condition*. Chicago: University of Chicago Press.

Arnheim, R. (1996). *The split and the structure*. Berkeley: University of California Press.

Association of American Medical Colleges (2001). Parents' education and income level of all medical matriculates: 2000. Washington, DC: AAMC.

Aswell, M. L. (1932). *The standard diary*. Private collection.

———, ed. (1944). *It's a woman's world: Stories from* Harper's Bazaar. New York: Whittlesey.

———, ed. (1947). *The world within: Fiction illuminating the neuroses of our time*. New York: McGraw-Hill.

Atwood, M. (1990). *Surfacing*. New York: Fawcett Crest.

Babb, L. A. (1999). *Ethics in American adoption*. Westport, CT: Bergin & Garvey.

Bakhtin, M. (1986). *Marxism and the philosophy of language*. Trans. L. Matejka and I. R. Titunik. Cambridge: Harvard University Press.

Barnard, R. Speaking places: Prison, poetry, and the South African nation. *Research in African Literatures* 32(3) (2001): 155–76.

Barthes, R. (1981). *Camera lucida*. New York: Hill & Wang.

Bartholet, E. (1999). *Family bonds: Adoption, infertility, and the new world of child production*. Boston: Beacon.

———. (2001). Adoption rights and reproductive wrongs. In S. E. Chase and M. F. Rogers (eds.), *Mothers and children: Feminist analyses and personal narratives*. New Brunswick, NJ: Rutgers University Press.

Batchelor, S. (1997). *Buddhism without beliefs: A contemporary guide to awakening*. New York: Riverhead.

Beckett, S. (1958). The unnamable. In *Three novels by Samuel Beckett* (pp. 291–414). New York: Grove.

Berger, P. and Luckman, T. (1966). *The social construction of reality: A treaty in the sociology of knowledge*. New York: Doubleday.

Bergler, E. On acting and stage fright. *Psychiatric Quarterly Supplement* 23 (1949): 313–19.

Bettelheim, B. (1989). *The uses of enchantment*. New York: Vintage.

Bhabha, H. K. (1994). *The location of culture*. New York: Routledge.

Block, A. (1997). *I'm only bleeding: Education as the practice of social violence against children*. New York: Peter Lang.

Bloom, H. (1977). *Wallace Stevens: The poems of our climate*. Ithaca: Cornell University Press.

———. (1998). *Shakespeare: the invention of the human*. New York: Riverhead.

Boler, M. (1999). *Feeling power: Emotions and education*. New York: Routledge.

Booth, W. (1988). *The company we keep: An ethics of fiction*. Berkeley: University of California Press.

Brink, A. (1979). *A dry white season*. New York: Penguin.

Britzman, D. (1998). *Lost subjects, contested objects: Toward a psychoanalytic inquiry of learning*. Albany: State University of New York Press.

Brown, R. My Africa: The politics of belonging in Nadine Gordimer's *The Pickup*. *Vogue* (September 2001): 494, 496.

Broyard, A. (1992). *Intoxicated by my illness*. New York: Clarkson Potter.

Buber, M. (1970). *I and Thou*. Trans. W. Kaufman. New York: Scribner (original work published 1923).

Bynner, W. (1980). *The way of life according to Laotzu*. New York: Perigee. University of California Press (original work published 1944).

Campo, R. (1997). *The desire to heal: A doctor's education in empathy, identity, and poetry*. New York: Norton.

Carlson, D. Cosmopolitan progressivism: Democratic education in the age of globalization. *Journal of Curriculum Theorizing* 19(4) (2003): 7–31.

Castaneda, C. (2001). Incorporating the transnational adoptee. In M. Novy (ed.), *Imagining adoption: Essays on literature and culture* (pp. 277–99). Ann Arbor: University of Michigan Press.

Chekov, A. (2003). A doctor's visit. In J. Coulehan (ed.), *Chekov's doctors* (pp. 174–82). Kent, OH: Kent State University Press (original work published 1898).

Chodorow, N. (1978). *The reproduction of mothering*. Berkeley, CA: University of California Press.

Cirigliano, M. D., and L. A. Lynn. Diagnosis and treatment of stage fright. *Hospital practice* 27(4A) (1992): 58–60, 62.

Clance, P., and S. Imes. The impostor phenomenon in high-achieving women: Dynamics and therapeutic intervention. *Psychotherapy: Theory, Research and Practice* 15(3) (1978): 241–47.

Coetzee, J. M. (1999). *Disgrace*. New York: Penguin.

Coleridge, S. T. (1993). *Kubla Khan*. In M. Mack, M. W. Knox, J. C. McGalliard, P. M. Pasinetti, H. E. Hugo, P. M. Spacks, R. Wellek, K Douglas, and S. Lawall (eds.), *The Norton anthology of world masterpieces* (vol. 2, pp 614–16). New York: Norton (original work published 1811).

Coles, R. (1986). *The moral life of children*. New York: Atlantic Monthly Press.

Colette, S. G. (1975). The secret woman. Trans. M. Crosland. In S. Cahill (ed.), *Women and fiction: Short stories by and about women* (pp. 36–41). New York: New American Library.

Conrad, J. (1986). *Heart of darkness* (ed. with an introduction by P. O'Prey). New York: Penguin (original work published 1902).

Coxhead, D., and S. Hiller (n.d.). *Dreams: Visions of the night*. London: Thames and Hudon.

Cronin, J. (1987). *Inside*. London: Jonathan Cape.

———. No unnecessary noises allowed, OK? *Ingolovane* 1 (n.d.): 8–12.

Culley, M., and C. Portuges, eds. (1985). *Gendered subjects: The dynamics of feminist teaching*. Boston: Routledge & Kegan Paul.

Cunningham, M. (1998). *The hours*. New York: Farrar, Straus, & Giroux.

Deb, S. (1995). *Scientific racism in modern South Africa*. New York: Cambridge University Press.

Deleuze, G. (1995). *Negotiations: 1972–1995*. Trans. M. Joughin. New York: Columbia University Press.

Deleuze, G., and C. Parnet (1977). *Dialogues*. Trans. H. Tomlinson and B. Habberjam. New York: Columbia University Press.

Deleuze, G., and G. Guattari (1988). *A thousand plateaus: Capitalism and schizophrenia*. Trans. B. Massumi. London: Athlone.

DeLillo, D. The art of fiction. *The Paris Review* 123 (1993): 277–306.

Delpit, L. D. The silenced dialogue: Power and pedagogy in educating other people's children. *Harvard Educational Review* 58(3) (1988): 280–98.

de Mello, A. (1992). *Awareness: The perils and opportunities of reality*. New York: Doubleday.

Derrida, J., and C. V. McDonald. Choreographies. *Diacritics* 12 (1982): 66–76.

Derrida, J. (1972). Discussion: Structure, sign and play in the discourse of the human sciences. In R. Macksey and E. Donata, eds., *The Structuralist controversy* (230–41). Baltimore: Johns Hopkins University Press.

———. (1976). *Of grammatology*. Trans. G. Spivak. Baltimore, MD: Johns Hopkins University Press (original work published 1967).

———. The principle of reason: The university in the eyes of its pupils. *Diacritics* 13(3) (Fall 1983): 9–33.

———. (2002). *On cosmopolitanism and forgiveness*. Trans. M. Dooley and M. Hughes. New York: Routledge.

DeSalvo, L. (1989). *Virginia Woolf: The impact of childhood sexual abuse on her life and work*. New York: Ballantine.

———. (2002). *Vertigo*. New York: Feminist Press.

de Saussere, F. (1959). *A course in general linguistics*. New York: McGraw-Hill.

Dewey, J. (1900). *School and society*. Chicago: University of Chicago Press.

———. (1938). *Experience and education*. New York: Macmillan.

———. (1966). *Democracy and education*. New York: Free Press (original work published 1916).

Dickinson, E. (1985). Poem #1129. In S. M. Gilbert and S. Gubar (eds.), *The Norton anthology of literature by women* (pp. 862–63). New York: Norton (original work published 1868).

Dillard, A. (1974). *Pilgrim at Tinker Creek*. New York: Bantam.

———. (1977). *Holy the firm*. New York: Harper & Row.

———. (1982). *Teaching a stone to talk: Expeditions and encounters*. New York: Harper-Collins.

———. (1987). *An American childhood*. New York: Harper & Row.

———. (1990). *The writing life*. New York: HarperPerennial.

Doll, M. A. Flight and fear: Introduction to Literacies. *Journal of Curriculum Theorizing* (Spring 2002): 107–108.

Eco, U. (1976). *A Theory of semiotics*. Trans. W. Weaver. Bloomington: Indiana University Press.

———. (1990). *The Limits of interpretation*. Trans. W. Weaver. Bloomington: Indiana University Press.

Ehrenreich, B., and D. English (1978). *For her own good: 150 years of experts' advice to women*. New York: Anchor.

Eigen, M. (2001). *Ecstasy*. Middleton, CT: Wesleyan University Press.

Eisler, R. (1987). *The chalice and the blade*. San Francisco: Harper & Row.

Eisner, E. W. (1979). *The educational imagination: On the design and evaluation of school programs*. New York: Macmillan.

Elam, D. (1998). P.S. "I love you": Umberto Eco and the romance of the reader. In N. Bouchard and V. Pravadelli (eds.), *Umberto Eco's alternative: The politics of culture and the ambiguities of interpretation* (pp. 185–207). New York: Peter Lang.

Eliade, M. (1961). *Images and symbols*. New York: Sheed & Ward.

———. (1990). *Symbolism, the sacred, the arts*. New York: Crossroad.

Ellsworth, E. Why doesn't this feel empowering? Working through the repressive myths of critical pedagogy. *Harvard Education Review* 59(3) (1989): 297–324.

Estés, C. P. (1992). *Women who run with the wolves: Myths and stories of the wild woman archetype*. New York: Ballantine.

Evans, P. (1996). *The verbally abusive relationship: How to recognize it and how to respond*. Avon, MA: Adams Media.

Fadiman, A. (1997). *The spirit catches you and you fall down: A Hmong child, her American doctors, and the collision of two cultures*. New York: Farrar, Straus & Giroux.

Fairbairn, W. R. D. (1954). *An object-relations theory of the personality*. New York: Basic.

Fanon, F. (1963). *The wretched of the earth*. Preface, J-P Sartre. Trans. C. Farrington. New York: Grove.

Fassinger, P. A. Understanding classroom interaction: Students' and professors' contributions to students' silence. *Journal of Higher Education* 66(1) (1995): 82–96.

Finch, Anne. (1974). The introduction. In J. Goulianos (ed.), *By a woman writt: Literature from six centuries by and about women* (pp. 71–73). Baltimore: Penguin.

Fine, M. (1992). *Disruptive voices: The possibilities of feminist research*. Ann Arbor: University of Michigan Press.

Flax, J. (1993). *Disputed subjects: Essays on psychoanalysis, politics, and philosophy*. New York: Routledge.

Ford, T. (1999). *Becoming multicultural: Personal and social construction through critical teaching*. New York: Falmer.

Foucault, M. (1980). *Power/knowledge: Selected interviews and other writings 1972–1977*. Ed. C. Gordon. Trans. C. Gordon, L. Marshall, J. Mepham, and K. Soper. New York: Pantheon.

———. (1982). Afterward: The subject and power. In H. L. Dreyfus and P. Rabinow (eds.), *Michel Foucault; Beyond structuralism and hermeneutics* (pp. 208–26). Chicago: University of Chicago Press.

Frank, A. (1995). *The wounded storyteller*. Chicago: University of Chicago Press.

Frank, M. Rosalind Russell. *Architectural Digest* (April 1992): 190.

Frazen, J. (2002). *How to be alone*. New York: Farrar, Straus & Giroux.

Freemantle, T. Nobel laureate's latest defies classification. *The Houston Chronicle*, November 21, 2003.

Freidson, E. (1986). *Professional powers: A study of the institutionalization of formal knowledge*. Chicago: University of Chicago Press.

Freire, P. (1994). *Pedagogy of the oppressed*. Trans. M. Bergman Ramos. New York: Continuum (original work published 1970).

Fugard, A. (2003). *"Master Harold"... and the boys*. In J. A. Stanford (ed.), *Responding to literature* (552–89). New York: McGraw-Hill.

Gabbard, G. O. Stage fright. *International Journal of Psycho-Analysis* 60 (1979): 383–92.

———. (1997). The vicissitudes of shame in stage fright. In C. W. Socarides and S. Kramer (eds.), *Work and its inhibitions* (pp. 209–20). Madison, CT: International Universities Press.

Gailey, C. W. (1998, April). *The search for baby right: Race, class and gender in U.S. international adoption*. Paper presented at the Wenner-Gren symposium New Directions in Kinship Study: A core concept revisited. Majorca, Spain.

———. (2000). Ideologies of motherhood and kinship in U.S. adoption. In H. Ragone and F. W. Twine (eds.), *Ideologies and technologies of motherhood: Race, class, sexuality, nationalism* (pp. 11–55). New York: Routledge.

Gallagher, K. No justice, No peace: The legalities and realities of amnesty in Sierra Leone. *Thomas Jefferson Law Review* 23 (2000): 149.

Gawande, A. When doctors make mistakes. *The New Yorker* (February 1, 1999): 48–54.

———. The learning curve. *The New Yorker* (January 28, 2002): 52–61.

Gergen, M. (1992). Life stories: Pieces of a dream. In G. Rosenwald and R. Ochberg (eds.), *Stories lives: The cultural politics of self-understanding*. New Haven: Yale University Press.

Gilligan, C. (1993). *In a different voice: Psychological theory and women's development*. Cambridge, MA: Harvard University Press.

Gilman, C. P. (1985). The Yellow Wallpaper. In S. M. Gilman and S. Gubar (eds.), *The Norton anthology of literature by women: The Tradition in English* (pp. 1148–61) .New York: Norton (original work published 1892).

Giroux, H. A. (1994). Living dangerously: Identity politics and the new cultural racism. In H. A. Giroux and P. McLaren (eds.), *Between borders: Pedagogy and the politics of cultural studies* (29–55). New York: Routledge.

Giroux, H. A., and P. McLaren, eds. (1994). *Between borders: Pedagogy and the politics of cultural studies*. New York: Routledge.

Gitlin, A. (1990). School structure and teachers' work. In M. W. Apple and L. Weis (eds.), *Ideology and practice in schooling* (pp. 193–212). Philadelphia: Temple University Press.

Gordimer, N. (1984). *Burger's daughter*. New York: Penguin.

———. (2003). Town and country lovers. In J. A. Stanford (ed.), *Responding to literature* (pp. 365–73). New York: McGraw-Hill (original work published 1940).

Gorra, M. After the fall. *The New York Times Book Review* 104(48) (November 28, 1999): 7.

Gough, A. Embodying a mine site: Enacting cyborg curriculum. *Journal of Curriculum Theorizing* (Winter 2003): 33–47.

Gough, N. Learning from *Disgrace*: A troubling narrative for South African curriculum work. *Perspectives in Education* 19(1) (2001): 107–26.

Gramsci, A. (1971). *Prison notebooks*. New York: International.

Green, A. (2001). *The dead mother: The work of André Green*. G. Kohon (ed.). New York: Routledge (original work published 1983).

Greene, G. (1993). Looking at history. In G. Greene and K. Coppelia (eds.), *Changing subjects: The making of feminist literary criticism* (pp. 4–27). London: Routledge.

Greene, M. The passions of pluralism: Multiculturalism and the expanding community. *Educational Researcher* 22(1) (1993): 13–18.

———. (1995). *Releasing the imagination: Essays on education, the arts, and social change*. San Francisco: Jossey-Bass.

———. Reflection. *AERA Division B: Curriculum Studies Newsletter* (Fall 2002): 2.

Grossholtz, J. (1984). *Forging capitalist patriarchy*. Durham, NC: Duke University Press.

Grumet, M. (1988). *Bitter milk: Women and teaching*. Amherst: University of Massachusetts Press.

———. (1992). Existential and phenomenological foundations of autobiographical method. In W. Pinar and W. Reynolds (eds.), *Understanding curriculum as phenomenological and deconstructed text* (pp. 28–43). New York: Teachers College Press.

Grunebaum-Ralph, H. (April 1997). *(Re)membering bodies, producing histories: Silence, collective memory and historical narration in holocaust survivor narrative and truth and reconciliation commission testimony in South Africa.* Paper presented at the meeting of the American Comparative Literature Conference. Puerto Vallarta, Mexico, 10–13.

H.D. (1983). The flowering of the rod. In Louis L. Martz (ed.), *Collected poems: 1912–1944* (pp. 577–612). New York: New Directions (original work published 1944).

Hamilton, E. (1942). *Mythology.* New York: Little, Brown.

Haraway, D. J. Situated knowledges: The science question in feminism and the privilege of partial perspective. *Feminist Studies* 14 (1988): 579–99.

Harding, E. M. (1963). *Psychic energy: Its source and its transformation.* With a foreword by C. G. Jung. Princeton: Princeton University Press.

Harding, S. (1991). *Whose science? Whose knowledge? Thinking from women's lives.* Ithaca, NY: Cornell University Press.

Hartmann, E. The concept of boundaries in counseling and psychotherapy. *British Journal of Guidance and Counseling* 25(2) (1997): 147–62.

Henderson, J. L., and M. Oakes (1990). *The wisdom of the serpent: The myths of death, rebirth, and resurrection.* Princeton, NJ: Princeton University Press.

Henderson-Holmes, S. (1990). Snapshots of Grace. In T. McMillan (ed.), *Breaking ice: An anthology of contemporary African American fiction* (pp. 331–42). New York: Penguin.

Highwater, J. (1981). *The primal mind: Vision and reality in Indian America.* New York: New American Library.

Hilfiker, D. Facing our mistakes. *New England Journal of Medicine* 310 (1984): 118–22.

———. (1985). *Healing the wounds.* New York: Pantheon.

———. Facing brokenness. *Second Opinion* 11 (1989): 93–107.

———. (1991). Mistakes. In J. Stone and R. Reynolds (eds.), *On doctoring* (pp. 376–87). New York: Simon & Schuster.

Hillman, J. (1975). *Re-visioning psychology.* New York: Harper & Row.

———. (1979). *The dream and the underworld.* New York: Harper & Row.

———. (1996). *The soul's code: In search of character and calling.* New York: Random.

Hirsch, E. D. (1996). *The schools we need and why we don't have them.* New York: Doubleday.

Huebner, D. E. (1991). *Educational activity and prophetic criticism.* New Haven, CT: Yale University Divinity School.

Ibsen, H. (2003). A Doll's House. In J. A. Stanford (ed.), *Responding to Literature* (pp. 663–718). New York: McGraw-Hill (original work published 1879).

Jampolsky, G. G. (1979). *Love is letting go of fear.* Berkeley, CA: Celestial Arts.

Jayasinghe, C. (2002, February 2). LTTE increases child conscription amid Sri Lana truce. *Indo-Asian News Service*. Retrieved February 2, 2002, from *http://in.news.yahoo.com/020202/43/1fb65.html*.

Johnson, S. (1981). *From housewife to heretic: One woman's spiritual awakening and her excommunication from the Mormon Church*. Garden City, NY: Doubleday.

Jones, M. G., and T. M. Gerig. Silent sixth-grade students: Characteristics, achievement, and teacher expectations. *The Elementary School Journal* 95(2) (1994): 169–82.

Joseph, N. (1986). *Uniforms and nonuniforms: Communication through clothing*. New York: Greenwood.

Joseph, R. (1998). Plight of Lankan women workers abroad. *The weekend express*. Retrieved February 2, 2002 from *http://www8.pair.com/isweb3/spot/sp0525/clip2.html*.

Jung, C. G. (1958). *The undiscovered self.* Trans. R. F. C. Hull. New York: Little, Brown.

———. (1969). *On the nature of dreams*. Trans. R. F. C. Hull. Collected Works, vol. 8 (pp. 281–97). Princeton, NJ: Princeton University Press (original work published 1945).

———. (1977). *The archetypes and the collective unconscious*. Trans. R. F. C Hull. Collected Works, vol. 9 (p. 1). Princeton, NJ: Princeton University Press (original work published 1959).

Kachru, B. B. (1995). The alchemy of English. In B. Ashcroft, G. Griffiths, and H. Tiffin (eds.), *The post-colonial studies reader* (pp. 291–95). New York: Routledge.

Kaplan, D. On stage fright. *Drama Review* 14 (1969): 436–38.

Kimmel, H. (2002). *The solace of leaving early*. New York: Doubleday.

Kincaid, J. (1992). *At the bottom of the river*. New York: Farrar, Straus & Giroux.

———. (1997). *Autobiography of my mother*. New York: Plume.

Kingston, M. H. (1996). No name woman. In S. M. Gilbert and S. Gubar (eds.), *The Norton anthology of literature by women: The traditions in English* (pp. 2239–47). New York: Norton.

Klein, M. (1975). *Melanie Klein: Love, guilt and reparation and other works*. New York: Delacorte.

Koehn, P. H., and J. N. Rosenau. Transnational competence in an emergent epoch. *International Studies Perspectives* 3 (2002): 105–27.

Kohn, L. T., J. M. Corrigan, and M. S. Donaldson, eds. (2000). *To err is human: Building a safer health system*. Washington DC: National Academy Press.

Kozol, J. (1991). *Savage inequalities: Children in America's schools*. New York: Crown.

———. (1995). *Amazing grace: The lives of children and the conscience of a nation*. New York: Crown.

Krall, F. R. (1994). *Ecotone: Wayfaring on the margins*. Albany: State University of New York Press.

Kristeva, J. (2001). *Hannah Arendt*. New York: Columbia University Press.

———. Forgiveness: An interview. *Publications of the Modern Language Association of America (PMLA)* 117(2) (March 2002): 278–87.

Kuschel, K-J. (1994). *Laughter: A theological essay*. New York: Continuum.

Labosky, V. K. (1991, April). *Case studies of two teachers in a reflective teacher education program: "How do you know?"* Paper presented at the Annual Meeting of the American Educational Research Association, Chicago.

Lacan, J. (1981). The eye and the gaze. Trans. A. Sheridan. In J-A Miller (ed.), *The four fundamental concepts of psycho-analysis*. New York: Norton.

LaCombe, M. Seeking forgiveness. *Annals of Internal Medicine* 130(5) (1999): 444–45.

Landry, J. Archetypal psychology and the twelve-step movement, *Journal of Archetype and Culture* 58 (Spring 1995): 1–20.

Lather, P. (2000). Responsible practices of academic writing: Troubling clarity II. In P. P. Trifonas (ed.), *Revolutionary pedagogies: Cultural politics, instituting education, and the discourse of theory* (pp. 289–311). New York: Routledge Falmer.

Leape, L. Special communication: Error in medicine. *JAMA* 272(23) (1994): 1851–57.

Lessing, D. (2003). Through the tunnel. In J. A. Stanford (ed.), *Responding to literature* (pp. 860–67). New York: McGraw-Hill (original work published 1955).

Levertov, D. (1975). A woman alone. In *Life in the forest* (pp. 16–17). New York: New Directions.

Levine, C. Life but no limb: The aftermath of medical error. *Health Affairs* 21(4) (2002): 237–41.

Levine, D. N. (1985). *The flight from ambiguity: Essays in social and cultural theory*. Chicago: University of Chicago Press.

Levi-Strauss, C. (1972). *Structural anthropology*. Trans. C. Jacobson and B. Schoepf. Hammondsworth, England: Penguin.

Lewis, M., and R. Simon. A discourse not intended for her. *Harvard Educational Review* 54(4) (1986): 457–72.

Liebow, E. (1995). *Tell them who I am: The lives of homeless women*. New York: Penguin.

London, J. (2003). To build a fire. In J. A. Stanford (ed.), *Responding to Literature* (pp. 842–54). New York: McGraw-Hill (original work published 1910).

Lorde, A. (1980). *The cancer journals*. San Francisco: Spinsters Ink.

Lowell, A. (2003). Patterns. In J. A. Stanford (ed.), *Responding to Literature* (pp. 657–59). New York: McGraw-Hill (original work published 1915).

Lyotard, J-F. (1979). *The postmodern condition*. Trans. G. Bennington and B. Massumi. Minneapolis: University of Minnesota Press.

Lyotard, J-F., and J-L Thebaud (1985). *Just gaming*. Trans. W. Godzich. Minneapolis: University of Minnesota Press.

Mairs, N. (1994). *Voice lessons: On becoming a (woman) writer*. Boston: Beacon.

Mansfield, K. (1985). The daughters of the late colonel. In S. M. Gilbert and S. Gubar (eds.), *The Norton anthology of literature by women* (pp. 1515–31). New York: Norton (original work published 1922).

Marshall, J. R. (1994). *Social phobia: From shyness to stage fright*. New York: Basic.

Massachusetts Medical Society Online. Retrieved from *http://www.massmed.org/AM/ Template.cfm?Section=Top_Stories 33.*

McCoy, K. (1998, April). *Marxisms, Morality, Intoxications, Politics.* Paper presented at the annual meeting of the American Educational Research Association. San Diego, CA.

McGee, P. (1992). *Telling the Other: The question of value in modern and postcolonial writing.* Ithaca: Cornell University Press.

McKenna, R. (1991). *Rollie McKenna: A life in portraits.* New York: Knopf.

McLaren, P. (1998). *Life in schools: An introduction to critical pedagogy in the foundations of education.* New York: Longman.

Merkin, D. A new man. *The New Yorker* (November 15, 1999): 110–12.

Mies, M. (1986). *Patriarchy and accumulation on a world scale.* London: Zed.

Miller, D. L. (1989). *Hells and holy ghosts: A theopoetics of Christian belief.* Nashville: Abingdon.

———. The death of the clown: A loss of wits in the postmodern moment. *A Journal of Archetype and Culture* 58 (Spring 1995): 69–82.

Mishler, E. G. (1984). *The discourse of medicine: Dialectics of medical interviews.* Norwood, NJ: Ablex.

Mokara, D. In R. Nessman, Playing host to U.N. racism conference, South Africa still wrestles with divisions. *Savannah Morning News,* August 26, 2001, p. 10A.

Moore, T. (1992). *Care of the soul: A guide for cultivating depth and sacredness in everyday life.* New York: Harper & Row.

Morris, D. Light as environment: Medicine, health, and values. *Journal of Medical Humanities* 23 (2002): 7–30.

Morris, M. (2000). Dante's left foot kicks queer theory into gear. In S. Talburt and S. R. Steinberg (eds.), *Thinking queer: Sexuality, culture, and education* (pp. 15–32). New York: Peter Lang.

———. (2001a). *Curriculum and the holocaust: Competing sites of memory and representation.* Mahwah, NJ: Lawrence Erlbaum.

———. Multiculturalism as jagged walking. *Multicultural Education* 8(4) (2001b): 2–8.

———. Curriculum as the undecidable. *Journal of Curriculum Theorizing* (Winter 2003): 3–6.

n.a. Centerpoint; A new modality for experiencing analytical psychology. Unpublished.

Nafisi, A. (2003). *Reading* Lolita *in Tehran: A memoir in books.* New York: Random House.

Nasar, S. (1998). *A beautiful mind.* New York: Simon & Schuster.

Nelson, H. L., ed. (1997). *Stories and their limits.* New York: Routledge.

NiCarthy, G. (1990). *Getting free: You can end abuse and take back your life.* Seattle: Seal.

Nicholson, L. Women and schooling. *Educational Theory* 30(3) (1980): 225–33. Noonday.

Nussbaum, M. (1997). *Cultivating humanity: a classical defense of reform in liberal education.* Cambridge, MA: Harvard University Press.

O'Brien, A. (2001). Transnational adoption narratives: The family as nationalist agenda. Paper presented at the Modern Language Association annual meeting, New Orleans, LA.

O'Connor, F. (1969). *Mystery and manners.* Ed. S. Fitzgerald and R. Fitzgerald. New York: Farrar, Straus & Giroux.

———. (1978). *The complete stories of Flannery O'Connor.* New York: Farrar, Straus & Giroux.

Omond, R. (1985). *The apartheid handbook.* Middlesex, England: Penguin.

Opie, I., and P. Opie (1974). *The classic fairytales.* New York: Oxford University Press.

Ostriker, A. (1999). Scenes from a mastectomy. In H. Raz (ed.), *Living on the margins* (pp. 175–200). New York: Persea.

Otto, R. (1958). *The idea of the holy: An inquiry into the nonrational factor in the idea of the divine and its relation to the rational.* Trans. J. W. Harvey. New York: Oxford.

Patmore, C. (1993). The angel in the house. In M. H. Abrams, E. T. Donaldson, A. David, H. Smith, B. K. Lewalski, R. M. Adams, G. M. Logan, S. H. Monk, L. Lipking, J. Stillinger, G. H. Ford, C. T. Christ, D. Daiches, and J. Stallworthy (eds.), *The Norton anthology of English literature* (vol. 2, 1723–24). New York: Norton (original work published 1854–62).

Pinar, W. F. (1992). Cries and whispers. In W. F. Pinar and W. M. Reynolds (eds.), *Understanding curriculum as phenomenological and deconstructed text* (pp. 92–101). New York: Teachers College Press.

———. (1994). *Autobiography, politics, and sexuality: Essays in curriculum theory, 1972–1992.* New York: Peter Lang.

———. (1995). Understanding curriculum: A postscript for the next generation. In W. F. Pinar, W. M. Reynolds, P. Slattery, and P. Taubman (eds.), *Understanding curriculum* (pp. 847–68). New York: Peter Lang.

———. (2000). *The gender of racial politics and violence in America: Lynching, prison rape, and the crisis of masculinity.* New York: Peter Lang.

———. "I am a man" The queer politics of race. *Journal of Curriculum Theorizing* 17(4) (2001): 11–40.

———. (2002). Strange fruit: Race, sex, and an autobiographics of alterity. In P. P. Trifonas (ed.), *Revolutionary pedagogies: Cultural politics, instituting education, and the discourse of theory* (pp. 30–46). New York: Routledge Falmer.

Pinar, W. F., and M. Grumet (1976). *Toward a Poor Curriculum.* Dubuque, IA: Kendall/Hunt.

Pinar, W. F., and W. M. Reynolds, eds. (1992). *Understanding curriculum as phenomenological and deconstructed text.* New York: Teachers College Press.

Pinar, W. F., W. M. Reynolds, P. Slattery, and P. Taubman (1995). *Understanding curriculum.* New York: Peter Lang.

Polo, Sir M. (1903). Sir H. U. (ed. and trans.). *The book of Sir Marco Polo the Venetian concerning the kingdoms and marvels of the East* (3rd ed., two vols.). Revised throughout in the light of recent discoveries by Henry Cordier. As quoted in J. Grossholtz (1984). *Forging capitalist patriarchy.* Durham, N. C.: Duke University Press.

Ponnambalam, S. (1983). *The national question and the Tamil liberation struggle.* London: Zed.

Pordzik, R. Nationalism, cross-culturalism, and utopian vision in South African utopian and dystopian writing, 1972–1992. *Research in African Literatures* 32(3) (2001): 177–97.

Quindlen, A. Goodbye, Dr. Spock. *Your Child, Newsweek, Special Edition* 136 (Fall/Winter 2000): 86–87.

Radin, P. (1956). *The trickster: A study in American Indian mythology.* New York: Philosophical Library.

Ragone, H. (2000). Of likeness and difference; How race is being transfigured by gestational surrogacy. In H. Ragone and F. W. Twine (eds.), *Ideologies and technologies of motherhood: Race, class, sexuality, nationalism* (pp. 56–75). New York: Routledge.

Rappaport, P. (1989). *A study of stage fright: Its history, its etiology, and an approach to treatment.* Digital Dissertations <*http://www.umi.com/dissertations/fullcit/8917309*>.

Ravitch, M. Fiction in review. *Yale Review* 89(1) (2001): 144–53.

Readings, B. (1999). *The university in ruins.* Cambridge: Harvard University Press.

Reitemeier, P. J. Musing on medical mistakes: A four-piece ensemble in search of an orchestra. *The Journal of Clinical Ethics* 8(4) (1997): 353–58.

Reynolds, W. M. (2003). *Curriculum: A river runs through it.* New York: Peter Lang.

———. (unpublished manuscript). *Talking about the generations: Curriculum studies, harlequins, pink panthers, and disarray.*

Rich, A. (1985). When we dead awaken. In S. Gilbert and S. Gubar (eds.), *The Norton anthology of literature by women* (pp. 2044–56). New York: Norton.

———. (1985). Taking women students seriously. In M. Culley and C. Portuges (eds.), *Gendered subjects: The dynamics of feminist teaching.* New York: Routledge (original work published 1978).

Rich, F. (2003). Review of the Yale Repertory Theatre Production of *"Master Harold" . . . and the Boys.* In J. A. Stanford (ed.), *Responding to literature* (pp. 589–90). New York: McGraw-Hill.

Richardson, L. (1990). *Writing strategies: Reaching diverse audiences.* Newbury Park, CA: Sage.

Rogat-Loeb, P. (1999). *Soul of a citizen: Living with conviction in a cynical time.* New York: St. Martin's.

Rorty, R. (1989). *Contingency, irony and solidarity.* New York: Cambridge University Press.

Rosenblum, B. (1991). Cancer in two voices: Living in an unstable body. In J. Barrington (ed.), *An intimate wilderness: Lesbian writers on sexuality* (pp. 140–43). Portland, OR: Eighth Mountain Press.

Roston, D. (1986). On studying anatomy. In *Poetry: A collection of poems written by medical students* (p. 23). Rootstown, OH: NEOUCOM.

Sacks, O. (1995). *An anthropologist on Mars: Seven paradoxical tales.* New York: Vintage.

Said, E. (1983). Opponents, audiences, constituencies and community. In H. Foster (ed.), *The anti-aesthetic: Essays on postmodern culture.* Port Townsend: Bay.

Salinger, J. D. (1966). *The catcher in the rye.* New York: Bantam.

Sardello, R., ed. (1995). *The angels.* New York: Continuum.

Savannah Morning News, December 10, 1999, A-1.

Schrijvers, J. (1985). *Mothers for life: Motherhood and marginalization in the North Central province of Sri Lanka.* Eburon: Delft.

Schwab, J. (1978). *Science, curriculum, and liberal education: Selected essays.* I. Westbury & Neil J. Wilkof (eds.). Chicago: University of Chicago Press.

Sedgwick, E. K. (2003). *Touching feeling: Affect, pedagogy, performativity.* Durham: Duke University Press.

Serres, M. (2000). *The troubadour of knowledge.* Trans. S. F. Glaser and W. Paulson. Ann Arbor: University of Michigan Press.

Sexton, A. (2003). Snow White and the seven dwarfs. In J. A. Stanford (ed.), *Responding to literature* (pp. 400–406). New York: McGraw-Hill (original work published 1971).

Sherwin, S. (1992). *No longer patient.* Philadelphia: Temple University Press.

Simpson, A. W., and M. T. Erickson. Teachers' verbal and nonverbal communications patterns as a function of teacher race, student gender, and student race. *American Educational Research Journal* 20(2) (1983): 183–98.

Slattery, P., and D. Rapp (2003). *Ethics and the foundations of education: Teaching convictions in a postmodern world.* Boston: Allyn & Bacon.

Small-McCarthy, R. (1999). From *The Bluest Eye* to *Jazz*: A retrospective of Toni Morrison's literary sounds. In C. McCarthy, G.Hudak, S. Miklaucic, and P. Saukko (eds.), *Sound identities: Popular music and the cultural politics of education* (pp. 175–93). New York: Peter Lang.

Smith, D. (1999). Journeying: A meditation on leaving home and coming home. *Pedagon: Interdisciplinary essays in the human sciences, pedagogy, and culture* (pp. 1–7). New York: Peter Lang.

Smith, D. E. (1987). *The everyday world as problematic: A feminist sociology.* Boston: Northeastern University Press.

Smith, M. L, and H. P. Forster. Morally managing medical mistakes. *Cambridge Quarterly of Healthcare Ethics* 9 (2000): 38–53.

Solinger, R. (1998). Poisonous choice. In M. Ladd-Taylor and L. Umansky (eds.), *Bad mothers: The politics of blame in twentieth-century America* (pp. 381–402). New York: NYU Press.

———. (2001). *Beggars and choosers: How the politics of choice shapes adoption, abortion, and welfare in the United States.* New York: Hill & Wang.

Sommers-Flanagan, R., D. Elliot, and J. Sommers-Flanagan. Exploring the edges: Boundaries and breaks. *Ethics and Behavior* 8(1) (1998): 37–48.

Sontag, S. (2001). *Where the stress falls: Essays.* New York: Farrar, Straus & Giroux

South Africa still wrestles with divisions. *Savannah Morning News,* 10A.

Spring, J. (1998). *Education and the rise of the global economy.* Mahwah, NJ: Erlbaum.

"Sri Lanka." Microsoft Encarta Online Encyclopedia, 2001. Retrieved February 2, 2002, from *http://www.msn.com.*

Stanford, A. F. (2003). *Bodies in a broken world: Women novelists of color and the politics of medicine.* Chapel Hill: University of North Carolina Press.

Steinberg, J. Clinical interventions with women experiencing the impostor syndrome. *Women and Therapy* 5(4) (1986): 19–26.

Stevens, W. (1951). *The necessary angel: Essays on reality and the imagination*. New York: Vintage (original work published 1942).

———. (1972).The man with the blue guitar. In H. Stevens (ed.), *Wallace Stevens: The palm at the end of the mind: Selected poems and a play* (pp. 133–49). New York: Vintage (original work published 1939).

———. (1972). The comedian as the letter *C*. In H. Stevens (ed.), *Wallace Stevens: The palm at the end of the mind: Selected poems and a play* (pp. 58–74). New York: Vintage (original work published 1922).

Stolberg, S. G. Bush urges a cap on medical liability. *New York Times*, July 26, 2002, A-16.

Stone, J. (1980). He makes a house call. In *In all this rain* (pp. 4–5). Baton Rouge: Lousiana State University Press.

Stoskopf, A. The forgotten history of eugenics. *Rethinking Schools* 13(3) (1999): 76–80.

Taubman, P. Teaching without hope: What is really at stake in the standards movement, high stakes testing, and the drive for "practical reforms." *Journal of Curriculum Theorizing* 16(3) (2000): 19–34.

Thiong'o, N. W. (1995). The language of African literature. In B. Ashcroft, G. Griffiths, and H. Tiffin (eds.), *The post-colonial studies reader* (pp. 285–90). New York: Routledge.

Tompkins, J. (1989). Me and my shadow. In L. Kaufmann (ed.), *Gender and theory* (pp. 121–39). Oxford: Blackwell.

Tong, R. (1996). *Feminist approaches to bioethics*. Boulder, CO: Westview.

Topping, M., and E. Kimmel. The impostor phenomenon: Feeling phony. *Academic Psychology Bulletin* 7(2) (1985): 145–55.

Treaster, J. B. Malpractice rates are rising sharply: Health costs follow. *New York Times*, September 10, 2001, A-1.

Trinh, Minh-ha, T. (1989). *Woman, native, other*. Bloomington: Indiana University Press.

Trudeau. G. Doonesbury. *Savannah Morning News*, August 8, 2003, 7A.

Trueba, H. (1989). *Raising silent voices: Educating the linguistic minorities for the twenty-first century*. New York: Harper & Row.

Turco, L. (1993). *Emily Dickinson: Woman of letters*. Albany: State University of New York Press.

U.S. Department of State. (2002). Retrieved December 19, 2002 from *http://travel.state.gov/orphan_numbers.html*.

Vendler, H. H. (1969). *On extended wings: Wallace Stevens's longer poems*. Cambridge: Harvard University Press.

Verghese, A. (1995). *My own country*. New York: Vintage.

———. (1998). *The tennis partner*. New York: HarperCollins.

Vogel, A. (1974). *Film as a subversive art*. New York: Random.

Waitzkin, H. (1991). *The politics of medical encounters*. New Haven: Yale University Press.

Waldenfels, H. (1990). *Absolute nothingness: Foundations for a Buddhist Christian dialogue*. Trans. J. W. Heisig. New York: Paulist.

Walsh, T. (2001, June/July). Rising malpractice rates add to physicians' fiscal pressures. *MassMed.org* (Massachusetts Medical Society Online). *http://www2.mms. org/vitalsigns/junjul01/top1.html*.

Warren, R. P. (1971). In H. Adams (ed.), *Critical theory since Plato* (pp. 981–92). New York: Harcourt Brace Jovanovich.

Wear, D. On white coats and professional development: The formal and the hidden curriculum. *Annals of Internal Medicine* 129 (1998): 734–37

———. (2005). Teaching respect and empathy: A case study of the formal and hidden curriculum of cultural competency. In D. Wear (ed.), *Professionalism in medicine: Critical perspectives*. New York: Springer.

Weaver, J., A. Anijar, and T. Daspit (2003). *S F Curriculum, Cyborg teachers and youth culture*. New York: Peter Lang.

Weingart, S. N., R. M. Wilson, R. W. Gibberd, and B. Harrison. Epidemiology of medical error. *BMJ* 320 (2000): 774–77.

Welsford, E. (1966). *The fool: His social and literary history*. Gloucester: Peter Smith.

West, C. (1988). Interview with Cornell West. In A. Ross (ed.), *Universal Abandon*. Edinburgh: Edinburgh University Press.

Whitaker, M. Thinking contextually about accountability. *The Teacher Educator* 39(4) (2004): 267–80.

Wilde, O. (1960). *De profundis*. New York: Philosophical Library (original work published 1905).

———. (1993). *The picture of Dorian Gray*. New York: Dover (original work published 1890).

Will, G. Uncivil overreachers in both parties vandalize American politics. *Savannah Morning News*, August 3, 2003, 9A.

Willeford, W. (1969). *The fool and his scepter: A study in clowns and jesters and their audience*. Evanston: Northwestern University Press.

Williams, A. Towards the biologics of cultural production: The literary politics of Thomas Mofolo. *Alienation: Journal of the Centre for the Study of Southern African Literature and Language* 6(2) (1999): 5–23.

———. (2000). The postcolony as trope: Searching for a lost continent in a borderless world. *Research in African Literatures* 31(2) (2000): 179–93.

Williams, P. J. (1991). *The alchemy of race and rights*. Cambridge, MA: Harvard University Press.

———. (1998). *Seeing a color-blind future: The paradox of race*. New York: Farrar, Straus, & Giroux.

Williams, T. T. (2000). *Leap*. New York: Pantheon.

Wilson, W. (1939). *Alcoholics Anonymous*. New York: Alcoholics Anonymous World Services.

———. (1953). *Twelve steps and twelve traditions*. New York: Alcoholics Anonymous World Services.

Winnicot, D. W. (1987). *Home is where we start from: Essays by a psychoanalyst.* New York: Norton.

Witman, A. B., D. M. Park, and S. B. Hardin. How do patients want physicians to handle mistakes? *Archives of Internal Medicine* 156 (1996): 2565–69.

Wolf, S. M. (1996). *Feminism and bioethics: Beyond reproduction.* New York: Oxford University Press.

Wolff, C. G. (1988). *Emily Dickinson.* Reading: Addison-Wesley.

Woolf, V. (1938). *Three Guineas.* New York: Harcourt Brace Jovanovich.

———. (1955). *To the lighthouse.* New York: Harcourt Brace Jovanovich (original work published 1927).

Worell, J., and P. Remer (1992). *Feminist perspectives in therapy: An empowerment model for women.* Chichester, England: Wiley.

Wu, A. W., S. Folkman, S. J. McPhee, and B. Lo. How house officers cope with their mistakes. *Western Journal of Medicine* 159 (1993): 565–69.

Yeats. W. B. (1959). The second coming. *The collected poems of W. B. Yeats* (184–85). New York: Macmillan (original work published 1921).

Young, I. (1990). *Throwing like a girl.* Bloomington: Indiana University Press.

Young, R. J. C. (1993). Freud's secret: *The Interpretation of Dreams* was a Gothic novel (206–31). In L. Marcus (ed.), *Sigmund Freud's* The Interpretation of Dreams: *New interdisciplinary essays.*

Index

197